Hide Little Boy

A Veteran Paratrooper and ex-SAS
Reservist's Journey of a Psychopathic
Upbringing, Brutality in Her Majesty's
Forces, Discarded and Gaslighted by the
Church of England, before Lifesaving
Therapy with a Horse Called ISIS.

Paul Parks

First paperback edition October 2020

Book design by Publishing Push

ISBN 978-1-913704-81-0
ISBN 978-1-913704-82-7

Published by PublishingPush.com

Contents

Introduction

Corrie ten Boom once said, 'Never be afraid to trust an unknown future to a known God'. I have this phrase written in the front of my Bible, to remind me that however life seems, however difficult life is, I always have hope. Life is never perfect, marriage or relationships are never perfect, but when you add a debilitating mental illness into the mix, perfection seems to be an unreachable destination.

Paul and I have been married now for over 17 years, and for 14 of those years, we lived with the 'shadow' of PTSD. I say shadow, as, for 14 years, we didn't know what PTSD or Complex PTSD (CPTSD) was or how its symptoms played out in our lives. We, or more accurately I, knew that something was not right, knew that my lovely, caring, beautiful husband could change at the flick of a switch and then afterwards, have no idea or understanding of how he had been. No-one wanted to help or understand, and for many years, I felt totally isolated and alone, yet not willing to give up on a man that I knew was extraordinary in his compassion and love for people, yet was also damaged. Paul and I have come from completely different backgrounds, upbringings and life experiences, yet we firmly believe that God brought us together.

Paul did not choose to have PTSD; we did not choose to have PTSD as part of our marriage, but it was. The divorce statistics surrounding PTSD and CPTSD are, to say the least, disheartening, but there is hope; hope for a marriage or relationship which will come out the other side stronger than ever. We have, and this book is testament to, an unswerving faith, a determination to see justice and a deep, deep love and commitment.

Introduction

I know that for Paul, this has not been an easy book to write, but it needed to be written. Not just as a 'cathartic' exercise for him, but as a way of getting out there the reality of living with a mental illness and the effect that that illness can have on loved ones and families. As a way, too, of highlighting the stigma and shame that still surrounds mental illness and the ignorance and hypocrisy of Institutions that, quite frankly, should know better.

Our hope is that this book will not just be an interesting story of how difficult life can be for some people, but that it will, in some way, be a catalyst for change; change that is so desperately needed, to ensure that families like ours don't suffer in the way that we have suffered, and that no more military veterans decide that the only way out of their suffering is suicide.

As you read this book, my prayer is that you will see the 'real' Paul, the man that God chose and created him to be, the man that I fell in love with and chose to stand by.

As a student at University, I loved the music of Amy Grant, and in one of her songs she sings:

'When the weight of all my dreams is resting heavy on my head and the thoughtful words of help and hope have all been nicely said. But I'm still hurting, wondering if I'll ever be the one I think I am. Then you gently re-remind me, that you made me from the first and the more I try to be the best the more I get the worst, and I realise the good in me is only there because of who you are. And all I ever have to be is what you've made me.' ['All I Ever Have To Be' by Amy Grant]

If you are suffering from PTSD or any other debilitating mental health illness, or you are caring for and supporting someone who is suffering, then I hope that this book is an encouragement that there is hope, and yes, there may be many obstacles to overcome, but there is hope.

Lois J Parks
September 2020

In writing this book, I have been as authentic and factual as possible. In order to accurately recount some of the stories from my life, I felt it was necessary to include language which some people may find offensive.

Paul Parks
September 2020

PART ONE

'The Blue-Ringed Octopus'

1959 – 1975
Age: 0 – 16

"There can be no keener revelation of a society's soul than the way in which it treats its children."

Nelson Mandela

Kenya, Africa.

'This is me!'

The blue-ringed octopus: An exquisitely beautiful sea creature, less than 5 inches in diameter but which holds venom 1,000 times stronger than cyanide and has enough of it to kill 26 humans in just minutes.

My mother: Stunningly beautiful with a captivating personality, short in stature but with the ability to devour and destroy anyone who came across her path.

My father: Never met him and know very little about him. I know that he was of Indian origin, a Sikh, a very handsome and distinguished-looking man and a successful businessman who ran a haulage business in Nairobi, Kenya in the 1950s/60s.

I am told I was conceived on a hillside in the shadow of Mount Kilimanjaro. My mother, married to Larry (one of her many husbands), was, at the time running a hotel/brothel in Nairobi City. Her 'career' had been, and would always be, that of a 'madam'.

I am one of four children, all to different fathers. Teja, her lover and my father, was, she told me later, the love of her life, the only man whom she had ever genuinely loved. As the emotion of love was something that did not come naturally to my mother, I have no idea whether or not her feelings for my dad were any different to the 'feelings' that she had for the countless other men that came in and out of her life and mine.

Whilst my conception may have been gloriously romantic, in a setting worthy of a 1950's Hollywood Blockbuster movie, my life as a child was anything but.

Westcliff on Sea, Essex, UK

'Lost Budgie, Lost Boy'

It was a sunny day with a clear blue sky, and I must have been only about 4 years old. At this time, we lived in a house in Westcliff on Sea, Essex. I was running up and down the cliff paths, skipping and playing on my own and enjoying my own imaginary world, when an elderly lady stopped to talk to me. I had seen her before, coming in and out of one of the terraced houses a few doors down from our house. She was a sweet and nice lady with grey hair, and she wore black glasses with thick lenses. With a slight croak in her voice, which revealed to me that she was sad and on the verge of tears, she bent forward to say something to me.

"Could you please help me, little boy? My budgie has escaped, and I can't find him!"

I nodded my head and began to walk around the cliff footpaths with the elderly lady. We walked up and down the paths on the cliff's hill and along some roads. There was no sign of the budgie. Eventually, the elderly lady gave up and went back to her house, disheartened and sad. I became determined to find the budgie for this lady, as I thought that the budgie would be in danger and all alone. I continued to walk up and down and all around the Westcliff paths looking in bushes and listening to see if I could hear the budgie. I kept up the search for hours until I, too, became despondent and tired and I made my way home. For me, the lost budgie, even at such a young age, reminded me of my feelings of being lost, hollow and empty.

When I arrived home, I noticed two full milk bottles on the front doorstep. In an attempt to please my Mum, and with joy in my heart, I picked up the two milk bottles and pushed open the front door which was already slightly ajar. I ran down the hallway hoping to see a smiling face, thanking me for my kindness, cherishing me and appreciating me. Maybe the void and empty hole in me would flee, just like the budgie had if I impressed my mum, and she would thank me with a cuddle. Just maybe? At this tender age, I was very aware of the deep, dark feelings I had, grief for the loss of something, but not knowing what I had lost.

Suddenly, I tripped and fell. I had been running at such a speed that I flew into the air and landed on the hard, tiled floor in the hall with my whole body outstretched. My arms were fully extended and the two milk bottles smashed and broke in my hands, with the glass cutting deep into the flesh of my left hand. Blood began spurting out of my hand like a water pistol; there was a gash which took nine stitches to repair, and I still have the scar as a reminder to this day. At this moment, I became aware of the feeling of shock, a feeling I had had many times before, but on this occasion, I became aware of a feeling that was very distinct from before. Little did I realise at the time, but that feeling would become another acquaintance of mine. Shock and the experience of terror were to be my nemesis throughout my life; my Achilles heel. Of course, shock and terror also introduced me to their bedfellow, fear!

Shock, terror and fear would be the portrait of the pilgrimage that I would journey. My journey; my pilgrimage to holiness. A journey of many moments of being brutalised, and many moments of living in terror. Brutalizing my soul, brutalizing my mind, brutalizing my spirit, and brutalizing my body. Shaped, hammered, and moulded into holiness.

Leigh on Sea, Essex, UK

'Blood'

I must have been about 5 years old, and I had just come downstairs one morning. Reaching the bottom of the stairs, I turned immediately right which led directly into the living room which, in turn, led into the kitchen, both rooms separated only by glass partition doors. Straightaway, I was confronted with a scene which could have been lifted right out of an 18-rated horror movie. Only this was no movie. This was reality; the reality of my life and the trauma of my childhood experiences.

Within a few seconds, an explosion of distressing and harrowing emotions rose up inside of me, leaving me choked and stunned and frozen to the spot. Horror, repulsion and panic; I was unable to move. My feet were like lead, so extremely heavy. I felt trapped. Blood was splattered all over the glass partition doors. Keith, my mother's latest boyfriend, had his back to the worktop and my mum was in front of him. Streaks of blood were spurting out of Keith's chest onto the glass. I could see puncture wounds in Keith's chest. Blood, deep red blood, was everywhere.

I was staring at my mother's hand, which was raised high above her head, and gripped tightly in her fist was a long-bladed kitchen knife. At that moment, her head turned towards me and her eyes met mine. I could clearly see the whites of her eyes and the murderous rage in them. Her arm froze above her head, my presence stopping her from thrusting the knife downwards once more into Keith's chest. Keith turned to look at me, to see what had prompted this break in the vicious attack being inflicted on him; his eyes met mine. I didn't see fear, just defiance and loathing;

defiance towards my mum and loathing towards me. The three of us were frozen, suspended in a still moment of bizarre human deprivation and feeble humanity. I felt like I was being held in some sort of time warp; everything was motionless, floating, stagnant. I was numb, dazed, disorientated and hollow. I was a child. I was isolated and alone, and I was just a child.

I walked back up the stairs and curled up on my bed in the foetal position. I didn't dare close my eyes for fear of what images may be there; instead, I just stared into the blankness of my existence.

"Aaaaaaaaaaah!" I screamed but in total silence. My pain was silent. My familiar friends re-appeared; sadness, anxiety and fear. I cried and cried and cried.

'Sparkles'

Waking up at about five in the morning, I was excited knowing there was a small packet of fireworks downstairs. I had never seen a firework display, and I was eager to witness one first-hand. Everyone was in bed asleep, and experience had taught me that my mum would not be getting out of bed for ages. I could not hold my excitement any longer. I crept down the stairs and into the living room. On the table, there was the packet of fireworks; it was as if it was calling me by name. The anticipation was just too much and I opened the box. Its contents revealed to me a colourful fusion of various-shaped fireworks, their colours bright, exciting and enticing.

Picking out a triangular volcano-shaped firework, about five inches in length, I wondered what surprise it would reveal. Not able to contain my anticipation anymore, I took the volcano into the kitchen and searched for the matches we used to light the gas cooker. Once I found the matches, I needed to work out how to light the fuse. Should I hold it in my hand and see the flame?

Should I place it on the table? I soon realised I couldn't physically hold the firework and strike a match at the same time!

Frustrated, I noticed the fireplace in the living room. I placed the firework carefully in the middle of the fireplace pit and aimed it up the middle of the chimney. This would be fun! Aged 6, I had no idea of the mechanics of a chimney and so did not know that a chimney has an internal curve to cause the draw of smoke, or that the flue had a cap placed on the top of the chimney. Naively and innocently, I thought the chimney was a hollow tube from top to bottom with the top opening up to the sky. Eagerly, I lit the firework and stepped back.

Instantly, flashing and glittering yellow sparks spewed upwards, about eight inches high into the chimney. Wow, this was amazing! Suddenly, the volcano erupted, firing green, red, and blue fireballs up into the chimney. Fireballs were ricocheting off the draw-bend in the chimney and being re-directed into the living room. Mayhem was all around me, with the fireballs bouncing off walls and furniture. Panic-stricken, I ran around the living room dodging the discharging fireballs and desperately trying to extinguish them with a cushion. At the same time, I was trying to keep as quiet as I could.

"When will it stop? The noise will surely wake Mum up!"

Burst after burst, zoom after zoom, the fireballs flashed by me. Finally, the triangular volcano-shaped firework fizzled out.

Panicking, I quickly realised I had to act swiftly to conceal what I had done and the mess it had made. I opened the back door to get rid of the smell and threw the charred pillow out into the rubbish-filled garden. There was no way it would be noticed, camouflaged amongst the piles of rubbish. I scraped the charred black patches on the carpet and cleaned the hearth. The carpet was so old and heavily patterned that I thought I had a chance my mum would not notice the damage.

As it was, my mum didn't rise from her bed until early afternoon, and guess what? She never noticed a thing. The smell had disappeared, and I had deep-fried some bacon for my breakfast which helped to disguise the smell of the firework. The other fireworks in the box were never used and eventually joined the ever-increasing mountain of rubbish in the garden.

A close call! At least I saw a firework.

'Not my birthday party'

Although it was a private, member's only adult drinking club, I was allowed to sit downstairs on my own, on a soft chair. The room I was in was just about big enough for a small coffee table and a couple of soft chairs. The door to the room led directly onto the stairs which led up to the drinking club bar and dance floor. The date was the 24th of August, my birthday, and also my older sister Amber's birthday, although Amber was thirteen years older than me. Amber was celebrating her birthday with a party upstairs, drinking and dancing the night away. I obediently sat on my chair downstairs, totally alone, for the whole evening and into the night. From early evening, adults of all ages passed by me on their way up the stairs and into the party. Some stopped to say hello. Some asked me what I was doing sitting there, and I told them I was waiting for my mum who was upstairs at the party. I had strict instructions to sit downstairs, not to move or leave the building.

Time passed by very slowly. I know that I was there until at least four in the morning, as I recall asking some of the people what time it was as they were leaving. An older man responded by saying, "It's four in the morning and you should be in bed!"

With the innocence and naivety of a child, I did mention to some of the people that it was my birthday too, and to my delight, some, who were rather merry with drink, searched their pockets for small change and gave me a few pennies wishing me 'happy birthday'. Others just staggered down the stairs, passed by me and out of the front door as if I were invisible.

Neither my mother nor my sister ever came downstairs to check on me for the whole night. I was given no food or drink or anything to keep me amused; I just sat with my own thoughts and sadness. As I write, I can recall that as a child, I never had a birthday party. I never even received one birthday present, and I certainly never got to experience the joy of blowing out the candles on a birthday cake whilst friends and family sang 'Happy Birthday' to me.

I was always different from the other children. I carried this sadness, stigma, disgrace, shame and guilt of always being different from 'normal'. It was lonely and embarrassing to be me. My young soul endured life in the shadows of shame.

'Run Paul, Run!'

Screams; harrowing screams! Blood-curdling screams! My mum shrieked whilst standing still in the middle of the living room looking up at the unfolding scene with pure delight. Delight? Why delight? She was unable to conceal her satisfaction, her visible satisfaction, in the smirk of self-gratification spreading across her face. I turned my gaze from my mother to the scene at the top of the stairs. Thud! Thud! Thud! The sound of police batons smashing into Keith's skull. Keith was now no longer just another 'boyfriend', he was my stepdad.

Blood was pouring and spurting out of Keith's head, splattering the staircase walls and soaking his once-white shirt. A ferocious struggle was taking place between six policemen and Keith. The light on the ceiling above shone brightly on Keith's blood-soaked shirt; the red blood glistened like gloss paint. Keith stood about three-quarters of the way up the stairs, clutching the bannisters with two hands, refusing to budge. Two policemen stood on the steps above him, hammering blows onto the top of his head with their batons. The sound of each strike was dull and muffled, like the noise of a hammer smashing open a watermelon. The other two policemen were standing on the stair below Keith, hammering their batons onto his hands in an attempt to force him to let go of the bannisters. Another two policemen were trying to pull him down the stairs by his feet. Even though I was only a little boy and most men looked big to me at that age, Keith was huge, a colossus of man, as strong as three men; a rock that could not be moved. He looked down at my mum with a triumphal smile and eyes full of menace. I sensed that the chaos and terror before me had been well-orchestrated by a proficient, experienced composer; my mum! Shrewd in her performance, she shrieked in a high-pitched scream, filling the atmosphere with panic and hysteria. I reminded myself that I was awake; I was breathing, although I was gasping for air. My muscles were tight, my body felt like a lead weight, and my face grimaced, reacting to the menacing bedlam before me. I was suffocating with fear!

"Paul! Paul! Get Paula and run, get Paula and run, runnnnn!" my mum screamed at me.

I looked down at the floor in front of me and I saw Paula, my younger sister, who was about 10 months old, sitting on her bottom, wide-eyed, confused, stoic and motionless. Panic, fear and terror stopped me from moving. I was completely frozen to the spot. I tried to move; I wanted to move, but my body wouldn't respond.

My mum screamed at me again, hysterically, "Run, run! Get Paula and run!"

Willing my feet to move, I stepped towards Paula, picked her up and, cradling her in my arms, I ran. As I ran, I kept repeating over and over, "Please don't catch me, please don't catch me!"

Terror overwhelmed me. I couldn't look back; fear of being caught by Keith motivated me to run as fast as I could. The feeling of being caught at any moment was nothing less than terrifying, making me sick to my stomach. The front door to our house was open. I ran outside holding Paula in my arms. The street was dark; it was night-time. I ran into the darkness and across the road into a shop doorway. It was pitch black and I cradled Paula in my arms and crouched down in the darkness. My back was against the shop door. I felt sure no one would find us there. We were in complete darkness, about six feet away from the pavement and across the road from my house of terror. If I peeked, I could still see the front door of our house where the hall lights were on.

Peering out of the darkness and cradling Paula, I could see more police vans and police cars pulling up outside our house. A few minutes later, Keith was wrestled out of the front door. It took multiple policemen to attempt to restrain him. I could see fear in some of the policemen's eyes, and gloating brutality in others. I could hear shouting, swearing; threats from Keith to the police, "I'll kill you I will!"

Keith got his arms free from the grasp of several policemen and managed to smash his fist into the face of one of them. The policeman's two feet left the ground, and in what looked like a reverse swimming dive, he was propelled backwards into the air and landed in a jelly-like heap, unconscious. Like a ball attached to an elasticated string, the brawling huddle between Keith and the policemen extended away from the rear of the police van, then retracted back. The struggle seemed to be never-ending. Finally, Keith was wrestled into the police van and driven away. All I could hear were the sounds of Keith banging and kicking the side walls of the van and shouting, "I'm going to kill you, pigs! I'm going to kill you, pigs!"

Shock, fear and terror struck me dumb. My mouth was wide open; I couldn't seem to shut it. My eyes were fixed, glazed over by the shock of what I had just witnessed. Paula was still stoic, silent and motionless. I comforted her the best I could and she fell asleep cradled in my arms. I was sitting on my bottom in the dark, numb, feeling lost, alone and petrified. Policemen and policewomen with torches were walking up and down the road in front of me. They were going in and out of the front door of my house. I kept still and silent. Hiding and staying silent made me feel a little safer. After what seemed like an hour or so, the light from a torch began to creep towards our hiding place; the beam was coming from the direction of the footpath. Suddenly, a light shone into my face and I squinted with the pain of its brightness. I could see the silhouette of a policewoman. She was walking towards us very slowly, holding the torch at arm's length in front of her. The torch found my face. The policewoman spoke very gently to me, "It's ok, don't worry; it's ok, don't be scared, I will help you".

The policewoman gently bent over and asked me to give her Paula. I noticed that she had a police hat on; a cap. The policewoman lifted Paula from my arms and gently held out her hand to me. She reassured me by saying, "It's ok, I won't hurt you."

I reached up and took hold of her hand and we walked out into the street and the light.

Fifty years later, I returned to the same street with my wife, Lois. I was able to show her the exact spot where Paula and I had hidden, the exact house where I had experienced so much violence and felt the exact fear that I had felt fifty years previously. I was only a child.

Now, as an adult recalling this event, I have three unanswered questions: Why did my mum not take Paula to safety? Why did she not protect me and take me to safety? Why did she put all that responsibility on me?

Anglesey, Wales, UK

'Haunted house'

A massive, exceptionally old Rectory was another of our temporary homes, situated on the outskirts of a Welsh village on the Island of Anglesey, off the coast of Wales. The Rectory was positioned next to a little ancient church, which was surrounded by many neglected and overgrown graves. On the other side of the Rectory, the top of a large garden crypt protruded out of the ground, but this was a rather unusual crypt as it had steps at one end leading to the underground chamber in which the caskets were buried. The top of the crypt and the steps down were surrounded by trees, so much so that it was difficult to find unless you knew where it was situated.

The Rectory itself was very isolated, a fair distance from the village community, and the front of the house was reached by following a long driveway to the front door. A high wall, around 10 feet high, enclosed a small orchard to the right of the house, and the only way to access this orchard was through a wooden door which was permanently locked. Behind the house were old stone stables which no longer housed animals, just an assortment of various rusting garden tools. The inside of the house consisted of many rooms, all with extremely high ceilings, and as you walked through the house it felt like you were negotiating a rather strange maze. It was not a pleasant, hospitable house; to a young boy, it was a very daunting and scary place with a decidedly eerie atmosphere. We found out later that the residents of the local village believed that the house was haunted.

My mum found the story of the Rectory being haunted fascinating, and not long after we moved in, she told me, a little boy, about an experience she claimed to have had in the house. She described in great detail, a devil-like figure rising up out of the floor and appearing at the end of her bed. She said that the figure was so real and distinct to her, in the same way a person would be in daylight. She told me how she woke up in the middle of the night and saw this gruesome devil-like figure coming up out of the floor at the end of her bed. The devil was snarling and growling at her, and a green cloud began to fill the bedroom. My mum said she knew the devil-like figure wanted to hurt her. According to her, the presence of this beast stayed in the bedroom for a considerable amount of time.

Listening to this story I became so fearful, and I never felt safe in that house, especially at night-time when trying to get to sleep.

Why would any mother deliberately cause such fear in a child?

'Little Blue Piano'

A second-hand little blue toy piano about 12 inches in diameter was given to my mum to give to me for my birthday. I longed to play with this little piano. The scratches on it did not matter to me. I thought it was a wonderful toy. When we moved into the Rectory, my mum had placed the little blue piano on top of an incredibly old dusty full-size upright piano which had been left by the previous occupants. I was not allowed to touch or play with the little blue second-hand piano. So, I just sat on my bottom and stared up at it with anticipation and excitement, like a dog patiently waiting to be given a treat. Now and then, when the moment felt right, I would ask if I could play with the piano. The answer was always, "No!"

On one occasion, however, to my utter surprise, she begrudgingly agreed to let me play with it, sarcastically saying, "Alright then, you can have the bloody piano".

15

However, there was, as always, a price to pay! I first had to endure a bombardment of abuse from her, "You little shit, you nag, nag, nag. You make me ill. You make me sick. Have the fucking piano."

The little blue piano was then pushed forcibly into my hands, but instead of joy and excitement, I now felt guilt and shame; the pain was excruciating. I pressed my finger on one of the keys, but the sound only made me flinch. I couldn't deal with the thought of my mum hearing that sound; it just filled me with dread.

I never played with the little blue second-hand piano again. I could not face the shame of what I, according to my mother, made her feel like. This feeling of shame and guilt clung to my mind and body my whole life. I was a disgrace for asking to play with the little blue piano.

'Ysgol' ('School')

School! Wales! Memories of misery, loneliness, racial abuse and stigma which I endured for a whole year whilst attending school in Anglesey. I was seven years old. Lessons were taught in Welsh and only in Welsh. The school was about 500 metres from our home, the Rectory. It was a small stone building with a little tarmac space at the front and a grass play area on a slight incline at the rear of the school. All pupils of various ages within the primary age range were taught and seated in the one and only classroom that the school had. We sat behind our single-seated desks in rows facing the teacher and blackboard. At this point in my life, my skin tone was much darker than it is now, and it was obvious that I was mixed-race; I was a little mixed-race Indian boy living in a small Welsh village! I stood out like the proverbial sore thumb in this school. I was completely different in appearance to all the very white Caucasian children in my class. Coloured, black, Indian and Asian people were not so common in the UK, and especially Wales, in the 1950s and early 1960s.

Mixed-race children had a powerful racial stigma projected onto them in this era, and to be mixed-race and illegitimate was just too much for most people to tolerate. The reason for this racism was due to a cultural view, held by much of society, that it was vulgar for a white woman to have had a sexual relationship with a coloured person; an Asian person or someone of African descent. I knew, and felt from a very young age, people's utter disgust with my mum because she gave birth to me, a mixed-race child, and disgust with me, because I was, through no fault of my own, mixed-race. I experienced the revulsion in people's eyes and faces when I noticed their top lips curl up and their eyes squint slightly, sneering at me, projecting their hate and racist thoughts onto me. I understood these 'vibes' from people from early on in my experience and knowledge of life. Many times, I would overhear conversations about me, and the word 'bastard' was almost always used.

Some of the adults would have their disparaging conversations about me in my presence, speaking loudly enough and with the deliberate intention that I would hear exactly what they were saying. Others, more covertly, would whisper behind a hand, point a not-so-hidden finger or deliberately turn their back to me. I was known as the little half-caste Asian bastard; I disgusted them.

I recall, as I was growing up, that I would shrink into myself whenever I heard the word 'bastard' used as a swear word or in general terms of conversation. I hid myself. I hid the colour of my skin. I became fearful of the shame of being mixed-race and being different. I would melt into the background, fearing exposure and disgrace. I never revealed my shame of being mixed-race and a 'bastard' to anyone, and, until recently, never dealt with the effect that this had on me as a child and into adulthood.

I suffered this racist discrimination from my teacher and her assistant throughout my year's attendance at this school. They too had vile conversations about me and my 'whore of a mother'. Yes, they called my mother a whore within my earshot, and interestingly always spoke in English during these conversations, when the rest of the time they spoke almost always in Welsh! I know what they were saying about my mum was true, but it still cut me to the core, and I felt such deep shame and what I now know to be depression. On a good day, they would just refer to my mum as 'that distasteful woman living in the Rectory'! I feared each day; I was anxious every morning and frightened as I made the lonely walk to school. I never confided in anybody about the way I was treated by the teacher, her assistant, and the other children. I was deeply embedded in shame and embarrassment, and I accepted that this was the way life was going to be for me.

My mum, unlike other parents, never asked me how my day at school was, or showed any interest in my life really. I trudged to school and back each day. Every day was the same. If I had been older at the time, I probably would have run away. In fact, I know I would have run away. However, I sat each day behind my desk, compliant. I was ignored from the start of the school day until the end of the school day. I either coloured or just sat there staring into space most of the time. I wasn't able, or given the opportunity, to learn Welsh, and I sensed that the teacher was hoping we would quickly move away from the village.

At break times I would walk around the grass area on my own with my hands behind my back. No-one dared play with me; I was completely socially ostracised from the school community. My only friends were depression, melancholy and sadness. I never had the opportunity to play, I just walked around lonely and sad. Strangely, though, this did not seem odd to me; I was used to this way of life. I knew no different.

I do remember one moment of joy, one moment of recognition, in the whole year I was at this school. It was a moment that lasted for all of five minutes! Winter had come and a heavy and full downpour of snow had covered the grass playing area of the school with a foot of soft snow. At playtime, all the children ran around throwing snowballs and enjoying the snow, while I did my usual thing and played on my own. I went to the top of the play area and began to build a snowman on my own. This playtime was extended to allow us to play for longer in the snow, and I quietly got on with building my snowman. I was, as usual, ignored and not bothered by any of the other children. Eventually, I finished my creation. He was fantastic! He was as tall as me with a large round body and a smaller round head. He was such an impressive sight, and I was so proud. A twig for a nose, and small stones for eyes, mouth, and ears. I added a final touch by placing my hat on top of his head. I stood back to admire my work and a stillness emerged over the playground.

The teacher had come out into the playground to call and gather us back into the classroom. It turned out to be a timely and unique moment. The children stopped playing and turned their attention to my finished snowman. I turned to look down the slope wondering why the children had gone silent. The handbell had not yet been rung to call the end of play and return to class, and in front of me, as I looked down the hill, I was confronted with the sight of all the children smiling at my handiwork; staring at my snowman.

My teacher seemed surprised that I was able to craft something so good, and she too stood still looking at my snowman. A moment, one moment in a year of misery. A smile, one smile in a year of misery came my way.

The teacher rang the bell and noisy children filled the silence once more. I walked down the hill, sad to leave my snowman, my friend. Of course, I knew that the smile was really for the snowman, not for me, but it gave me some feeling of pleasure all the same.

'Bread of Life'

I always wanted to try and please my mum in a vain attempt to earn her love and affection, something which, sadly, I now know would never have been possible.

On one occasion, she asked me to walk to the local village shop to buy some bread. I say local, but it was a good ¾ of a mile away from our house. Although it was quite a long walk for a small child on his own, I enjoyed having the time alone to daydream with no stress or fear. Stress and fear always filled the atmosphere wherever we lived in the world, whatever house we lived in.

Skipping along in my own temporary and peaceful world, I arrived at the shop. I paused for a moment before entering the building, in order to get my courage up to ask for a loaf of bread. There were barriers to cross; it wasn't as simple as just going into a shop to buy a loaf of bread! Firstly, I didn't speak the language; Welsh was the first language of the majority of people in the village. Secondly, I knew I would face the usual attempt by the shopkeeper to hide her utter contempt for me. I was, after all, the little half-caste boy, the son of the whore who lived in the Rectory. We were the talk of the village and I knew it.

With my courage built up, and a 'you can do it' attitude in my head, I entered the shop, endured the looks, bought the bread, and began my walk home. In a carefree slow walk back along the country road, the hunger pangs in my stomach somehow seemed to know that I was carrying a loaf of bread. My walking pace slowed down, and guilt overcame me as I contemplated opening the loaf of bread and eating a slice. "Just one slice. Surely one slice would be OK?"

The hunger pangs increased, and I just couldn't wait any longer. I opened the loaf of bread and gobbled down a delicious slice of bread. Straightaway, I felt the relief from the hunger cravings in my stomach; bliss! I then ate another slice of bread, then another slice, then another and another. I found myself on the corner of the long driveway leading to the Rectory, suddenly gripped with fear, dread and guilt. I could clearly see the Rectory, but I could not move. In a vain attempt to cover up my 'crime', I tried to re-wrap the half of a loaf of bread that remained. I stood on the corner of the driveway for what must have been an hour and a half, frightened and full of guilt. I did not want to go home with only a quarter of a loaf of bread. Wide-eyed, frozen to the spot, sad and alone, I stood on the corner.

I didn't know it at the time, but this event in my life, 'the bread' event, was to become a gentle whisper in my ear. It was the beginning of a spiritual journey which, later on in my life, I would become aware of. The 'bread event' was one of the many callings, the many gentle, very gentle whisperings in my ear of a spiritual journey that I was not in sync with until a dramatic spiritual awakening event in my thirties. This spiritual awakening opened my heart to realise and know, that even as a little boy, I was known in my fear, I was known in my loneliness, I was known in my pain, and I was known in my hunger. Hunger not just in the physical sense, but for the bread of love, the food of comfort, and the satisfying full tummy of security.

Right now, however, I was standing on the corner, confused and helpless. Eventually, I came up with a plan. I would say the bread bag must have had a hole in it and that the bread fell out on my way home. I was sure this was a good explanation, and so I made my way up the driveway and into our house. Mum was nowhere to be seen. I walked around the house to find her to voice with confidence my concocted explanation, but she was nowhere to be found. She'd gone out and no doubt had forgotten that I even went to the shop. I put the bread on the side in the kitchen, and nothing was ever mentioned about the missing bread.

'Kane & Abel'

A lane next to the Rectory spiralled its way through the countryside, journeying up and over an old bridge with a fast-flowing river beneath it, to a vast expanse of farmland. At this time, my brother Mark, who was 12, older than me by five years, was living with us. For some reason, unbeknownst to me, he hated me. He was cruel and premeditated in his behaviour towards me, behaviour which could be regarded at its best as over the top, and at its worst, sadistic. At times, his behaviour towards me threatened my life. For me now, as an adult who has undergone extensive psychological therapy, I can see that my mother's psychopathic influence on his early development had damaged Mark to the core of his being.

Although I knew that Mark was always trying to get me into trouble, he was my older brother and, in a strange way, I looked up to him and wanted to please him and earn his approval.

One day, Mark invited me to go on a walk with him; nothing unusual with that, and I didn't have much else to do, so I agreed. It was a hot summer's day and the sky was bright blue, but Mark seemed to be more interested in getting to our destination than admiring the scenery, and at times I had to jog to keep up with him. Experience should have told me at that point, that he had something planned, something that would probably end up being dangerous for me! We walked down the lane near to our house until we arrived at a bridge which spanned a fast-flowing river, and the water beneath it thrashed around as it passed under.

Mark began skipping up and down the road between the two stone walls which formed the sides of the bridge, and I immediately joined in, copying the antics of my older brother. This was fun! Occasionally we would stop to look over the walls to see the rapids, twirling and bubbling as the river gushed along, looking like it was in a frenzy, hurrying to get to the other side of the bridge. I was intrigued and mesmerized by this power of nature. We started to skip again, and then, without notice, Mark abruptly stopped skipping. We were on opposite ends of the bridge, facing each other, a bit like cowboys about to embark on a quick draw showdown. We just stood still looking at each other. I did not know what to make of it; it was weird.

The look on Mark's face had changed from one of playful fun to distaste and hate, and I knew that it was directed at me. He could not hide it. A smile spread across his face, not one of joy, but a malicious, spiteful smirk. I knew this meant danger. In my mind, I needed to please him, to keep him happy, to stop anything bad happening to me. Yet again, fear was my friend.

Mark climbed onto the bridge wall to my left as I was facing him; this was the side of the bridge facing upriver. The river flowed rapidly downstream towards and under the bridge from this side. On top of the bridge wall, there was a capping made of smooth rounded concrete, about seven inches in diameter. Mark walked up and down the wall with his arms held horizontally out to each side of him, as though walking a tightrope. He had always been a good climber, and I was impressed with his ability to do this. I merely stood still, fearful and watching his every move. Then he stopped, looked down at me and said, "You try."

I didn't move; I didn't want to try! Mark continued to walk up and down the wall saying, "Look, it's easy! Come and have a go."

"No!" was all I could utter.

Mark was insistent that I have a go, and so I succumbed to his invitation. As I was quite small, in order to climb onto the wall, I had to sort of belly-flop myself over the top and I found myself staring at the rapids beneath me. I was stuck in this position for a while, my arms dangling over the bridge on the river side and my feet hanging over the road side. Mark jumped off the bridge and helped me to get up onto my feet by holding my hand. He continued to hold my hand as I walked up and down the bridge wall a few times. I was nervous; I absolutely hated heights, and still do. Somewhat ironic, I know, as years later I made a living parachuting out of aircraft!

I asked Mark to help me down, and tears began to flow down my face. He ignored my pleas, and when I was halfway along the wall, he suddenly let go of my hand.

"Do it yourself," he said.

I immediately began to lose my balance and fell off the wall feet first towards the water. For a short while, I managed to grab on to a couple of large stones sticking out of the bridge wall and shouted for Mark to help me. I clung to the stones, scared of falling into the water, but Mark just peered at me over the wall and did not attempt to rescue me.

I started to fall towards the water, my whole body outstretched vertically, my hands grazing the wall as I made my descent.

I crashed into the rapids sinking deeper and deeper, my eyes wide open. White bubbles pounded around me with an explosive noise. It was not dark, but light, as I was spun around, flipped upside down and forcibly pushed from side to side by the power of the rapids, deep under the water. I couldn't swim; not that the power of water prevented me from swimming, but I had not yet learnt to swim. It seemed like an eternity that I was under the water, being pushed in one direction until suddenly, I was flung up out of the water and onto a mud bank on the other side of the bridge further downriver. The upper part of my body lay on the mud, whilst my lower remained in the water. I lay there dazed and exhausted, all my strength depleted. I probably looked dead. Eventually, I lifted my head to look back towards the bridge and saw Mark peering at me, scrutinising me. Our eyes connected, then he just turned and walked away. He knew I could not swim. Gradually, inch by inch, I made my way up the riverbank, back to the bridge and started my walk home. Soaked, shocked and resigned to the fact that this was my life, and there was no way out of it.

'Pigs!'

We were made aware that long before we moved into the Rectory, an awful tragedy had taken place on the nearby farm which had even come to the attention of the national news. A little boy had been visiting the farm which lay just over the bridge near to the Rectory, and had been attacked, killed, and eaten by a herd of pigs. I had overheard a conversation between adults about the incident, but mainly around the issue that no-one had ever been held accountable for this tragic accident, and that there was anger that the farmer was still allowed to farm pigs. Mark knew all about this tragic news story, and he also knew how to get to the farm.

One day, after much persuading and nagging, Mark convinced me to go with him on an adventure. Our mission was to see how close we could get to the farm with the child-eating pigs! Mark and I walked down the country road, over the bridge, and down onto the riverbank. Making our way up-river, about a hundred metres along the riverbank, we came to a field and stopped. This was the point where we could see the farm, and more importantly, see the pigs. From the riverbank, the distance between myself and Mark and the pigs was about the size of two football pitches. The pigs were running free near and around the farm's barn. We could clearly see them nuzzling their noses in the ground, rolling around in the mud and grunting and snorting loudly as they foraged. They were a lot bigger than I expected; to a seven-year-old, they were gigantic-looking beasts!

My brother persuaded me to follow him so that we could get closer to the pigs, so we began walking, in pace, side by side. The field was slightly uphill, and as we got closer and closer, Mark kept reassuring me that everything was alright.

"I'm scared. I want to go back!" I whispered over and over again, each time becoming less of a whisper and more frantic.

"Keep going!" he whispered.

It seemed that the pigs were not remotely aware of, or bothered by, our impending presence. They were too distracted by eating and rolling, and doing things that pigs like to do! I, on the other hand, was absolutely terrified. I kept my focus securely fixed on the pigs, watching to see if they spotted us, so much so that I did not notice that Mark had dropped behind me. I was very close to the pigs now, these huge, aggressive beasts. I looked behind me, only to see my brother running as fast as he could back towards the riverbank, leaving me totally alone, except of course for the pigs!

I stood completely still. I did not want to disturb them or draw attention to myself; I was frozen to the spot!

Suddenly, one of the pigs looked up at me and screeched a shrieking squeal which acted as an alarm to the rest of the herd. I had startled and surprised at least 10 enormous pigs! I turned and sprinted towards the river, but my running fuelled the pigs to begin running towards me! The fear of being caught by the pigs was nauseating. All I could hear was snorting, squealing and the squelch of hooves in the mud as they galloped to catch me. They were closing in on me! I could hear them getting closer, I could feel them getting closer. I knew that if I fell or tripped, I would not have time to get up again. Feeling the hot breath of a pig on the back of my leg, I made it to the river and hurled myself down the bank and into the water. My brother was nowhere to be seen; just pigs on the riverbank like an army waiting to attack. Mark had left me to be trampled and eaten by pigs. He had led me there to die a horrible death.

I waded down the river, staying in the water until I got to the bridge. The pigs did not leave the riverbank, but thankfully, they stayed out of the water. When I got to the bridge, I climbed back up to the road and made my way home, soaking wet, tearful, and utterly alone. I knew better than to tell my mum what had happened; that would only have provoked Mark. She wasn't at home when I got there anyway, and probably wouldn't have been interested. I learnt a valid lesson that day; never, ever to trust my older brother again. But would I?

'I dare you!'

Mark and I were home alone; not exactly a recipe for success, for me at least! My mum had gone out for the day, and foolishly, yet again, I succumbed to Mark's request to play a game with him. I did not think I had a choice when I was home alone with him. He could get very cruel towards me, so I complied. The new game Mark was excited about, and introduced me to, was 'hanging out from a first-floor window'!

I followed Mark up the stairs and into Mum's bedroom. He opened the sash window. The window opened out to the front of the house, and he climbed up onto the windowsill, grabbed the ledge and lowered himself down and onto the outside of the house. He then just hung there facing the wall of the house, fully stretched out with his body vertical to the ground. A fall to the ground would mean potentially life-changing injury or death. As it was such an old building with very high ceilings, the drop from the first floor was huge. Mark hung there for five minutes then climbed back into the bedroom. "Right! It's your go," he ordered.

I hated heights and insisted that it was too dangerous for me, but with the assurance that Mark would help me and hold my hands, I rose to the challenge. Reluctantly and helplessly, I climbed onto the ledge. My bottom sat on the ledge with my feet and legs dangling on the outside of the window. Mark helped me to slowly turn and grab onto the windowsill while I lowered myself out of the window to a hanging position. I constantly pleaded with Mark not to let me go, as I lowered myself inch by inch until I was vertically outstretched and fully hanging, just holding onto the window ledge by my hands.

At that moment, when I was fully outstretched, Mark quickly lowered the sash window down onto my fingers. My fingers were clinging tightly onto the windowsill, and he pushed the window down firmly enough to stop me falling and tight enough for me to be completely trapped and hanging from the window. I soon realised that he had left the bedroom because he did not answer my cries for help. I hung on the outside of the wall with my face and body pressed against the wall. I was sobbing and whimpering. The pain in my hands and fingers was immense, and at some point, I must have slipped into unconsciousness. I came to, shocked and disorientated, as I was dragged up from the outside of the house wall by Keith and laid on my mum's bed. I was awake but my hands had no feeling in them, and I began to open and close my fingers to help the circulation flow again.

After a little rest, I got up and went downstairs to get myself something to eat. The 'window' event was never discussed. I never knew if Mark was punished. The only time the 'window' event was talked about was many years later in a conversation I had with my mum when she asked me if I remembered it. I said I did and that was the end of that conversation. Never mentioned again.

'Garden of Eden'

It was around 9 o'clock at night and, true to form, my mum had gone out for the night. Mark, my brother, had cajoled me into following him outside and into a high-walled orchard which was located next to our house. I recall that the sky was clear and very dark that night, with many constellations visible. Mark led me, without speaking, to the far end of the orchard, and then, without warning, he turned and ran swiftly to the only gate that led in and out of the orchard. He slammed the gate shut, locked it from the outside and ran away. I was completely trapped! The walls surrounding the orchard were made of Welsh stone and were about eight feet high. The gate, which was the same height as the walls, was made of solid wood and impenetrable. My eyes, which had by now adapted to the darkness, scoured the area in the vain hope that there might just be another way out.

The darkness and quietness were haunting, and I turned to run towards the gate, shouting for help as I ran. I banged repeatedly on the gate, pleading for my brother to come back and let me out, all the time petrified that something, someone, would come out of the darkness and hurt me. I didn't dare turn my head around to see if it was safe; instead, I just kept banging on the gate, shouting, crying and sobbing with fear. I was just a child. Eventually, I accepted that no-one was going to come for me; no-one was going to rescue me. I turned around to face the darkness and eeriness of the orchard; tall trees loomed high above me appearing dark and creepy in the gloomy ambience of night. I've no idea how long I sat with my back against that gate, alone and terrified, falling in and out of sleep, utterly engulfed by fear.

At the time, I had rarely been inside a church, only to attend my mum's many weddings; sadly, bigamy was another of her 'traits'. On this night, however, I found myself walking around the orchard in the dark, and one of the few Bible stories that I knew from school, was the story of Adam and Eve. As I walked around in the darkness, the story began to unravel in my mind. I saw Adam and Eve in amongst the foliage. I saw the temptation between them. I saw God speaking to them. I knew this was God, and the experience I was having was real to me, but I had no idea about the Bible, faith or the church. This experience just became part of my memory. It was real and it happened. Weird? Maybe, but I remember the bright colours of the scene and the authenticity of my interaction with this event.

While I recount and write about my experience and fear in the orchard, I have come to realise and know in my heart that God was with me in my fear, comforting me, keeping my mind occupied with the story of Adam and Eve!

Eventually, I couldn't hold sleep back and woke up in the morning light of daybreak. Still locked in the orchard; still alone.

My mum eventually came and unlocked the gate, and I was able to leave the orchard and the Garden of Eden story. Well, not leave the story, but continue to walk forward in life in my journey. There was no cuddle of reassurance from my mum, no shock from her at the realisation that her young child had spent all night alone, outside in a locked orchard; no recognition that her actions, staying out all night and leaving me with Mark, had caused such trauma and suffering for me. To her, I sensed it was no big deal; to me, it was damaging.

Now, as an adult, seeing things through the eyes of someone who has, in therapy, processed many traumas and come out the other side, I do believe that this experience in the orchard was part of the ongoing call on my life from God.

Also, this experience was to be a mirror of the consequences for me of the way in which my mum chose to live her life, and the influence and effect that that had on my life going forward. Trauma became my menacing, malignant and cancerous existence for many more decades of my life.

'Someone's watching over me'

As a child, I rarely had baths; it wasn't high on the list of priorities for my mother! While we lived in the Rectory on the Island of Anglesey, on the rare occasions that I was given a bath, it was usually outside in a grey tin bath. Once or twice, I can recall having a bath inside in the large bathroom which was in much need of repair and decoration. Various pipes and electric wires were visible all around the bathroom, revealed in between the many broken floorboards.

On this particular day, I entered the bathroom and noticed an old rusty mobile gas fire was lit and the smell of gas was strong. My mother had run a bath for me, and taking off my clothes, I got into the rather cool water. I tried to warm the water up by turning the hot tap on, but this was unsuccessful; only cold water came out of the hot tap! I sat in the bath and an eerie feeling came over me. I was used to this eerie feeling in my life; it usually came over me when I sensed and perceived something bad was going to happen to me. I felt frightened in the bathroom. I got out of the bath and put a large towel around me, holding the towel over my shoulders as I walked down the stairs and into the front room.

Just as I sat down on the rug, I heard a loud 'bang', and the house seemed to physically shake. I just sat still on the carpet, not really knowing what to do. I heard my mum run upstairs to investigate; at that stage, she didn't know that I was downstairs! Being inquisitive, I made my way up the stairs to the door of the bathroom and, peering in, I could see that the whole bathroom was destroyed; everything was twisted and burnt. The porcelain sink had shattered and was all over the floor in numerous bits.

The gas fire was now just a mound of mangled metal laying all around the bathroom, and an enormous hole was in the wall that the gas fire had been close to, and there was another huge hole in the ceiling above. The smell of the burnt bathroom was overbearing. Amazingly, the bath was intact with just chunks of the top edge of the bath blown off. There were no flames as the force of the blast had blown out the fire at the same time. I looked at Mum and she looked at me. Our eyes connected but she did not seem too upset. I struggled to comprehend what had happened and what could have happened had I stayed in the bath. I really did not know how I should be feeling, but what I did know was that the explosion would have killed me. I went back downstairs to the front room and laid on the rug, curled up in my towel. I assumed the foetal position and fell asleep.

Years later, I wondered if the explosion in the bathroom was purely due to my mum's incompetence and neglect, not keeping me safe by using an old dodgy, rusty gas fire, or if there was something darker at play with regards to me and my life.

'Ceiling Collapse'

The reception room in the Rectory had high ceilings, tall skirting boards and crumbling sculptured coving covering the area where ceiling and wall met. Sitting on the floor on the round worn-out rug in the middle of the room, I stared out of the window, daydreaming, content in my own world of thoughts. This was something I did regularly, to escape my surroundings and the mistreatment I suffered at the hands of my mum and brother. Out of the blue, I became aware of a somewhat eerie sensation, disturbing, frightening and not part of my thoughts or dreams. It was an overwhelming sense that something bad was about to happen. I had come to realize, at a young age, that I became aware of trouble happening before it happened. Now, as an adult and after three years of therapy, I have come to understand that this 'awareness' was extreme hypervigilance; having lived in an environment of fear and abuse, I always needed to check my environment to see if it was safe.

The eerie sensation persisted. I got up off the carpet and made my way through the house to the doorway of the kitchen. There wasn't actually a door to the kitchen, just an open doorway. I stood in the doorway and saw that my mum was cooking something on the old gas cooker located on the far side of the kitchen; I suppose she was about five metres away from me. Her back was to me and she could not see me, so I shouted, "Mum!"

She did not hear me, so again I shouted, "Mum!"

She still did not hear me. On my third attempt, she turned her head towards me and then immediately turned back to what she was doing, responding only with the instruction, "Go away!"

For some weird reason, I didn't go away; I needed to get my mum to come to me. I shouted louder and louder, attempting to be so annoying that she would leave what she was doing and come to me. Tersely, and with obvious annoyance, she turned around. She walked briskly towards me with a gait that told me I was in for it! I stepped back a few paces from the doorway, backing away from the threat coming my way. Mum was two steps away from the doorway when there was a deafening crash; the kitchen ceiling had completely collapsed and fallen onto the floor of the kitchen, and dust and debris were everywhere. My mum had been hit with what looked like a piece of concrete debris on the back of her lower leg, slicing into her calf and forming a couple of deep wounds. Blood started to flow down her leg, but she was still able to walk, and other than the leg wounds, seemed OK. When the dust settled, we were able to investigate the damage to the kitchen; it was a complete mess. The gas stove, which my mum had been cooking on seconds before the collapse, was completely crushed into a V shape. She would have been killed instantly, and if I had not stayed in the doorway, I too would have been killed.

'Return to Anglesey'

In 2006, Lois and I and one of our children visited Anglesey whilst on a family holiday in Wales. I was keen to know if the Rectory was still there and if I could remember how to find it. To my surprise, the Rectory was still standing and had not changed at all. We stood at the end of the long drive, debating whether we should go and knock on the front door, when a man walked towards us. He asked us if we needed something, or if we were looking for someone, and I explained that, as a child, I had spent time living in the Rectory.

Immediately, he said he remembered my family, and that he was relieved to see that I was alive. As that was a rather strange comment to make, I asked him why he thought that I might be dead. He told us that the rumour in the village was that because we all disappeared overnight, we had all been killed. He had half expected to find our skeletons buried somewhere in the garden!

The truth of the matter was that we had done another 'midnight flit'! We had emigrated to Canada.

London, Ontario, Canada

'Strangled'

Instantly, like a spring retracting, I sat upright in bed, waking from my sleep stupor. Before I could open my gunged-up eyes, I sensed an eerie, sinister and unnerving aura in the darkness. I could hear a gurgling sound, a sound like a toilet had just been flushed and was semi-blocked. The sound became louder and louder. A light was on in the hall; I could see the yellow strip of light peeking under the bottom of my door. "What on earth is that strange noise?" I muttered to myself, as I slowly crept towards the door and opened it.

Slowly, leaning forward with only my head extending out into the hall, I looked towards what I believed to be the source of the sound. I could see right into my mother's bedroom. A sense of horror flooded over me, and my stomach immediately began to heave. The door to my mum's room was wide open and the light was on. Keith was strangling my mum. He was on top of my mum, on his knees, straddling her with one knee on either side of her torso. Leaning forward with both of his hands wrapped around my mum's throat, he was crushing the breath of life out of her. Her arms flopped lifelessly. Mum's left arm hung over the side of the bed, nearly touching the floor, limp; her seemingly lifeless right arm had flopped onto the right side of her body on the bed. To me, she looked dead. I could still hear the peculiar gurgling sound; it was becoming fainter now, fading. I screamed, "Mummmm!" Keith turned his head and looked venomously, as he had done many times before, straight into my eyes. It was obvious there was murder in his eyes; heartlessness, mercilessness, he was in a rage and beyond rational thought. Without thinking, I switched from being an observer to entering the bedroom of revulsion. I jumped onto the bed and onto Keith's back and started hitting him, punching him, shouting and screaming, "Leave her alone! Get off her! Get off her!"

Keith kept his left hand locked around my mum's throat, and at the same time, turned his head and body to the right to look at me on his back. With his right hand, he grabbed me by the throat, squeezed his fingers together and lifted me off his back and into the air. I hung in the air held up by his single hand around my throat, with my legs and arms dangling helplessly. Keith bent his right arm as if preparing to throw a shot putt and threw me out of the bedroom door and onto the landing. I smashed onto the floor, dazed and gasping for air. I must have been thrown about ten feet. I lay on my back, motionless and unable to move. Disorientated, I gathered myself together and ran down the stairs, fumbling with the door handle in a panic to open the front door. I was totally terrified. Was Keith coming after me? I couldn't open the door. Finally, with a mixture of adrenaline and horror filling my body and mind, I managed to open the door and run out of my house. I sprinted to a neighbour's house and banged repeatedly on their front door, shouting and screaming for help. Lights went on behind their front door, and the door was opened by a man I knew; his name was Jim. He and his family had immigrated to Canada on the same ship as us. I ran inside their house shouting and screaming, "Keith is killing my mum! Keith is killing my mum!"

Jim and I both ran from his house into mine, up the stairs and into my mum's bedroom. Jim wrapped his left arm around Keith's neck and tried to pull Keith off my mum, but Keith was too strong. He continued to strangle her. I kept shouting at Keith, begging him to leave her alone and to stop. Thankfully, Jim's wife had called the police, and eventually, they managed to drag Keith off my mum.

I watched her being put onto a stretcher and taken to hospital in an ambulance. Jim and his family invited me to stay with them at their house. I have no recollection as to where Paula or my other siblings were at that time; I just know they weren't in the house.

A few days later, I was asked to visit my mum in hospital to encourage her to get better as I was told she had said she wanted to die. I sat by her bed and talked to her for many, many hours over many, many days, trying to encourage and convince her to live. I just wept and wept, begging her to live. This was my life, always.

'Shotgun'

"Just stand there and look at the end of the road to see if Keith is coming!"

"Why, Mum?"

"Because he is coming with a shotgun to kill us."

My mother then calmly walked away from me and into the other room.

"Mum, Mum, where are you going? Please Mum; don't leave me here. Mum!"

"Shut up; stand there and tell me when you see Keith's car coming."

"But Mum!"

"Shut up! I'm going to phone the police."

My mother casually walked out of the living room and left me completely on my own.

The living room of this house had a large window which looked out over a wide-open and flat piece of wasteland. The turning into our road was about 500m from our estate, the Cascade Estate, and it was possible to see cars turning into the estate from our window.

Alone in the living room, my left hand was gripping and squeezing the arm of a chair and my right hand was covering my mouth. I stared out of the window and waited for the sight of Keith's car turning into our road. I really needed the toilet; I wanted to poo and I didn't know if I could hold it in! Tears trickled down my face; I was panic-stricken and frightened. I couldn't move. I couldn't move my feet. I did not want to move in case I missed Keith's car. I didn't want to let my mum down; I must not let my mum down. I forced myself to stop the tears leaking out of my eyes and down my face. I just stood there, waiting, watching, staring and completely alone. Time passed very slowly; had it been 10 minutes? Felt like ten hours. My Mum popped her head into the living room for a few seconds just to ask me if I'd seen anything yet, and then disappeared again. I shouted out as she was leaving the room, "Mum, should we run?"

Her response was clear; "No! Stay there! Keep watching!"

Fear overwhelmed me; dread filled my body and my thoughts; again, I was frozen. I knew what Keith was capable of, and I knew that he would not hesitate in shooting my Mum or me. I wanted to run; I so desperately wanted to run, but I do as I am told - I follow orders.

There was no sign of Keith's car, and I could hear my mum on the 'phone pleading with the police to hurry because Keith was coming to shoot us. Mum's voice went silent, and I heard the front door open. The house was quiet; I was on my own. I had no idea where she'd gone, I just knew she was not here. I had an overwhelming urge to cry out, shout out, scream out, but I was not able to. Fear had frozen my voice box. Silently, inwardly, my whole being was screaming, "Somebody, please help me! Help, help, help me! I do not want to be shot. I'm just a child!"

I was still standing in the same place in the living room, petrified I might have missed Keith's car; I had not moved.

As quickly as she went out, my mum returned and came into the living room where I was still standing on duty. "Mum, Mum, what's happening?"

"Don't worry, the police stopped him way before he reached our road." Her response was carefree and unconcerned.

As I write this and recall that event, I just want to shout, "WHY? WHY? WHY DID SHE DO THIS TO ME?" To question, "Mum, were you using me again? Did you induce all that fear in me? Did you make me experience such terror and dread so that I could tell the police how scared I was?" To confront her, "You did! You inflicted pain and fear on me so you could use me to have Keith put in jail!"

I did tell the police how scared I was, but I didn't implicate my mother. For many weeks and months after this event, I constantly stared in the distance at the road where it turned into our estate, still worrying, still imagining Keith coming to shoot me.

'Wimber'

As a young child, I remember some of the many adults who frequented our house and watched the news on our black and white TV. They would shout and swear at the TV and make disparaging comments about the people in the news. I felt greatly disturbed by their gossip and hate-filled venom, and it saddened my heart. I remember getting so angry with them once that I foolishly interrupted some adults. They were all standing in the front room, running down a person in the news, having just finished criticising one of their friends who had been caught by the police. I, too, had been listening to the news and their conversation. I angrily interrupted and told the adults, "There must be a reason why people do these things! Something must make them do it! Maybe it is not their fault?"

I stood still; a silence came over the room and everyone looked right at me. Every person disregarded my comments, including my mum. I felt guilty and alone and went outside and into the woods for solitude.

Around this time, I was sitting on my own in the front room. The TV was on, although I was not watching it until I heard a man begin to speak. He was being interviewed on a talk show, and I got up off the carpet and stood in front of the TV to listen. For some reason, I was intrigued by him. I stood listening to him for ages; I was mesmerized! I do not remember a lot of what he said but it was a significant and profound moment in my young life. Years later, I recognised that the man was John Wimber. John Wimber had had an enormous influence on the Christian Charismatic Movement and revival in the 1980s and his ministry is still influential to this day. I believe I was drawn to John Wimber on the TV, at that noticeably young age, because of a spiritual connection, but at the time, had no idea why and what this connection was.

'A kind smile'

I have various periods of amnesia and a sense of being lost in a world of chaos throughout the primary school phase of my life. Although, from the recollections I have, loneliness is a recurring theme. When I was about eight years old, I attended a school in London, Ontario, just for a few months. We were living in a house which was about seven miles from the nearest primary school. I had no friends at this school; I never had time to make friends in schools or neighbourhoods because we moved house, town or country with an alarming frequency. Most of the moves were so that my mum could avoid a court hearing, arrest or some other less formal consequence of her fraudulent/illegal activities.

Despite having no friends, I have positive memories of this school. I really liked the teacher and she seemed to like me, so my time in her classroom felt safe. She often smiled at me and reassured me. Having moved schools so frequently, I could not do the same work as the other students, such as maths and writing, so she let me colour. She would gently and unobtrusively, so as not to draw attention to my academic inabilities, give me some of her time. She tried to get me started on reading, something that no other teacher before her had even bothered to try, and I adored her and cherished the morsels of time she gave to me. This was the only time, during my school life, that I can recall not being fearful of being asked questions in class as, inevitably, I would not know the answers. She never put me in that position.

Filled with enthusiasm, I got myself up in the mornings and began the long walk to school. Although more than 3 miles long, the walk was easy to navigate because it was a straight walk along a busy 'A' road with just one turn into a housing estate where the school was situated. After school, I repeated the walk, but this time made various detours in and out of shops in the shopping mall, to deliberately delay getting home. I didn't always go to school; if my mum was having a 'bad' day, I would be obliged to stay home and take care of her. I would make her endless cups of tea and sandwiches, while she lay in bed, apparently depressed. I was fully aware, however, that the real reason was that she had only come home in the early hours of the morning after a night of partying! She either had a hangover, or she was too tired to get herself up for the day.

One day, on my walk to school, I was walking on the pavement minding my own business, when my teacher pulled up beside me in her car. She leaned across from the driving seat and opened the passenger door. I looked into the car and saw her big smile and her big round glasses enhancing her soft and kind eyes. I hesitated and stood still. "Paul, would you like a lift to school?" she asked whilst leaning over so I could see her, and she could see me. I got into the car and she drove me to school. We did not talk as I think she did not want to overwhelm me with questions, but I sensed that she understood that life was difficult for me. Unfortunately, we moved house again soon after, and I missed so much this person who had shown real care and concern towards me, although it was at a distance.

'Humiliation'

For some reason, my mum found it enjoyable and funny to deliberately humiliate me. I remember on one occasion; I was playing outside in a communal grassy area at the back of one of the houses we lived in when Mum called me to come into the house. Amber, my older sister and one of her boyfriends were standing beside my mum laughing and giggling at me, as I stood on the backdoor step looking at them.

"What is it, Mum? What do you want?" I asked.

The three of them were lined up in front of me, standing side by side and facing me. They looked like they were hiding something behind them. Still giggling, they stepped aside from each other and looked in the direction of the kitchen. I looked to see what they were looking at and I saw a sanitary towel hanging from the top of the kitchen door. At the time, I didn't know what it was, but I could see it was covered in deep red liquid which was dripping onto the tiled floor. The three of them, Mum, Amber and her boyfriend, broke into hysterics. I walked up to the sanitary towel and asked what it was. This made them laugh even more hysterically, which added to my confusion and subsequent humiliation. I had an idea the sanitary towel was something that women used, but I did not know what it was for. As I approached it, I noticed it was covered in what I thought was blood, and I felt sick to my stomach. The three of them by this point were laughing uncontrollably, staring at me, then looking towards the sanitary towel, then back to me. I was totally confused.

I went upstairs to get away from the humiliation of the three of them laughing at me, and when I came downstairs some hours later, Amber and her boyfriend had gone and the 'soiled' sanitary towel had been thrown in the bin.

The next day, I asked my mum about it and whose blood was on the towel. Her response was short and sweet, "Don't be stupid, it was ketchup!"

It was only when I was much older that I realised what a sanitary towel was, and what it was used for. This may seem like a rather strange story to recount, but it exemplifies the bizarre and somewhat disturbing and childish behaviour of my mother and what I was constantly subjected to by my only parent.

The consequences for me of being subjected to utter humiliation by three adults left a deep scar of loneliness which I've carried all my life.

'Gouge his eyes out!'

It was about 1.00 am, and numerous adults of varying ages had been arriving at my mum's party since about 8.00 pm. Young, trendily dressed men and women, middle-aged men and women, people from a diversity of backgrounds. All were coming for the same thrill - the excitement of an 'adult' party. We had been living at this location for a few months now, a large bungalow in Suburbia, London, Ontario. Our sojourn there wasn't to last much longer. Loud music blasted up the stairs from the basement; the front door was wide open, and all the lights in the house were on. Cars continually pulled up and parked outside, eventually filling the whole street. I, a child, sat in the kitchen on a stool and watched the flow of people continuously walking through our front door and into the basement as if lured by the sound of the music. Occasionally, someone would notice me, but only to ask me where they should go.

Things changed when three very tall, well-built, rough and scary-looking men walked into the house, had a whispered conversation between themselves and walked down the stairs to the basement party. I was curious, and quietly followed them down the stairs. It was an exceptionally large, long room, which had been decorated, carpeted and furnished with chairs and couches all around the perimeter. I stopped my descent a few feet away from the bottom of the stairs, far enough down to give me a view of what was going on, but not so far that my presence was obvious. I leaned my back against the wall; I was in the basement; I was at the party. Music was blasting loudly. The room was packed with adults dancing, smoking and drinking. People were kissing and, blatantly, without any sense of shame at all, indulging in sex on the couches and chairs.

The three noticeably tall men mingled with the people on the dance floor; however, their demeanour was not one of pleasure, but of threat and menace. Without warning, the trio began hitting and punching people who were within their reach. Chaos erupted all around me. I was scared, frozen to the spot with my back glued to the wall behind me. People were screaming, panicking and running to get up the basement stairs and out of the bungalow. My eyes were wide open, as was my mouth as the scene unfolded in front of me. A man, a small man, who I knew to be one of my mother's many boyfriends at the time, attempted to attack one of the aggressors by jumping on his back. In an instant, the noticeably larger man reached over his back, grabbed my mother's boyfriend by the hair and threw him over his shoulder onto the floor in front of him, leaving him dazed, helpless and on his knees. The large man then grabbed the smaller man's head with both hands, put his right thumb into the small man's eye and squeezed his left eye out of its socket. Screaming and screaming, the small man fell to the floor, curled up into the foetal position and did not move. These men were professionals, too big and too strong for anyone. I hadn't moved from my spot at the bottom of the stairs. I couldn't move. I wanted to move; I wanted to get away from the images in front of me, but I couldn't.

By now, people were hysterical, fighting to get up the basement stairs and out of the bungalow. Time seemed to have stopped. Slowly, I walked up the stairs and out the front door. I stood there taking in the scene; police cars, people screaming and crying, ambulances arriving. It was dark outside, and I stood under the faint light of a streetlight. I was still, silent, quiet, shocked. No-one came to me; no-one comforted me.

Eventually, I made my way back into the house and to bed, not wanting to close my eyes for fear of what I might see.

The next day, I asked my mum about her friend, and why the men did that to him. Emotionless, she just fobbed me off saying that Keith sent them around. I wanted to know how he was, the man who had his eye gouged out; I was so, so sad for him because he was actually a nice man, one of my mother's many boyfriends that I actually liked. My mum didn't answer me, just asked me if I saw it happen. I told her I did. She ignored me. At that point, I realized that that man was hurt and damaged for life because he knew my mother and she didn't care.

For many years, and even today, I feel a sense of guilt about the man losing his eye, a sense of unfairness and injustice for a kind man. A sense of outrage for him.

'Goal!'

Throughout my life, wherever I've lived, I have carted around with me two trophies, both won by me for playing football! For some reason though, I only have one memory of playing football, although I must have played countless matches. I can clearly remember scoring a goal; it was the winning goal and it won my team not only that match but the championship! I remember dribbling the ball around four or five players on the opposite team until I was in front of their goalie, about three feet away from him. I popped the ball past him and into the right side of the goal. GOAL! One of the trophies was a team prize, for winning the championship, and the other was an individual prize awarded to me, for scoring the most goals that season. Although I have always known, because of the trophy, that I had scored the most goals that season, I can only remember scoring that one goal. I cannot remember anything else of that football season, just that!

I do, however, remember the presentation evening. My coach had told me that I had to attend the presentation. At that point, I was totally unaware that I had won a prize! If my coach hadn't insisted that I attend, I know I would not have gone, as my family didn't do that sort of thing. Indeed, the thought of attending the presentation filled me with fear and dread. What if my mum wanted to come? How would she dress? How would she behave? What if she didn't want to come? Would I be happy to go on my own?

The decision was made for me, as my mum told me, not surprisingly, that she wouldn't be going and that I must go on my own.

I had suffered an injury in-between the end of the season and the presentation evening, and my right leg, from below the knee downwards, was in a hard cast which meant I had to walk with the help of crutches. I made my way to the presentation evening, on my own and on my crutches. My coach sat me at the top table, and a large audience of adults and children were sat in neat rows in front of us. I hated sitting at the top table. I felt very exposed, like everybody was looking directly at me. I was awarded, along with my teammates, a small trophy for winning the championship, and I felt very proud to be part of the team. Then, my coach started telling everyone what an outstanding season I had had, and that I was the top goal scorer that season. This was unbearable for me. I was confused, embarrassed and, for some reason, I felt ashamed. As soon as the trophy was presented to me, I had an overwhelming need to get out of the venue; looking back now I would say that I had some sort of panic attack. I could not stand the crowd and the praise, so I left and hobbled home on my crutches. Both trophies were inscribed with the surname that my mum was using at that time. I had so many surnames at different stages of my childhood that I never really had a clear identity!

Pembroke, Ontario, Canada.

'Toilet Roll Flag!'

"Hurry! Hurry! Pack anything you want to take, but just hurry!" Agitated and flustered, the contagious panic in my mum's voice grasped hold of me once again. Here we go again! On the run, having to disappear yet again. My heart sank once more, and sadness and melancholy overshadowed me. Outside was a U-Haul trailer attached to our old banger of a car.

Swiftly, the trailer was packed, and we were on the road. Destination: Pembroke, Ontario. This was going to be a day's journey. We were driving on the highway and passed the city of Toronto. I was sitting on the back seat of the car, the only one of my siblings who had been entrusted to the care of my mum at the time. I looked in the driver's rear-view mirror and saw a scene which summed up everything about my life perfectly. Flying high behind us was a symbol of my life, an emblem, a flag soaring high above the road in the slipstream of our car. Out of the top of the U-Haul trailer tailgate, a long white flag of toilet roll waved at all the cars on the road. The toilet roll was swaying from side to side, up and down, dancing in the wind, rising and falling above the trailer. The toilet roll had unrolled itself to about 15 feet in length. I shouted, in a tone mixed with humour, cynicism and despair to my mum, "Look! It's our flag flying". We shared a rare moment of joy together, as we laughed and laughed at the sight of the toilet roll. This was the flag that symbolised our lives. This toilet roll flag proved to be true time and time again throughout my life.

Eventually, we arrived in Pembroke. Mum had already pre-arranged for us to stay with a family, but this family was rather peculiar and different. The mother of this family was one of my mum's latest friends. I can't remember if everyone who lived in the house was actually a member of the same family, but the house was filled with young adults and teenagers. This was a family that today would probably be labelled as underclass and dysfunctional. I particularly remember a young male adult who dressed in women's clothing and had very blond bleached hair. He was always practising his impersonations of glamourous Hollywood actresses and singers. I asked him why he did this, and he told me that he liked to enter talent shows. I had never seen anyone like this before, and as a small boy, I remember feeling confused and somewhat guarded in his presence.

Attached to their house was a large shed-like building with mattresses inside. The young adults and teenagers spent most of the day going in and out of this shed. This shed, however, was where I was made to sleep at night, totally on my own. I slept on one of the three old mattresses on the floor, and there was a hook on the door to lock it. I made sure I locked the door every night, and lay in the dark and cold, but felt somewhat safe knowing that that the door was 'locked'. In reality, the simple hook would not have afforded any protection against unwanted guests, but as a scared naive child, it gave me comfort.

I noticed there were many visits to this house by some dubious-looking acquaintances of the family. We had only been in Pembroke and living with this family for a few weeks when my mum attempted to commit suicide. She was taken to hospital and I was left to live with this strange family and their even stranger acquaintances.

After a few days in hospital, I was asked by the hospital doctors, yet again, to go into the hospital to see her and talk to her. For the second time in my short life, I was having to try and persuade my mum to consider living, to convince her that life was worth living and not to give up. Obligingly, and out of duty, I did as I was asked. I sat by her bedside talking to her and encouraging her for a few days. She lay very still, and she seemed deeply, deeply depressed. She looked terribly ill.

Eventually, my mum returned to our 'home', and life, according to our family insignia, that is, the toilet roll flag, carried on. This was a life spent witnessing my mum manipulate everyone; friends, doctors, welfare officers, boyfriends, her family and me. I realise now, today, in 2020, that my mum's attempted suicide was probably to persuade the Pembroke Welfare Office to give us, my family, a house to live in.

'Bedtime Rats'

Very soon after mum came home, we were given an incredibly old house to live in. The house was grey on the outside and there was a lot of scrap metal in the garden. Rats ran freely around, both outside and inside the house. Whilst we were living in Pembroke, Paula, my youngest sibling, returned to live with us.

The house was a detached, incredibly old wooden structure, made from upright two-by-four planks of wood nailed together at a vertical angle, the same way a boundary fence is constructed. There was no cavity wall to separate the inside from the outside of the house. It looked like a shack that an African American family might have lived in, in a poor Southern State a hundred or so years ago.

During our time living in this particular house, I was only too aware of the sordid relationship that my mum was having with the head of the Welfare Department in Pembroke. I remember that he was a rather short man, with a large round stomach, and his greasy hair sported the ubiquitous 'comb-over' of a man of his age, desperately trying to cover his bald patch. Whenever he and I bumped into each other, his attempt to smile at me did not betray his true feelings, and it was clear he really just wanted to say, 'Get out of my sight, you little shit!' I knew he didn't want to be confronted during his disgusting, sleazy visits to my mother.

Throughout the short time we lived in this house (shack), I slept on a mattress on the floor, but at least I had my own bedroom. Sleep was difficult because of the rats; the countless rats. At night-time, in the darkness, I would lay awake on my mattress just staring at the ceiling, trying desperately to fall asleep. It was impossible. The rats would begin scurrying around the perimeter of the house as soon as it became dark, and I could hear them through the wooden walls. They had no fear, and after a few minutes, they would begin to enter the house through nooks and small holes they had chewed and created over time.

In the early days of living in this house, I would lie awake on my mattress and turn the light on. Even with the lights on, though, the rats would still scurry around, afraid of nothing. When they came close to my mattress, I would attempt to scare them away by banging a long stick near them. It is interesting, and somewhat sad, how a young boy can adapt and get used to his surroundings. Eventually, despite the rats, I would get so tired that I would just fall asleep. I always woke up when the rats ventured to scuttle over my body, and at times, dash around my head! To me, some of the rats were the size of a cat!

I decided that I needed to come up with a plan to rid our house, and my bedroom, of the rats. Naively, I thought I could shoot them all, and I set about carefully putting my plan in place. I had a high velocity .22 pellet gun. It was one of the strongest pellet guns around at the time, and it was a very handy implement for someone who lived in a rat-infested house. My plan was concocted, now all I needed to do was carry out my mission!

Each morning, at around 2 am, I would hear the sound of the rats beginning their night-time escapades in my room. As soon as the scurrying intensified, I would switch on the light and begin shooting at the startled rats. Some of them would be stunned by the light for a second, and this gave me the chance to get a good shot. Some of the rats would be defiant and keep running around even though they were in full view. Later that morning, I would collect, and throw onto the garden rubbish heap, the carcasses of the two or three rats that I had killed the night before.

This way of living didn't bother me; I just accepted our living conditions, as I had no other choice. We were not part of any community; we were always on the outside, on the edge of society. The embarrassment and shame that I constantly felt was, in reality, my mother's shame which I internalised. We were weird; different to any other family that I came into contact with.

'Pam's Parties'

My mum was the queen of 'adult' parties. Her outfit of choice for these debauched gatherings was a very tight-fitting catsuit, which left nothing to the imagination. She also always wore a cat ears headband to compliment her outfit! At many of these gatherings, my mum was the only female in a room full of men. Not all the parties were men only, but many of them were. Bizarrely, the content of the party was, for the most part, very corny, consisting of silly games involving water. People would end up being absolutely soaked with water in the house. My mum enjoying pushing the men with childish antics and teasing them. The men did nothing to retaliate; it seemed the sight of my mum in her catsuit seemed to indulge their pleasure. I preferred to stay in my bedroom while these antics were going on.

On one occasion, I decided to creep downstairs to see what exactly was going on. What I witnessed was crazy! My mum caught me observing what was going on, and instead of sending me back to my room with a 'thick ear', she made me join in with one of her silly games. I told her I did not want to, but she insisted. I had to sit down in the middle of a line of adults on the floor while they threw water over their heads and onto the person behind. I got soaked, and as soon as I could, ran upstairs to my room. Debauchery describes these parties; shame describes my inner soul.

One early morning about 5.00 am, I made my way downstairs and Mum was sitting in the front room surrounded by several Marines in uniform. They all looked fit and strong with their noticeably short regulation haircuts. Mum looked straight at me, and I could see that she was furious that I had come downstairs at that particular moment. It was obvious that the Marines weren't expecting a young boy to walk in on their gathering, and as I made my way back upstairs, I heard them saying that they needed to leave. I have no idea what I disturbed, but it was sure to be something perverse, something sexual, or maybe Mum just got a kick out of leading the Marines on. Yet again, it was I who felt the shame, humiliation and embarrassment, not my mother!

'Hatred'

It was wintertime in Pembroke, and when I could be bothered to, I would catch a yellow bus at the end of our drive to a small country school. I was very much aware that the headteacher at this particular school did not like me at all. She was an older lady, with short grey hair and glasses. She did not like my mum and did not hold back from overtly showing her utter contempt for both my mum and me. I was the only mixed-race child in the class, and whilst my ethnicity obviously made the headteacher uncomfortable, the main object of her repugnance was my mother. My mum's reputation very quickly became renowned in the small hunting town of Pembroke. My mum's shame became my shame; I carried the shame that she was either blissfully unaware of or too arrogant to care about. I suspect the latter was the truth. I clearly sensed the headteacher thought I was a bad influence in the school, although I never did anything to justify why she should feel this way about me. She made me feel like I was infecting the school, like I was a disease. Nevertheless, the sneers on her face, whenever she looked at me or talked to me, were evident.

She was not only the headteacher, but the teacher of my class. Almost every day that I attended school, I would end up in the corridor being punished. My punishment was always the same; I had to stand in the corridor holding my hands behind my head with my back to the wall. To stand still, utterly humiliated, whilst teachers and pupils walked by me. Many punishments came my way for not knowing answers to questions or simply just looking the wrong way at her. I know I switched off and looked out of the window, escaping into my own daydream world for most of the time. Daydreaming, however, resulted in punishment. A public scolding in front of the class and then dismissal to the corridor. Many times, I was even held responsible for other pupils' bad behaviour going on around me. I became acutely aware that some of the girls in the class thought I was cute, and would often have fits of giggles in my presence. This infuriated the headteacher even more and she would scold me for their giggles and make me stand in the corridor for most of the day.

One day in winter, on the playground, a long area of ice had become a slide for us children to play on. It was great fun; we would run towards the start of the ice patch and jump on with two feet and slide to the end. On this particular day, I began my run, jumped onto the ice and started to slide. Halfway through my slide I lost control, and flipped completely into the air, landing on my forehead, causing a gash. As it does with head injuries, blood began to pour out. All the headteacher did was scold me, and it was left to another teacher to administer first aid to me, which consisted of giving me a bandage to hold on my head. I suspect now, with hindsight, that I had concussion, as I had an awful headache for the rest of the day and kept being sick. My punishment for falling on the ice? I had to stand in the corridor, holding the bandage on my head!

'For sale! $1,000'

Pembroke was a hunting town in Ontario, situated Northwest of Ottawa alongside the beautiful Ottawa River. Most days, from our house, we would hear the wolves howling, and in springtime, the bears would wake from their hibernation, and, to satisfy their hunger, would come and scavenge through our garbage bins. During the hunting season, many cars would drive through town with a trophy moose or deer strapped triumphantly to the roof of their car.

Peter was a multi-millionaire. He owned most of the town that we lived in, including the refuse company that served the whole town and surrounding area, and the car speedway track. The speedway track, which promoted banger racing, drew hundreds of eager spectators each week.

As a small boy, banger racing was exciting and enticing and I looked forward to my visits to the speedway. One evening, I had been sitting on the seats in the stand, but as it started to rain,

I decided to shelter in the area underneath the stand with many other people who had the same idea. The stand was a layered sequence of seats joined together, stepping up in height to the top seat about 10 rows up. It became really crowded underneath, so I decided to take a walk around and look at the various food and souvenir kiosks. The rain became much more intense and soon it was absolutely pouring down. Suddenly, there was an enormous crashing sound, followed by agonising screams; screams of both panic and pain. The stand had collapsed right onto the people sheltering underneath, and the people who had been sitting on the seats were now piled on top of the mangled mess of metal and bodies. It was a horrible scene. Many children were hurt, and I could easily have been one of them. Many people suffered life-changing injuries that day, and sadly some lost their lives. I can still remember the screams, the sound of hysteria; it was deafening. I stood in the rain some thirty metres away, still, and silent.

Peter, the owner of the speedway, came and found me, and drove my mum and me back to our house. During the drive, he told my mum in a very matter of fact way that he was not worried, that he would blame the company that built the seating stands and sue them. I remember thinking about the people; what about the poor injured men, women and children?

Peter was another of my mum's lovers; she was his mistress, his 'bit on the side'. My mother linked up with Peter soon after we moved to Pembroke; she was well practised in quickly determining those who had money, power and influence, and who might be an asset to her. Peter, on his own and sometimes with his business partner, would often speed into our driveway in his open-air Dune buggy. They would be loud and lairy and filled with drink. Mum would 'entertain' them, and then they would go on their way.

Peter's wife was sadly not able to have children, although, at the time, I was not aware of this. One day, Peter asked me if I would like to earn some money mowing his lawn, something that I was really glad to do. I realise now that it was a ruse, an excuse to get me to go to his house, because he already had a paid gardener. His property and land were so large and extensive that he needed a full-time gardener and handyman. I gladly agreed and went to his house which was on the edge of the Ottawa River, about one hundred metres in distance from a bridge spanning the river, which formed the border separating Ontario from Quebec.

Peter's house was huge, built in the shape of an octagon. The Ottawa River flowed at the bottom of the garden, and Peter's single-engine plane with water floats was parked on his private river jetty. The house had a long window, about 20 metres in length, which looked out over the garden and onto the river. At the time, I did not know but each time I mowed the lawn, Peter's wife was secretly watching me.

One day, I accidentally blocked the lawnmower and it completely stopped working. As I looked up at the big house, I saw her watching me. I was worried that she would be annoyed that I had broken the lawnmower, so I played for time, trying to fix the mower, bluffing that I knew what I was doing! Eventually, Peter's wife came out to me and helped me get the mower going again.

On another occasion, Peter's wife came out to me, brought me a drink, and sat and talked to me before I needed to get back to work. I had absolutely no idea that my 'job', mowing the lawn, was merely a ploy to help Peter and his wife come to a decision which, in turn, would force me to make a decision that no child should have to make.

Peter's wife had become very fond of me, and wanted to adopt me! The first I knew about this was one day when I was walking along a road in Pembroke. Peter's long white limousine pulled up beside me and stopped. Peter and my mum were inside; my mum was sitting in the front passenger seat and Peter was driving. I remember the streak of brown chewing tobacco running down the outside of the car where Peter spat the tobacco out of his window.

I was invited into the limousine, and sat on the back seat, in the middle. We began to drive. It felt a bit weird, like a sort of interrogation was about to happen, with Peter repeatedly looking at me in his rear-view mirror. Was I in trouble? Something was definitely not right. Nothing much was said, other than small talk from Peter; "How are you, Paul? Do you like mowing the lawn at my house?"

My mum, who had not engaged in conversation with me, suddenly turned around and looked at me. Her left arm rested on the top of the chair, and she rested her chin on her arm. She looked at me, and then said, "Would you like to go and live with Peter and his wife?"

There was no run-up to this question or sugar coating of it; just a simple, matter of fact question. She went on to explain, "You could become their son and Peter would send you to a very good school. If you do this, Peter will give me 1,000 dollars. You would be looked after very well, and I'm sure we could see each other sometimes. Remember Paul, Peter will give me 1,000 dollars if you say yes."

I sat in the back of the limousine, completely stunned and shocked. Once again, depression, anxiety and fear enveloped me. In my head, I was repeating, "Shit! Shit! Shit!"

"Paul! Peter will give me 1,000 dollars if you say yes."

I was absolutely dumbfounded. I had been enjoying a lovely day, away from our house, just roaming around the town on my own, in my own world; then Bang! Once again, I was devastated. I did not know what to say; I did not know what to do. I was completely confused. My mum was staring at me, willing me to say 'yes', with a big false forced smile on her face, a smile and expression that kept saying, "Say yes, please say yes."

I had no interest in money or business; I was a kid, trying to get by. I thought 1,000 dollars would be good for my mum, as it was a lot of money. Peter was now staring at me in the rear-view mirror, his eyes connected with mine, and I tried to avoid his gaze by looking frantically from side to side, not knowing what to do or say.

My first thought was that my mum needed me, she needed me to look after her. I did not really understand how I was feeling, and I felt pressured and manipulated, powerless and alone, abandoned by own my mum.

With all the confidence that I could muster, I said, "No!"

I guess that felt like the safest thing to do at that moment.

"I want to stay with my mum."

A few minutes later, I was asked to get out of the car. They dropped me off back in town, and then just drove off as if nothing had happened.

The decision I made that day has confused and deeply troubled me all my life. I had no-one to discuss the decision with. I don't know if I did the right thing for my mum because I presume she never got the 1,000 dollars, and I don't know if I did the right thing for me. Certainly, my life would have been very different if I had agreed to the 'sale'. I would have wanted for nothing materially, and I know that Peter's wife would have loved and cared for me as the child that she so longed for.

Even now, I can't quite get over the fact that my mum, my own mother, was willing to sell me for 1,000 dollars.

'Groomed'

As a youngster and teenager, I was always very physically fit and enjoyed any sport that I had the opportunity to have a go at. I particularly enjoyed football and ice hockey! The opportunity arose, via a contact of my mum, for me to join a wrestling team. I had no experience of wrestling, but it seemed like a good idea so I thought I'd give it a go. We met in the evening and were taught by a male coach and his assistant, who was also male. The training involved full-contact wrestling, and eventually, fighting bouts in tournaments at weekends. I wasn't too impressed with the outfit we had to wear, as it was a very figure-hugging tight leotard!

During our training meetings, the coach and his assistant would teach us the various wrestling holds and techniques, and the rules that we had to follow. The coach, who I guess was about forty years old, was a big man with a very large stomach, not very athletic looking at all! His assistant was much younger, somewhere in his late twenties and was extraordinarily strong and fit.

One evening, during training, I noticed the assistant looking at the coach, and the coach nodding his head as if giving permission for something. Little did I know at the time, but the 'signal' between the coach and his assistant was an indication that 'the coast was clear'. Everyone else in the wrestling team was distracted by practising moves, holds and techniques with each other on various training mats scattered around the gym. I hadn't been allocated a training partner that night, and I realise now I was purposely not given a partner to enable the opportunity for the assistant to engage with me. The assistant came over to me, grabbed hold of me and wrestled me to the floor. Nothing unusual in that; we were, after all, at a wrestling training session.

However, what followed was nothing to do with wrestling, but more to do with the sexual perversion of the assistant and the coach. The assistant put me in a wrestling hold position which meant that my genitals were positioned tight against his face and mouth, and I was unable to move. I was then subjected to an act of sexual abuse, and I could not move. The hold he had me in, combined with his strength, held me in that position for what seemed like forever, but in reality, was probably about twenty to thirty seconds. I felt totally disorientated and scared. I felt such shock, disgust, shame and anger, but there was nothing I could do. Eventually, he released me, and I stood up. I was so confused as to what had just happened.

"Why didn't the coach help me?" I thought to myself. I was only about 10 years old.

Then, not even having time to get my head together, he grabbed me again and threw me into the same wrestling hold with my genitals pressed against his face, and committed the same act. Again, I was restrained, and I could not move. Total terror and helplessness overwhelmed me. The coach was standing about five feet away, and I could see that he saw what was going on, but he did nothing about it. As soon as the assistant let me go, I stood up and began to gather my things together to leave. I was so confused and I felt the terrible feeling of being violated.

Naively, I went to the toilet for a pee before I made my way home. I went to the urinal which was furthest away from the entrance door to the toilet. The assistant came into the room and stood by the door and stared at me. I remember his beard and the glasses he had on. I stood there, frozen, not moving. I was still peeing. I did not attempt to try and leave the toilets because I would have to walk towards him. He continued to stare at me and just stood there. I felt like his prey. I felt his evil desire to abuse me some more. The corridor just outside the toilets began to get noisy with people going up and down, and he saw me look at the door, realising that if I was to shout, I would be heard. He walked out of the toilets.

I waited a while, mustering up the courage to approach the toilet exit door. I opened the door to the hall, ran down the corridor and out of the building. I never went back to the wrestling club again.

This is the first time that I have ever been able to speak of this horrific incident in my life.

As an adult, I realise now that I was groomed to join and take part in the wrestling team.

'Drowning'

About a mile from our house in Pembroke was a small dam, and below the dam was a fast-flowing white rapid river. The dam continuously released the water into the extremely fast-flowing river. A group of us boys, aged between 10 and 18, would jump into the river at the point where the water was released from the dam. This was an area of white-water whirlpools and angry swirling rapids. We would take turns to jump off the dam feet first into the whirlpools. The force of the whirlpool would hold you underwater, constantly spinning you around until it eventually spat you out further down the river and into the fast-flowing rapids. We would ride the fast-flowing rapids lying on our backs, being pushed downriver for about a half a mile until we came to a bend and the river flow slowed down. At this point, we were able to climb out of the river and onto the bank. To an eleven-year-old this was quite a thrill, adrenaline flowed and there was no real recognition of just how dangerous an activity it was!

On one occasion I jumped into the dam, and as usual, I was tossed and turned in the white bubbles of the whirlpool under the water. On this occasion, however, I did not move forward down the river and had no opportunity to come up and out of the water. I got weaker and weaker, and at the same time, not going anywhere. One of the group, who was 18 years old and about 18 stone in weight, jumped into the whirlpool to help me. He came underneath me in the whirlpool and thrust me up out of it and into the air. I landed about five feet further down the river and began the journey down the rapids towards the bend and safety.

On another occasion, I was moving quite smoothly downriver, being pushed by the rapids, but I was too close to the edge. A long thick tree trunk had fallen into the river, and it was blocking my way forward. I was being pushed by the rapids towards the log, and my only option was to reach out and try and grab onto it. I hit it with quite a force and ended up with my chest pinned to the log, my arms stretched over the top and my feet and legs extended underneath with my body forming the shape of the letter U around it. The rapids were so powerful and strong, I was completely trapped and could not move. Gradually, my head was being pulled lower and lower towards the waterline, and I could feel myself slipping down under the water, still pinned against the log. As the water covered my mouth it became more and more difficult to breathe, and I was quickly running out of strength to continue to hold my head above the water. I was sure I was going to drown.

Out of the corner of my right eye, on the riverbank, I saw a man trying to reach out to me. He battled the rapids and reached his hand out to mine. Very slowly, inch by inch, he pulled me in and onto the riverbank. As I lay there catching my breath, he warned me about the dangers of playing in that particular stretch of water, then just disappeared. I looked for him everywhere to thank him, but he had completely disappeared. Maybe that day I had a guardian angel?

Ottawa, Canada.

'You're surrounded!'

"Get some of your stuff and pack quickly! You've got ten minutes. Hurry! Hurry! You've got ten minutes. Come on, get moving." Mum kept whispering this to me over and over again, quietly so that no-one else would hear her. Straightaway, I knew we were on the move again. My gut feeling was right; we would never stay any length of time in one home, or one community, ever. It was never to be. As usual, I just kept quiet, did what I was told and got on with it. I packed some underwear, t-shirts and a pair of jeans into a garbage bag. No toys; I don't recall ever having any toys or ever receiving a birthday or proper Christmas present of any value.

It was night-time and dark as we loaded the boot of our car. We drove through the night and I sat in the back of our old car, miserable and glum. This was my life; I knew nothing else. I could not be bothered to ask where we were running to yet again. Running from town to town and country to country was normal for me. It would be the last time I saw Pembroke, Ontario, my latest home out of dozens and dozens of homes. Well, not home exactly; I never had a home as such, just places I stayed in for a short while.

Several hours later, I was lying in bed staring into the dark, confused and muddled in thought. We were on the run again and we ended up at the house of another of my mum's friend's, Pat, who lived in Ottawa, Ontario. Suddenly, out of the quietness of the night, a megaphone broke the silence with a forceful and commanding voice, "This is the police. You are surrounded; your house is surrounded." The policeman bellowed through his megaphone, "You are surrounded. Open the door!" I jumped out of bed and ran into the living room. My mum and Pat were standing opposite each other, staring at each other in total silence. We were now all gathered in the living room; my mum, her friend Pat whose house it was, Paula and myself. Mum tentatively pulled the living room curtains slightly apart and peered out to see if the police were in the back garden as well. I could see she had 'the look' in her eyes; I had seen many times. She was going to attempt to make a run for it. She closed the curtains and her head dropped slightly. I knew then there must be policemen in both the back and front gardens. We were surrounded and Mum knew it. There was no way out.

Pat, her friend, kept telling her that she should give up and let the police in. It was not in my mum's DNA to do this. Mum paced the living room up and down. Suddenly, my mum flashed a look at her friend and said, "You called the police, didn't you?"

I remember Pat looking to the floor and saying, "It was the only thing I could do".

"Let them in," my mum said, defeated.

Pat opened the front door and the police came into the house. I looked down the long hall and past several large policemen streaming into the house, and I could see the darkness of the night outside. Frightened by the sight of these enormous men coming towards me, I had an overwhelming desire to run, but I couldn't move. I knew this feeling. It was the frozen, terrifying and helpless feeling; this feeling was one of my best friends. The notion of running to hide immediately disappeared the second I was grabbed from behind by two female immigration officers in plain clothes. In all the commotion, Pat had also opened the back door to allow more of the policemen and immigration officers to come into the house. One of the female immigration officers stood to my right with her left hand on my shoulder and her right hand gripping my wrist. The other one stood to my left with her right hand on my shoulder and her left hand gripping my wrist.

Within seconds, I was bundled out of the front door of Pat's house and put into the back seat of a black saloon car with the two officers seated either side of me. In front and behind of the saloon car were police cars with their blue flashing lights twirling and dancing, lighting the whole street up. Neighbours were now standing in their front gardens, on their front doorsteps, looking out of upstairs windows, watching the commotion, watching us, watching me. I was taking all this in when I saw my mum, arms behind her back, her wrists restrained by handcuffs, being bundled out of the house by two immigration officers. Mum was put into a black saloon car in front of the car I was in. Paula, my younger sister, was carried out of Pat's house by another immigration officer and put into a third black saloon car parked immediately behind the car I was in. The police cars drove off with their blue flashing lights turned off, and I noticed the night had become dark again.

The performance ended; the audience of neighbours began to drift back into their houses and upstairs curtains were drawn closed. I felt so deeply ashamed and embarrassed to the core of my soul. I just wanted to hide. I could feel my 'friends', depression and melancholy, overwhelming me again as I sat in the back seat of the car. I was very used to this feeling.

We drove to a building that looked to me like a prison. Iron gates opened and a security guard checked the ID of the driver of the car that I was in. Once we were inside the building, I was taken to a brightly coloured room with toys in a box and locked in the room on my own. The room was comfortable. I never saw my mum again that night, and I spent the night completely alone. At some point, a lady came into the room with blankets and sheets and made a bed up for me on a couch. I did not sleep much that night. I played with the toys, and every now and then, someone would look through the window of my room to check on me.

Early the next morning, I was given some toast and a drink of orange. I remember being really hungry and wolfing it down; I have no idea when I had last eaten. I finished the toast and orange and then I was swiftly marched out of the building by the female immigration officers and put into the back of an unmarked black saloon car once again. A very tall plain-clothed female immigration officer sat next to me in the back seat, and two male immigration officers sat in the front of the car, one in the passenger seat and one in the driver's seat. The three officers did not talk to me at all on the exceptionally long drive from Ottawa to Toronto airport. All I could do was look out of the car window and stare at the countryside flashing past me, feeling scared, gloomy and very alone. The journey from Ottawa to Toronto airport took many, many hours. We had one toilet stop on the way to Toronto, and I was escorted from the car to the toilets and back to the car by the very tall female officer. I was not given anything to eat or drink on the whole journey.

Finally, arriving at Toronto airport, we were driven through the airport's security gates to the bottom of the steps that led up to the open door of an aeroplane. We waited at the bottom of the aeroplane's stairs. I was surrounded by the three immigration officers. A black saloon car pulled up with more officers and my mother in it. My mother got out and we were reunited. A third car pulled up and Paula exited the car with female immigration officers holding her hands, one on each side of her. I asked what was happening and my mum told me we were going to return to England. Another car pulled up and Keith, who we had not seen for some time, got out to say goodbye. To this day, I do not know exactly why Keith turned up at the airport, or how he knew we would be there. I do recall a conversation with my mum many years later in which she claimed that the Canadian authorities had found out that she had not declared that she had been arrested once in England for stabbing Keith. My gut feeling, however, is that we were more than likely deported because my mum was fiddling the welfare state, or defrauding an insurance company or some other financial scam, and had been caught. Mum often did this sort of scam; fraud was her thing. Weirdly, Keith said goodbye to us all, and then the immigration officers escorted us onto the plane and to our seats. All the other passengers stared at us, curiously. On the flight, I remember sitting by the window of the aeroplane, not speaking and trying to work out why we were going back to England and what my mum had done, yet again, to get us into trouble.

We landed in England at Heathrow Airport; we were met by some more plain-clothes immigration officers. They escorted us to a minibus which was parked on the tarmac. In the dark of night, combined with the neon lights of London, we were driven from Heathrow Airport to a refugee hostel. The refugee hostel was an enormous, incredibly old, mansion-like house, surrounded by tall trees, somewhere in the suburbs of London. A long driveway led up to the refugee hostel. We entered the hostel and a smell suddenly hit us. It was an overwhelming smell of damp and mould. I could taste and feel the toxins in the air and in my throat when I inhaled.

The gloomy atmosphere of the hostel was perpetuated by poor lighting. We were given two rooms on the bottom floor, a big lounge room and one bedroom. The lounge had a fireplace and some incredibly old wooden furniture. Accommodated in the other rooms of the hostel were families from all over the world; African families, Chinese families, Indian and Pakistani families. No-one attempted to talk to each other. *Simon, my mother's current, and noticeably much younger boyfriend, had flown over from Canada to England to be with us. He came and lived with us in the refugee hostel. I remember peeking through the lounge door one night to see him breaking up some of the old wooden chairs to burn on the open fire for heat. We had less and less furniture as time went on.

Southend-on-Sea, Essex, UK

'Weirdo!'

I have calculated that from the age of 5 to 16, I attended around twenty-five, if not more, different schools. Some schools I attended for a month or two, and some schools I attended for a little longer. My attendance, however, was intermittent during my time at all these schools. There could be a gap of several months between me attending one school and joining another. The changing curriculums, languages and countries of the schools I attended seriously inhibited my chance of an education. School was a negative and lonely existence for me and arriving at a new school always brought problems for me. Firstly, I was mixed-race, so I would immediately become the target of those with racist tendencies. Secondly, although I was of slim build, I was very fit and strong, and at high school, I was seen as a threat by the school 'hard men', so would end up having to fight to establish my 'ranking' in the school. I tried to avoid these encounters; I didn't by nature want to be involved, but groups of pupils would always come looking for me.

My earliest recollection of a fight was actually at primary/ elementary school when I was quite young, and I learned to fight back. The school bully confronted me after school, supported by many of his friends who formed a circle around me and him. I just went mad. I exploded with anger and rage and fought back when he attacked me. The fight ended with him flat on his back and me walking off victorious, leaving his friends standing in dismay. This was the beginning of many fights at many different schools for me.

After our deportation from Canada, we eventually ended up living in Southend-on-Sea, and my mum took me, in the middle of the day, to join a comprehensive school. I had no idea of the British school uniform tradition, or of the teenage culture of the time that your choice of clothes made you 'cool'. I must have been about twelve years old. The path leading up to the main reception of this particular school was sandwiched between two two-storey buildings, which housed many classrooms. As I walked, some girls hung out of the windows and started to shout down at me and my mum as we walked along the path. "It's Donny Osmond," they shouted. I did not have a clue what this was all about, but I did have an inclination that this would cause problems for me with some of the boys at the school.

I walked down the path wearing huge Canadian snow boots, jeans and a Canadian duffle coat. I was totally embarrassed and began to dread the inevitable fights to come. My mum, on the other hand, walked with her head held high, enjoying the attention, dressed in a skirt which was just short enough to cover her underwear and a top which left absolutely nothing to the imagination!

I started attending the school the following day, still wearing my noticeably big and embarrassing snow boots. It did not take long for the first fight to come my way at this school. I was walking around on my own during the lunch break, looking totally out of place and somewhat weird, quite different from everyone else. A group of about ten boys came up to me and began the routine I was well used to by now.

"Where you from, weirdo? Why do you talk like that? You think you're a hard man, don't you?!"

Then the 'main' guy attacked me, throwing a few punches and a few kicks. He and I launched into a full-blown fight which resulted in neither of us winning and the fighting stopped. Eventually, they would go their way and I continued my walk around the school grounds, on my own, looking weird.

My stay at this school didn't last very long and soon we were on the move again, this time to the West Midlands.

Coventry, UK

'My Mum's a Prostitute'

Derelict terraced houses boarded up with plywood nailed to the windows and front and back doors, brownfield open spaces full of old bricks and rubble surrounded this last terrace row of Victorian houses awaiting demolition. We lived in one of the only two remaining houses that were deemed habitable, or more accurately, just about liveable in, and my family and the family immediately next door to us were the only residents. Our house was right in the middle of a row of about fifty terraced houses, all of which were earmarked for demolition. These houses were just one street away from Coventry City football ground, and it was an area renowned to be Coventry's red-light district.

The front door to the house opened directly onto the pavement and street. Our next-door neighbours were hostile towards us; they were a family with a tough reputation. The mum was large and threatening; the dad was equally as large and equally as threatening and it was rumoured that he was a white supremacist. Their two grown-up sons were, just like their parents, large and threatening and fully-fledged Skinheads. They wore Oxford Bags trousers which were turned up to display Dr. Martens boots. One evening, I was sitting in the front room when a huge rock came flying through our front room window, smashing the window and splattering glass all over me before landing on the floor directly next to me. Panic-stricken, I sat still on the floor for a few moments, and then tentatively opened the front door to see one of the 'boys' from next door running away down the street, laughing loudly. I knew this family did not like my mum and her friends prostituting themselves on the front door of our house. I guessed this was the reason for the rock.

One evening at about 11.30 pm, I was sitting in the front room watching TV and suddenly, without warning, the front door flung wide open and slammed into the wall. My mum tripped over the doorstep and fell face down on the floor. Soon she was shouting and crying, all the time lying on the floor on her side. Black eyeliner was smudged down her face, her top was ripped, and to those who didn't know her, she looked like she had been attacked. My gut feeling, however, told me straight away that this was not real, this was my mum and she was up to something! Of course, a young boy must go along with the act; what else could I do? Being manipulated was something that I knew all too well. Mum started shouting at the top of her voice, "They tried to rape me! They tried to rape me!" Repeatedly, she screamed the same accusation. I, in turn, screamed at my mum, asking her what had happened, what was going on. I didn't really know how I should behave in this situation; I was confused and conflicted. "Should I be compassionate? Yet, I feel like, I know I am being manipulated. Should I play Mum's game and be concerned?" In actuality, I did what I had learned to do; absolutely nothing. There was nothing I could do; I was always powerless in these 'mum games'. Mum's outburst then turned to the real reason for this bizarre and cruel spectacle, *Simon. She had obviously used *Simon enough and wanted rid of him. *Simon, who had travelled over from Canada to be with her after we were deported, was much younger than her, rather naive and I think a little simple. A few minutes into this shocking and disturbing performance by my mother, *Simon walked innocently through the front door. Seeing the terrible scene in front of him, he appeared genuinely shocked to see the condition that my mum was in. He just stood there, mouth wide open, holding a bottle of Guinness in his left hand. Mum then started to scream at him, "You left me! You left me, you fucking bastard! They dragged me into a car and tried to rape me, but I escaped!"

Mum kept shouting at him, blaming him because he had left her alone to pop into a shop to get a bottle of Guinness for her. *Simon started to apologise over and over again saying, "Pam, you told me to get you a bottle of Guinness, you told me to leave you and go and get the Guinness." *Simon's eyes were like a window to his soul; he, like many before him, was broken. He looked at me, not knowing what to do or say, other than sorry. It was obvious that he was concerned about me, concerned about me witnessing this tragedy. I could see also that he knew that all was not right, that everything did not add up. She was doing what she always did, trying to turn me against *Simon, trying to get me to blame him for what had apparently just happened to her. She kept saying to me, "Look what a bastard he is to leave me. It's his fault this happened to me."

"But I was right behind you, Pam. I only popped into the shop for a minute; I was right behind you! I didn't see a car. I definitely didn't see a car!"

It was obvious that mum was making the whole story up, and having been exposed as a liar, she attacked in the only way that she knew best; she screamed and screamed abuse at *Simon, belittling and shaming him. *Simon submitted to silence, dazed and confused.

I had always found *Simon to be OK during the short time that he was part of my life. Indeed, when we were in Canada, he often lent me his Snowmobile and I used to travel around the wild woods on it during the winter. I suppose he had been seduced by my mum sexually; I formed this view because of the antics everyone could hear coming from their bedroom.

I calmed my mum down, playing her game, and went to bed. *Simon slept on the couch. He returned to Canada a few days later.

Our evening routine changed when *Simon left us. Mum and three other prostitutes would tout for business on the front doorstep of our house. One lady was a rough loud-mouthed forty-something heavy smoker with black curly hair. Another was heavily overweight, in her thirties (although looked much older), and I remember she always seemed to have a bag of chips in her hand. The third prostitute was a young girl, just seventeen years old, a trendy and kind person. She was very pretty. I remember her telling me all about her boyfriend, and how he would go to see Coventry football team play at the stadium down the road. Mum and the two older ladies would stand on the doorstep engaging in various conversations with men who drew up in their cars, sometimes laughing and giggling on the doorstep. I would sit in the middle room of the house. The door to this room was left open, and I could see through into the front room and the front door. The women took turns to go and get into the cars that drove up and down our street. When one of them came back to the house after their 'work' was done, they would walk past me into the kitchen and make a cup of tea. Every time my mum walked past me, she would look at me with a stare of indignant denial. I sat there listening to the laughter and banter they had with their customers. The seventeen-year-old girl often walked around the house with the little clothes she wore, undone. She never seemed to bother to do them up in between clients. Usually, even on a school night, I would go to bed about 11.30 pm, while the red-light community played out on my front door.

'Voodoo dolls'

Throughout my childhood years, many men came in and out of my life, some merely as boyfriends of my mother and some as stepdads. I came to notice a distinct pattern in her relationships with men. Initially, she would make them feel like they were the most amazing men in the world, showering them with trite yet ego-boosting words. Sexual encounters were constant and noisy! I even recall a wooden plaque that she put on the wall over one of her husband's side of the bed, which read something like, 'what the mind can perceive the body can achieve.' This was, in her eyes, some sort of ridicule of this particular husband. Inevitably, her attitude towards the 'man of the moment' would turn into something bitter and destructive. Her change of attitude towards them became one of evil intent. She would regularly add poison to their food, just enough to make them really sick, not kill them. Her language, descriptions and semantics of them changed as well; the men became objects rather than people. She would refer to them as "the it" or "the thing", and I was given strict instructions not to use or refer to them by their names, just the 'label' she had now given them.

The derogatory name-calling would then progress to using voodoo dolls. Mum would sit me down at the dining table and make me watch her make the dolls as an effigy of her present husband or boyfriend. Once finished, I would watch her sticking pins into them and putting them on the mantlepiece. On one occasion, Mum convinced me just how bad one of her boyfriends was, and encouraged me to help make one of the dolls and stick pins into it. Such was her power and control over me, but I was only a child. I felt so guilty about my actions afterwards because, in reality, this one was not a bad man.

Southend-on-Sea, Essex, UK

'Alpha Male'

School life for me was purely about existing and surviving. It had very little to do with education or development; it was purely an existence. The existence became a little easier and less lonely when I tagged along with the 'hard' boys. I soon learned that every school had a group of bully boys, a friendship group that most people would choose to avoid. At that time in Southend-on-Sea, the 'hard' boys predominantly belonged to one of two opposing subcultures - Skinheads or Teddy boys.

As happened at almost every secondary school (and some primary schools) I attended, a rite of passage was for me to engage in a fight with the school's 'Alpha Male'. It was no different at the second comprehensive school I attended in Southend-on-Sea, a Catholic School. I soon found that the school hard man, *Pete, wanted to pick a fight with me. I didn't know it at the time, but the fight that I was to have with him in the common room at school was a test, a test to see if I had what it took to become a member of his gang; an initiation, so to speak.

We both stood facing each other in the middle of a large communal area inside the school building, an area that was large enough to accommodate fifty or so students. Although *Pete was a student at the school, he had the appearance of a young adult aged around twenty years old; his masculinity had developed far quicker than the rest of us. I also knew he was highly intelligent, as he had sought me out prior to this, when I was on my own, to question and drill me. I was, to be honest, rather shocked and surprised when he picked the fight with me, but after the fight was over, it was obvious

79

to me that it was another way in which he was checking me out, assessing me to see what I was made off. There were no teachers around, and I immediately noticed that some members of his gang had strategically positioned themselves by the two entrances to the area to prevent unwanted spectators and to warn my aggressor if a member of staff was coming. *Pete was a strong and experienced bare-knuckle street fighter. I had already witnessed him knocking kids unconscious with a single punch, and I knew I could not match him physically in a fight; he was too big and too strong for me. I needed this to be my 'David and Goliath' moment! The fight began, and powerful punches rained down on me. They were considered and intelligent punches. I covered my face and head with my forearms and bent forward. I realised that if I tried to lift my head and start punching back, my face and head would be exposed to unrelenting punishment. The only thing I could think of doing was to wait for a gap, a momentary break in the punches which would enable me to throw myself at him and grab onto his neck. My plan then was to hold on until he either tired, or I was rescued by a teacher. All the time, we were surrounded by a circle of students, shouting, chanting and baying for blood. I seized my opportunity and jumped towards him, clamped my arms around his neck and yanked him as close as I could with all of my might. Now all I had to do was hold on for dear life. Ironically, it probably looked like we were hugging each other tightly!

This was my only hope, that he would tire and I could seize the opportunity to run away and out of the school. He tried to punch me in the head, but he could not lift his arms. He tried to pull me off him, but my grip was too tight. We staggered around the room bumping into people, furniture and walls, looking like boxers who could not break from each other in the ring. This went on for a good fifteen minutes, and even when we fell on the floor, I still hung on to him for dear life. This spectacle increasingly enthused the watching crowd, who became louder and louder with their shouts and chants; this time, however, the shouting and clapping were for me! Fortunately for me, the loud clapping and shouting attracted the attention of a teacher who came into the room to see what was going on and was confronted with the image of myself and *Pete rolling around on the floor with a circle of spectators around us. As soon as my opponent saw the teacher, he let go of me and I let go of him.

Not wanting to inform on each other, when asked by the teacher what we were doing, we simply responded that we were merely play-fighting, a lie that was backed up by the circle of spectators. I'm sure the teacher knew exactly what was going on. *Pete had a fierce reputation not just with the students but with the staff also, but it made his life easier to believe our story. He merely told us off and said that in future we should do that sort of thing outside, before quickly leaving. *Pete smiled at me, and in front of the gathered crowd, affirmed me with a simple nod of the head and "You're OK".

I had not received much affirmation in my life, mainly the opposite, so to me, this felt good, really good; it made me feel valued and important. This was not a situation where the other students would turn to favour me, as *Pete was too well-liked and feared, but it gave me credibility.

'Gangs'

*Pete was part of two prominent gangs in Essex. One gang was a street-fighting gang mainly made up of youths and young adults, and the other was a predominantly adult gang who undertook armed robberies and other such serious crimes in the Essex area. For me, I had passed the test, and it became a case of 'if you can't beat them join them', so I became involved with the street-fighting gang, one which wasn't particularly affiliated to either of the predominant subcultures.

The gang only allowed members who were tough and loyal; their ethos, it seemed, was to simply engage in fights with rival gangs. I soon realised, however, that this gang was also the 'training gang', the precursor to the adult gang. Members were groomed to prepare them for promotion to the adult gang and involvement with much more serious crimes including armed robbery. The younger members, however, often became the fall guys in such situations. *Pete acted as a 'recruiter' at school, and that had been the reason for provoking a fight with me.

Every member of the street gang had to have a personal weapon of choice, and mine was a bike chain and a flick knife. Flick knives were immensely popular in the 1970s. Every time we were summoned for a fight, we had to ensure that we had and used our weapons. On one occasion, we met up together and made our way to the rendezvous point for the fight with the other gang. There was an equal number of people in each gang, although the members of the other gang were slightly older than us, young adults in their early twenties, whilst we were predominately fifteen and sixteen. Arriving at the rendezvous, there was no hesitation or pause; we ran straight at them and they ran straight at us. I swung my chain at the guy who was running at me. He had no weapon. He was running so fast that the chain completely missed him, swung around his back and hit me in my left arm. A brutal fight commenced between us all. After only a few minutes, it became obvious that we were at a disadvantage and we began to withdraw. We walked backwards whilst continuing to fight our attackers. A couple of our guys had been hit with baseball bats and were bleeding profusely from their heads and holding their arms limply. Backing up, we came to a road and the rest of my gang ran off, leaving me trapped, on my own and surrounded by our rival gang. No-one came to help me, although my gang colleagues stood further down the road watching to see what was going to happen to me. Encircling me, I was in the middle of all their gang members, expecting to be killed or at least seriously maimed. Their leader looked up the road at my gang, looked at me, and said "What a bunch of cowards!"

Then, he swung a single punch at me which caught me on the chin and knocked me into the air. My feet left the ground and I ended flat on my back. To my surprise, the whole gang just turned and walked away, muttering, "Fucking cowards!" as they left.

After this fight, I began to make excuses when I was called on by my gang's members, although I knew I could not make excuses for long, and soon joined in again. The fights became more and more bloody, and the psyche of the members more and more destructive. Two of our members hung themselves, and I realised that life was getting really threatening for me belonging to this gang and out of control.

Once I was at a shop on my own when a rival gang recognised me. I walked out of the shop with my head down hoping I would be left alone. They quickly surrounded me and pinned me against a brick wall. The leader got his knife out, pushed it against my throat and started a verbal onslaught of what exactly he was going to do to me; "I'll spill your guts and cut your throat." The look in his eyes was more than terrifying; it was a look I would come to see many more times in my life. He moved his knife towards my eyes, and the threats began again; "I'm going to cut your eyes out, punk!"

Both of my arms were held pinned to the wall by other gang members and my legs were spread apart, with my face held tightly so that I could not move it.

"Fuck face, you hear me? I'm going to cut your eyes out. You're a member of *Pete's gang, aren't you?" he asked.

I denied it and denied knowing anyone called *Pete. His eyes got crazier looking and I could see that he was building himself up to cut me.

"Come on, let him go. You heard him; he is not a member. Let him go," a voice from within the gang instructed.

The guy held his knife a few moments more, then I was released and allowed to go. I fell to my knees with relief.

'Tattoo'

It was a requirement of gang membership that each member had to have a tattoo. At school, I agreed to allow another gang member to ink a tattoo on me in a cubicle in the boy's toilet. There was no sterilization of needles or precautions taken, I merely stood in the toilet cubicle with shirt off, whilst a boy not much older than me began clumsily inking the top of my left arm. Unbeknownst to us, the headteacher was doing a toilet spot check, and he saw two pairs of feet under this particular cubicle! He shouted and demanded that we open the door immediately, which we did, and he was confronted with two of us standing together in the cubicle, me with the top half of my body naked. My tattooist hid his needle and ink in his pocket. We were very loudly instructed to go immediately to his office. I went in first; the headteacher was seated behind his desk and his secretary stood beside me directly in front of the desk. Without any conversation, he stood up and told me to hold my hands out in front of me. In his hand, he was holding a cane, which he raised above his head and smashed forcibly down onto my left hand. The pain was excruciating. My relationship with this man had been difficult from the start of my time at this particular school; he thought I was dirt, mainly because of my mother's reputation and behaviour. He continued to smash the cane down onto my left hand another nine times. Then he turned his attention to my right hand, inflicting another ten lashes with equal force as had been inflicted on my left. I switched off from the pain. I was not going to give him the satisfaction of seeing me cry, absolutely no way. It became a mental battle between us, his loathing of me and my defiance of him. He ended by telling me that I was a disgusting evil little boy, and it became clear that he thought that myself and the other boy had been engaging in some sort of homosexual act. When he finished his verbal tirade, I calmly and quietly informed him that we were only tattooing my arm.

"Get out! Get out!" he shouted, and I was sent home straight away.

The next day the headteacher called me into his office, and I prepared myself for another caning. He stood me in front of his desk and asked me to show him the tattoo inking on my arm. When he saw it, he apologised and acknowledged that he had jumped to the wrong conclusion the day before. I left his office and the school chaplain asked to see me the next day. It was, at that time, a faith-based school, not that it made much difference to me, and therefore had a resident chaplain.

'Rescued'

The Chaplain spent a couple of hours talking with me. I found him to be understanding and to have a genuine concern for me. I never knew before this meeting with him that he knew so much about me. He knew all about my home life with my mum, about the gang I was in and the fights with other gangs. He even knew that I was being 'groomed' to join the Essex bank robbers' gang!

I listened intently to the chaplain. Other than the primary school teacher in Canada, I had never had anybody show concern for me in this way. To me, he was genuine; he had a genuine concern about where my life was heading and the consequences of making a wrong decision at this stage in my life. He wanted to help me escape my home life and gangs, and he suggested that the army would be a good choice for me to make and offered to help me join up. I was fifteen at the time and for the first time in my life, I felt I had a way forward. I became filled with excitement and hope. Here I had an escape route, an answer of how I could get away from the gangs, and more importantly leave my mum and the gutter life that we lived together.

At this time, I was working four jobs to help my mum with money. I had two morning paper rounds and an evening paper round, I worked in a scrap yard on a Saturday cutting up copper all day long, and on Sunday, I cleaned aeroplane toilets at Southend Airport. In the summer, I worked full time in a fish and chip shop, and I gave mum eighty percent of my money to help her pay bills. Most of it, though, went on whisky! I was so naïve and desperate to please and be affirmed by my only parent. I now know that this would never have happened, as she was incapable of such a response.

While I was listening to the chaplain, I realised that there was truth in what he was saying, and that my life was spinning more and more out of control. Unless I made a change now, I knew I would either end up dead or in prison for an exceedingly long time. My life had always been chaos and dysfunction, but now I was older and I wanted something different. I was sick of the shame I carried,

I was sick of the life that I led, I was sick of having no role model or guidance in my life. My mum had no idea how to parent, nor did she have any desire to learn how to. She encouraged me to become sexually active from the age of fourteen and would invite girls to stay over. Weirdly though, every morning after a girl slept over, she would come into my bedroom, demand that I get out of bed and beat a broom over my back so hard it would break into two bits, as punishment for being so shameless! This became a bizarre ritual for both of us.

With a lightness in my heart, I went back to see the school chaplain and agreed that the army was the way forward for me. He told me to go to the army careers office and that he would give me a reference. Excited about the prospect of this new start, I had already visited the army office a couple of times on my own, and had been told that the best regiment in the British Army was the Parachute Regiment. My mind was made up; I was going to be a Para!

I went to the Army Careers office in Southend-on-Sea and scraped through the written test (my literacy skills were very poor) with the help of the Army careers sergeant. I would not have succeeded without his help; even basic writing and maths skills for me were more or less non-existent. A few weeks later, I was asked to attend a day of selection at Sutton Coldfield, and I happily caught the train there. The day evolved around further written tests and maths tests alongside some physical tests. I loved the assault course and physical tests, not so much the maths and writing ones! I know I failed the maths and written tests; however, I beat most of the other applicants in the running and physical tests. I think I was hardened, toughened up by my life with my mum and the gang I was in. At the end of the selection day, I went for my final interview with a Paratrooper Major. This interview was important; this would either get me accepted to join the Junior Parachute Regiment or rejected. He asked me just one question, "What would you do at night if you were asked to go out for a drink, but you were ordered to stay in the barracks?"

I knew the right answer was to say, "I would stay in, Sir". Though this answer sold it for me, I went on, rather cheekily, to ask him how long it took him to be sitting where he was with the pips on his shoulders. He smiled at me and just told me that I would hear in a few weeks with the result of my application. As promised, a few weeks later, I received a letter saying that I had been accepted to join the Junior Parachute Regiment and I was to start in August 1975.

PART TWO

'Utrinque Paratus' – Ready for anything!

1975 – 1981
Age: 16 – 22

"And each man stands with his face in the light of his own drawn sword, ready to do what a hero can."

Elizabeth Barrett Browning

Southend-on-Sea, Essex, UK

'Suitcase'

Standing on the platform at Southend-on-Sea mainline railway station, I waited patiently for my train. I felt a mixture of trepidation, excitement and anticipation about the new life adventure I was about to embark on. I felt free! I was finally getting away from the influence and power of my mum, her life choices and depravity, and hopefully stopping the downward spiral of my life.

Mixed in with this feeling of freedom came the inevitable guilt; guilt that I was abandoning my mum and betraying the members of the gang. "How will mum cope without me? Surely, she'll be lost without my help and support? What trouble will she get herself into? Will she somehow continue to have a negative influence and hold on my life?" These thoughts raced around in my head.

No doubt, whilst I was away, she would ruin some more men's lives, and for sure, some of the guys from my gang would end up either dead or in prison.

With all these thoughts swimming around in my head, I could not wait to get on the train and get away from Southend and my rotten life. Holding a very small and battered suitcase I had got from a second-hand shop, I stepped onto the train, ready to be transported to my new life.

Aldershot, Hampshire, UK

'Junior Para'

Other young hopefuls along with me were picked up from Aldershot train station and driven to Browning Barracks in a green army coach. We were all given a few days to settle into our new environment and to what would become a significant part of our lives, our bed spaces.

Our bed spaces were not just where we slept; they were places of scrutiny, where we meticulously cleaned our kit and tidied our lockers, only to have everything inspected and lambasted by our Corporals, whilst we stood silently to attention at the end of our beds. Pretty much all we did throughout the first few days was go to breakfast, lunch and dinner, and get measured for our uniforms and army boots.

Every morning we got up for a Muster Parade at 8.00 am. At this parade, we were checked to see how well we had shaved, and if we could actually shave properly. I had never shaved before and had never been shown how to shave. I personally thought I did not need to shave; little did I know about army standards! On the second morning, during parade, a Sergeant leaned forward towards me and held his face a few inches from my face and demanded to know why I had not shaved. I told him I had never shaved before and did not think I needed to as I didn't have any facial hair. He pulled me out to the front of the three rows of new recruits, pointed at my face and bellowed, "See this, this is bum fluff! All bum fluff needs to be shaved every morning!"

"What was bum fluff?" I wondered.

After the parade ended, one of the lads came up to me and asked if I wanted to learn how to shave. He explained to me that I had exceptionally fine, light hair on my face, which was hardly visible, but was what the Sergeant called 'bum fluff'. He sat me down in a chair and a few of the other guys gathered around to watch *Tony teach me how to shave. I think there were quite a few guys there that day who learnt how to shave! This was probably my first experience of the camaraderie that the army gives you, and the start of my membership in this new family.

I sat in a chair and *Tony put some shaving cream on my face and began to give me a shave with a cheap disposable Bic razor. I was amazed at just how smooth my face felt afterwards. Some of the guys who had been watching the shave then went with me to the NAAFI, and we all bought a razor each and some shaving cream. From that point on, I would be expected to shave every morning for the rest of my time in the army, the only exception being later on in my army career when I began covert operations in Northern Ireland.

The next ritual to be endured was an army haircut! We had, of course, heard rumours about just how short our hair would be, and I for one wasn't looking forward to it! A long line of us stood outside the army barbers. Each time a new recruit exited the barbers with an army regulation crew cut, the rest of us couldn't hold back our laughter. Many of us had long hair, and the change in our appearance was both dramatic and hilarious. The visit to the barbers gave us all some light relief while we were getting used to a new culture and a new way of life.

When our first payday came, we were all surprised and shocked. Our weekly pay was only three pounds each; the remainder was kept by the army, who saved it on our behalf so that we would have some money to go home with on leave. Very quickly the 'duckers and divers' amongst the recruits thought about ways to increase their income and bought cigarettes to sell to the smokers amongst us.

For the first time in my life, I had friends, friends who would look out for me, and I for them.

'Gymnastics'

Legally, we were told, we could not start the Recruit Company selection course until we were seventeen years old. Recruit Company was the selection course recruits had to pass to win the famous coveted Parachute Regiment Maroon Beret and Wings. Those of us who were not yet seventeen were given a choice as to what we could do whilst we waited to be old enough to start Recruit Company selection. We could either continue in the Junior Para stream of soldiering and adventure training, or we could join a gymnastics team where we would learn gymnastics and perform gymnastic displays at various tattoos and county shows for recruitment purposes. I joined the gymnastics team, but only because some of the friends I had made decided to join!

Training began. We trained all day, every day. We had four months of training to complete with the end result being that we would become a Junior Paras Gymnastic Display Team. I found gymnastics training difficult, as I was not a natural gymnast. Some of the lads excelled and became very proficient. To begin with, our training consisted of running at, and jumping over, a basic vault box horse and landing with our feet together and our arms stretched out horizontally beside us. This training progressed to running at trampettes, learning to launch ourselves off them and somersault over the horse, hopefully landing on two feet in a neat finish.

Eventually, six-foot-high metal vaulting tables were introduced to our training. We now ran at the small trampettes placed in front of the vault, bounced upwards and over the six-foot-high vaulting table and onto a large trampoline on the other side. Another six-foot-high vaulting table was positioned at the end of the trampoline, and we had to bounce off the trampoline and somersault over the vaulting table, landing on our feet on soft mats, continuing into a forward roll and ending with the 'standard' pose of two feet together, arms outstretched. Finally, two more trampettes and six-foot-high vaulting tables were added around the large trampoline, so that each edge was covered.

We practised and practised every day. Perfection was the goal. Sometimes, however, we were allowed free time to bounce on the big trampoline for fun.

During my whole time at Browning Barracks, which accommodated hundreds of trainee Paras at different stages of selection, I only came across one black guy, and he was with us in our Pegasus Gymnastics team. This guy was six feet three inches tall and well built. One day, we were having fun bouncing on the trampoline, and he was going higher and higher, much higher than anybody else could manage. Then it happened. He was descending from an extremely high bounce and had unknowingly crept over to the edge of the trampoline for his descent. He crashed through the springs and the force of his descent combined with his heavy bodyweight forced him to fall forwards onto the outer steel bar of the trampoline. This impact immediately broke his right femur; it just snapped! He was bent forward on his tummy, lying at a right angle over the outer steel bar of the trampoline, and let out a deafening high-pitched scream of agony. He was screaming in excruciating pain and at the same time, he was stuck. Watching him being removed from the trampoline was horrific; he was in so much pain. This was to be his last time as a member of Junior Para and the Pegasus Gymnastics team. A few months later, he was medically discharged before his adventure had even begun. I once saw him in Aldershot town centre sometime later, as a civilian, and he was walking with a permanent life-changing limp. I felt deeply sorry for him. His error made me switch on to the fact that I needed to look after myself and get through my year with Pegasus Gymnastics Team injury-free.

'Displays'

After four months of intense daily gymnastics training, we were ready to perform gymnastic displays in public. Our display was exciting to watch, and, what you would expect from the Parachute Regiment, dangerous. Four rows of eight Junior Paras lined up with one row behind each of the four small trampettes. Behind each trampette was a six-foot-high vaulting table, all leading to the large trampoline in the middle. Our Major gave a short introduction to the gathered crowd, and then we began! Each one of us looked to the right at the line of gymnasts near to us, and with a split-second gap, we each, in turn, would run at the trampette after the person to our right had begun his run. This began a flow of bodies hitting the trampettes, bouncing upwards and somersaulting over the vaulting table onto the trampoline, and over another vaulting table, securing, hopefully, a perfect landing on the mat on the other side! All four rows of gymnasts continued this sequence resulting in an exciting mid-air display of young gymnasts, somersaulting some ten feet into the air and missing colliding with each other by inches. It was a spectacular display. Of course, in training, there were many collisions, but when we performed live, if there was a collision, we just had to carry on no matter what. We could hear the gasps from the audience as they enjoyed the spectacle before them.

We performed gymnastic displays at various venues around England, Wales and Scotland, including tattoos, shows at County Showgrounds and village and town fairs. A high point for us was performing a display during the half-time interval at the 1976 FA Cup final held in the old Wembley Stadium. The final was between Southampton and Manchester United. Sometimes, the Red Arrows Aerobatic display team would perform at the same event as us, along with the White Helmet motorcycle display team.

Often, after we had completed our displays, queues of young girls would line up in front of us to get our autographs; we felt like film stars! After one particular performance at a town fete, we were loading our equipment onto the four-ton lorries and were about to board our coach back to the barracks we were staying in when our Major told us that we had all been invited to a disco later on that evening. This disco was being put on for us in a local school, however, this was a rather different school to what we were used to; it was a Girls' Convent Boarding School run by nuns! Whoever organised that must have either been very naïve or stupid! Our Major read the riot act to us, stating that no-one was to take advantage of any of the girls. We were gobsmacked. Why on earth were nuns inviting us to a disco at a girls-only school? You can imagine the banter that followed.

That evening, we got the coach to the convent, but only after another dose of 'the riot act' from our Major. Many of the girls were shy, but many were, rather surprisingly, unashamedly forward. Inside the disco, which was being held in their gymnasium, two nuns were stood at every entry and exit door. Outside of the building, our Corporals patrolled the ground, keeping an eye on each and every one of us. The disco was actually very boring, controlled and contained. At ten o'clock on the dot, the music stopped, and we all boarded the coach. At this point, the girls started hanging out of the dormitory windows waving at us. Some girls jumped out of the bottom windows and ran to the coach, waving and screaming goodbye. Our coach pulled away very slowly as the coach driver had to be careful not to run one of the girls over! By this point, some of the girls had become very emotional and were trying to stop the bus from moving forward. A truly weird and unexpected experience!

Glasgow, Scotland, UK

'Line Dancing!'

We once performed in Glasgow, Scotland. This was what we thought would be a unique experience for our team because our accommodation was a hotel, and the hotel was located opposite a lovely park. We were given some time off, so we mucked around in the park opposite the hotel for a while. We practised somersaults and played some football. A large group of young physically fit boys naturally attracted the attention of the local girls. This did not go down well with the local lads, and sure enough, Glasgow being Glasgow, that evening we had twenty or so local lads arrive at the hotel fully equipped with knives, calling us out to have a fight with them. Our Corporals called the police and they were dispersed. We, however, felt humiliated at having to stay in our rooms. The next night we were allowed to go out on the town. A few of us found our way to a disco located at the top of some dark stairs. I ordered a drink and turned around to have a look at the dance floor. I was tapped on the shoulder by a bouncer and told I was not allowed to stand still, that I had to keep moving. The bouncer told me this was to help stop fights happening. *Wow! This was a tough place*! I thought.

So, I began to walk in the flowing circle of men and women walking in one direction around the dance floor, with my drink in my hand. My buddies and I looked at each other and laughed. Everyone was walking around the dance floor in the same direction. This was really weird! Anyway, we did not stay long and left as we had a show to do the next day and we did not want any trouble. If we stayed, we knew there would be trouble.

Peterborough, Cambridgeshire, UK

'Show and tell! (Mum's way!)'

Unfortunately for me, on one occasion, our Pegasus Gymnastics Team were booked to perform a display at the Peterborough Showground's annual County Show. It was unfortunate because my mum lived in Peterborough at the time. The dread and fear that had once been a daily part of my life revisited me. I was sure my mum would do something to humiliate me.

A couple of days before the display, our team was practising on a piece of the showground designated for us. Then it happened. The thing I was dreading. My mum turned up! She was now in her early fifties and was wearing a skirt that revealed the bottom of her knickers and a shirt that revealed most of her breasts. Nothing was left to the imagination. She could easily have been escorted from the showground for soliciting. Imagine the scene; thirty sixteen-year-old Junior Paras, three Corporals, a Sergeant and a Major all stood watching as my mum saunters up to me, giving the whole Pegasus Gymnastics team a sleazily entertaining 'show'.

Embarrassment and shame overwhelmed me. My whole body became numb; it was just terrible for me. The Corporals were smirking and whispering to each other, and the lads were just standing, hormones raging with mouths wide open. I said and did nothing. I just fell straight back into the realisation that this is my lot, this is what she does to me, there is nothing I can do. As I had learned to do all my life when I lived with mum, I switched off and sank into deep depression and shame and tried to carry on.

We were performing at the Peterborough Showground for a few days. On a night off, myself and a couple of the guys went out for the evening. They persuaded me to drop into my mum's house for a coffee before we went back to our accommodation. It was about 10.30 pm when we arrived at her house. She opened the upstairs window, saw it was me and my friends at the front door and eventually came downstairs to open the door and let us in. My heart sank. She was up to her bizarre games again. When she opened the front door, she was wearing only a see-through negligée. The bottom of the hem of the negligée sat just below her bottom.

"Hi, everyone! Come in and I will make you some drinks," she said to the guys who were now, once again, open-mouthed and wide-eyed. We went into the house and sat in the front room. Mum turned the lights on which made her see-through negligée even more see-through! Nothing was hidden from the gawps of the guys. All her private parts could be clearly seen. Her breasts and her private parts. I hid my shame and embarrassment. I was trying to ignore the situation as I did all my life. Mum stood in the middle of the front room revealing her nakedness to my friends and behaving as though everything was normal by making conversation with the guys.

When we left, no-one made a comment directly to me about my mum, but the sly smirks and giggles going on between them cut me to the core of my soul. After our final display at the Peterborough County Fair, whilst we were packing up all our equipment, I overheard the Corporals talking about a night they had had at my mum's house. My mum constantly brought shame and embarrassment on me, and this had a long-lasting effect on me, especially with depression, something that I carried during my time in the army.

Interestingly, the depraved night my Corporals had with my mum saved me from a 'beasting', which is a form of punishment particular to the armed forces, later on in my time in the Junior Paras. My mum had managed to get herself onto the front page of a national tabloid newspaper. The paper had a full-length picture of her on the front page and the caption was something like, 'Looking for a Husband.' Underneath her picture were details of how to write to her if you were interested in meeting her. Incredulous, I know! Her campaign was successful and shortly after the headline, I was invited to attend yet another wedding. The paper wanted to do a follow-up story and stupidly, I agreed to have my photograph taken with her and her new husband. Even more stupidly, I wore my Junior Para Uniform for the photograph. I wore the distinguished Maroon Beret with the badge with the distinctive blue backing signifying I was a Junior Para. This photograph appeared on the front page of the paper. My mum and the editors of the newspapers thought including a photo of me in my Junior Para Uniform would make the story even more interesting for the readers.

When I got back to barracks, I was immediately approached by one of the Corporals who thrust the newspaper in front of me and looked at me with utter disgust. I had embarrassed the Paras! Why did I not get punished? This particular Corporal was one of my mum's 'visitors' during our time in Peterborough, and he knew that I was aware of this! This meant he did nothing to me; he did not beast me, as he wanted to keep his visit to my mum's house quiet. Nothing else was said to me about the newspaper article.

True to form, Mum destroyed her new husband after a couple of years.

Aldershot, Hampshire, UK

'Para Selection - Pre-Recruit Company'

My time in the Pegasus Gymnastics Team soon passed. The year was up, and the fun was over. I turned seventeen and began Pre-Recruit Company selection training. There is a long sequence of selection processes to pass before the coveted Maroon Para Beret and Para Wings can be awarded.

Firstly, I had to pass Pre-Recruit Company Selection. This was an intense short programme of runs, assault courses and ten-mile tabs (physical exercise unique to the military), to see if myself and the other recruits were up to the standard needed to be able to start Recruit Company Selection proper. When I started the Pre-Recruit Company selection course, I had great difficulty getting the right size army boots to fit me while I was being assessed. After completing one of the ten-mile runs, all recruits were told to lie on our beds while we had a foot inspection. This worried me. I had blisters on the bottom of both my feet. Two long blisters ran from the back of both of my heels, along the base of my feet and reached my toes. My blisters had burst open on the ten-mile run, and they were now red raw with a couple of layers of skin worn away. The raw area extended along nearly the whole length of the bottom of my feet. My fear was that the foot inspection would reveal the state of my feet and I would not be allowed to finish and pass the Pre-Recruit Company Selection Course. I was sure this would disqualify me from proceeding to the Recruit Company selection course proper. My blisters caused me excruciating pain all day, every day, but I had vowed to myself at the start that I was going to either pass the Para selection or go home in a box. There was no way I was going to let anything stop me, except death! Certainly not the pain of blisters!

We all laid on our beds with our boots and socks off, while our bare feet were inspected one recruit at a time. There was nothing I could do to hide the condition of my feet. The Corporal came to me, looked at my feet and said, "Fucking hell, Parks, what the hell are you playing at?"

"That's it, I am going to be sent home," I thought.

The Corporal beckoned our officer who was standing at the end of the barrack room with his hands behind his back surveying the foot inspection, to come over and look at my feet. I really thought this was the end for me now.

"Bollocks," I said to myself under my breath.

He looked at my feet, holding one foot in the air to inspect it more closely. He then asked, "Parks, do your feet hurt"?

"Yes, Sir, they do. I'm really sorry but I can't seem to find any boots to fit me, but it's ok, it's really no problem."

The officer told me to lay there and rest my feet on the end bar of the bed. He then said to the rest of the recruits, "You bunch of wankers, every one of you, come and look at Parks' feet! This is what we are looking for, you tossers! Guts! The ability to push through pain!"

I was embarrassed not only by the comments that the officer made but also by the humiliation of having the other recruits, my friends, file past me in order to inspect my feet! I became aware that the assessors had observed me limping for a few days, but I still finished the runs, assault courses and ten-mile tabs. What I thought was going to signal the end of my selection process, turned out to be one of the reasons why I passed Pre-Recruit Company! After the foot inspection, one of the Corporals was tasked with ensuring that I got correctly fitting boots from the Quartermaster.

'Para Selection – Recruit Company'

After I passed the Pre-Recruit Company Selection, I then began the selection process in Recruit Company. Every single moment of every day, morning and night, was assessed. Our Major, who had the ultimate responsibility for our selection assessment, walked around each day making notes in a small black book about each recruit. He never said anything. He just observed. At the end of each day, the training staff had a meeting to discuss which recruit had failed the day, or which recruit would receive a warning to 'buck up'. Recruits were only allowed one warning during the several months' selection process.

Each morning at 8.00 am we gathered for a Muster Parade. It was a time of considerable anxiety for me. In my thoughts was a mantra of, "Please, please, I hope I did enough to pass yesterday, oh God I hope I have."

I never knew who God was. I just said it. The feeling of having to go back and live with Mum filled me with utter horror and apprehension.

For Muster Parade, we would line up in three ranks and stand at ease. We then waited for a list of names to be read out. As we were all so anxious to remain on the selection course, most times it felt almost as if we were facing a firing squad! Most of us were escaping from something or someone, and the army was our only hope. If your name was read out, then that meant that you had failed the previous day's activities and were off the selection course. Those people were immediately marched up to their barrack room to pack their kit and were sent home. That was the end of their selection. On a few occasions, if the selectors thought someone might have a chance to be assessed again, that person would be held back for the next Recruit Selection Course. I always felt sorry for the people whose names were read out and wondered how they coped.

However, my empathy for the failing recruits soon changed over a short space of time, as my mindset became that of the Parachute Regiment. Weakness was frowned upon. I began to see the failing recruits as weak people and a waste of space. Waiting to hear if my name was read out each morning certainly motivated me to try my hardest each day. The mindset of being the best and disparaging other regiments gradually became my mentality. Each day the numbers on our selection course dwindled down and down. I was determined that I was not going to be one of them.

The Recruit Company Selection process was divided into four phases, and specific milestones had to be reached in order to continue on in the process.

The first phase was Pre-Brecon, the second was P-Company, the third was Advance Brecon, and the final phase was RAF Brize Norton. Everyone wanted to reach the final phase; at RAF Brize Norton we would be trained to undertake military parachute jumps.

'Phase one: Pre-Brecon'

This phase consisted of many fast-paced and gruelling runs, tabs and assault courses, which eventually included the addition of a Bergen (military backpack) on our back with ever-increasing weights in it. Much of this phase of selection was spent on exercises in Wales and particularly the Brecon Beacons and the Black Mountains. The exhausting hill and mountain tabs, carrying heavy weights, had to be completed within a stipulated time; there was no margin of error. In order to pass each day, we had to beat the times set. We were taught to handle various weapons, how to fire them and use them to shoot people. We practised on targets which had the profile and image of a person on it. Stripping and cleaning various weapons became second nature to each one of us recruits. Map reading and Field Craft such as camouflage and attacking the enemy with live fire (real bullets!) was practised and practised until we were experts at attacking and killing an enemy. Bayonet training assured the selectors that their recruits were well on the way to being trained killers. Thrusting a bayonet into the heart region of a straw mannequin and at the same time shouting, screaming and manifesting aggression, invoked in us a feeling that we were indestructible and this was designed to form and shape us, me included, into animal-like killers. A thirst for blood began to emerge from within, awakening our deep, hidden, reptilian and evolutionary desire and need to fight and kill to survive and kill to eat. After the initial thrusting of the bayonet into the mannequin, there was the purposeful twisting of the bayonet, pushing it upwards to do as much damage as possible to your enemy's heart and organs. Then, me and the other recruits would quickly put a foot on the mannequin in order to push the body away and at the same time pull the bayonet out of the body. This training was designed to create a blood lust towards an enemy; any enemy would do. In our noticeably young, vulnerable and easily programmed minds, we were very easily indoctrinated.

Hypothermia! A crazy state for your body to get in. On one of the Pre-Brecon tests, a tab and run loaded with a heavy Bergan and carrying self-loading rifles, I was trekking from one mountain peak to another mountain peak when I became ill with hypothermia. The symptoms of hypothermia began to be obvious on my descent down the final mountain of the test. I had no idea of the state I was in and my gradual deterioration. I was about three miles from the finish line when the symptoms began to escalate. I started goose-stepping and leaping into the air while running down the mountain, my legs flipping from side to side and in all directions. A Corporal, positioned on the side of the mountain on the home stretch of the test, saw my difficulties and came to me and started running down the mountain with me. He did not touch me or help me. He just said, "Parks, you can see the finish line from here! Look! Keep going."

This was a test I had to finish and pass or I would fail the course. I was dizzy and somewhat delirious, goose-stepping uncontrollably in a run, and now dragging my rifle behind me.

"Keep going, Parks, you're nearly there."

I could now see the two Land Rovers and the finish line about a mile in front of me. I remember shouting at the Corporal running beside me, "Don't you fucking pull me out! I'm going to make it."

I was now in a slouch position, walking and swaying from side to side and fighting the hypothermia with all my might. I was getting weaker and weaker and colder and colder, but I kept going. The Corporal had radioed ahead to get the army medics to stand by for me at the finish line. Finally, I reached the Land Rovers and the finish line. I collapsed and was stretchered to a barracks and stripped naked. I could not now move or help myself and I was shivering with my teeth chattering uncontrollably. The medics lifted me into a warm bath and one stayed to supervise me. After warming my body up in the bath, drying me off and putting me to bed with a cup of hot chocolate, I soon started to feel ok again. Coming back to my senses, my first thought was, "Had I failed the test?"

The next day at Muster Parade my name was not called out; I had passed the final test of Pre- Brecon.

'Phase two: P Company'

Next came the P Company phase of selection. This is renowned as being one of the toughest training courses in the military. This phase comprised of more intense and harder physical and fear-based challenges and tests. There were many punishing runs which we had to complete two or three times a day. Sometimes we were woken up in the middle of the night, given one minute to be downstairs in our running kit and be standing in three ranks ready to go on a run. If someone was too slow and did not get downstairs within the time limit, we were all sent back to our barrack rooms and given two minutes to change into whatever uniform they decided, such as full uniform or webbing and Bergen ready for a tab and get back downstairs into three ranks again. These changes of clothes, going up and down, back and forth to our rooms could go on for several changes of clothes. Eventually, we would go on a run.

When we got back from the run in the middle of the night, we would then be given thirty minutes to get our lockers tidied, army regulation standard, of course! This meant not having a single crease in any block of clothing laid out on our locker shelves. When the thirty minutes were up, we would stand beside our beds ready for the inspection. If one of the recruit's lockers was not up to standard, we would all be given one minute to be downstairs for another run and the whole process started again. These tests and the wearing down of us mentally and physically soon began to whittle down recruits and some recruits just gave up the selection process and quit. The process was part of the selector's aim to exhaust us physically and mentally for the challenges ahead of us in P Company.

Sprinting around the assault course on various occasions throughout the day soon became, for me, a case of mind over matter. Physical strength was depleted from me and being tired and worn out made executing the various tasks we had to do on the Trainasium even more dangerous and scary. The Trainasium is an army assault course set over 50 feet above the ground. I remember standing on two scaffold poles up in the air with no safety net underneath me. My legs were spread apart with one foot on each pole. It was a straight drop to the ground and one slip would mean certain death. The length of the walk along the poles from one end to the other was about fifteen feet. I shuffled along the parallel poles to the halfway point, then the Corporal shouted up to me and said, "Stand still, touch your toes then stand up and shout out your army number, rank and name."

Incredulously for someone who was training to jump out of planes for a living, I hated heights and I still do! Cringing, I made myself do the task. When I bent forward, I felt sick to my stomach as I stared down the fifty feet or so to the hard ground; this did not feel safe. There were other daring tasks to do on the Trainasium and thankfully I achieved them without any injuries to myself. Unfortunately, this wasn't the case for some of the other recruits. Many times, the Corporals would tell us to push through the pain barrier in whatever physically or mentally draining task we were being tested on. I began to question, "What was the pain barrier? Had I experienced it? Would I know it and feel it if it happened to me?"

The Corporals kept telling us, "Once you push yourself through the pain barrier, you can achieve all the tests thrown at you".

I soon experienced the pain barrier! Our last ten-mile run and tab to pass P-Company had to be done within a time limit, and this was a fast and agonising ordeal. At the end of the run-tab, we had to lift another recruit into a fireman's lift and sprint a couple of hundred metres to the finish line. Two miles from the end of this run-tab I hit the pain barrier. I became abruptly aware of excruciating pain over my whole body. Cramps in my leg muscles, cramps in my stomach and chest; I felt like my body was shutting down. The pain intensified into an overwhelming sensation, and I realised that this was it; this was the pain barrier. I stubbornly kept going. Now, I was just putting one foot in front of another. My face was screwed up in intense pain and I was in the front group of several recruits who were keeping up with the Corporal pacesetter. I knew that I had to keep up with the pacesetter as that would mean that I would make the cut off time. To pass the time limit we had to arrive at the end with him. I looked behind me and many recruits were spread out at different distances. I knew they would fail the test. The excruciating pain pervading my body was now making me start to fall behind the lead group. I was desperate. Seeing the lead group slipping away from me and trapped in my pain was terrifying. I seemed helpless. I could not keep up. It was impossible. Then, somehow, I shouted, "Fuck!" and I began to push through the pain barrier. Every fibre of my body and mind was screaming with pain, but I kept pushing on and through. I was barely running now. My body crashed! My legs felt like lead and I could only walk and shuffle my feet forward. I was determined to push through the pain, but the lead group was about a hundred metres in front of me now and some of the other recruits began to pass me.

Then, suddenly and unbelievably, the pain reduced and diminished. I got a second breath; I got energy. This, I realised, was the pushing through the pain barrier experience. I sprinted to catch up to the main lead group, reeling them in metre by metre. I caught them with about five hundred metres to the finish line, and there was no way the pacesetter was getting away from me now. We were stopped abruptly with four hundred metres to go to the finish line and were told to pick someone up in a fireman's lift. I picked up a fellow recruit and sprinted two hundred metres carrying him across my shoulders. Two hundred metres from the finish line we were told to change over and I was carried the remaining distance. This was an important task, carrying your cohort even when exhausted. It was instilled in us; we were never to leave anyone behind in a battle. I made it! I went through the pain barrier and passed the final ten-mile test of P-Company.

'Milling'

'Milling' in P Company is a sad and depressing memory for me. Milling is a test of aggression, courage and determination, but mainly aggression. We were forced to 'mill' quite a few times through the selection process.

Recruits were sized up with an opponent according to weight and height and then sat on benches forming a square around mats which effectively formed a boxing ring. The Captain, (officer), sat on a six-foot-high vaulting table, holding a blue flag in one hand and a red flag in the other. Recruits are either blue or red. When it was my turn to mill, my opponent and I stood up to commence battle. There are no rules in milling other than no kicking. There are no breaks in fighting and no referee to stop the fight. You either win or lose or draw. The only equipment was the boxing gloves that we wore. As soon as the Officer dropped his flags, our remit was to punch the hell out of each other, aiming for the head of your opponent, fighting with the mindset that your life depended on winning the fight and knocking your opponent to the floor. I was matched with Private Dunn as we were the same size and weight. We fought each other like demons, and every time we finished our fight and stood before the captain for his judgement of who had won, with the success criteria being who had shown the most aggression, it reminded me of the Roman gladiators in the Colosseum waiting for the thumbs up or down. Dunn and I drew with each other every time we fought; he never won, and I never won. We had a friendship filled with mutual respect.

Dunn was killed in Northern Ireland on the 27th of August 1979 aged just 20 years old, in the massacre at Warren Point. His company was coming to relieve my company on that day, that is why remembering milling is such a depressing thought for me. It so easily could have been me instead of Dunn losing his life that day. He was too young to die in such an atrocious way and was such a good guy. I will share more about the Warren Point Massacre later in this book.

'Phase three: Advanced Brecon'

After passing P Company, I progressed onto the third selection phase, Advanced Brecon. Advanced Brecon was exactly what it said, advanced, with more in-depth understanding of killing tactics. Along with this phase of training were more arduous, physical and mental tests, longer tabs and runs combined with longer and more tiring exercises in the field. Our ability to pick up and learn as well as apply these new skills were also assessed. All these tests and assessments could mean a pass or fail at any moment for each recruit.

We lived in the field for various exercises with little or no sleep for many days. We learned about ambush tactics, killing fields (a defensive position that is intended to allow the defending troops to incapacitate a large number of the enemy), prisoner rolls and search, and how to sneak up and garrotte guards in the silence of night. Along with this, we also learned how to sew escape and evasion equipment into our smocks, skirmish towards an enemy under live fire, and map read in the dark of night after days of moving between different locations for an assortment of tasks. Such a task might be lying in an ambush for a whole night, waiting for the enemy to enter the killing area. Another task might be snatching an enemy agent and capturing them for interrogation. Intertwined with this training and tests were long and back-breaking tabs over the Brecon Beacons.

The final test for Advance Brecon was to set up an Observation Post and log activity of an enemy compound. Unfortunately, it was now winter and heavy snow covered the ground to a depth of two feet and with below freezing conditions. Our Observation Post was made from snow, and it was a camouflaged sort of igloo. Myself and my cohorts knew this was the final hurdle of Advance Brecon so, even though we could not feel our feet and our toes were turning blacker and blacker, we were not going to quit.

'Phase four: Brize Norton'

Thankfully, I passed Advance Brecon and proceeded to the final hurdle, Brize Norton. It was at Brize Norton that my feet began to thaw out, and the pain was unbearable. A few of us had got frostbite and it took all our might to not scream with pain as our toes thawed out. Our Corporals soon became aware of our problem and we were ordered to go to the Brize Norton doctors to have our feet looked at. We were ordered to have bed rest for a week while our toes thawed out, and this did not go down too well with our Corporals! None of us lost any toes, but to this day, aged sixty-one, my toenails still fall off occasionally and I have problems with my feet.

Brize Norton was a completely different experience from the previous selection process. The RAF base was more relaxed; on the base was a bowling alley, bar and sports facilities, and the culture was very different from the army. Each day was filled with Military Parachute training, learning to para roll and carry on our person all the equipment we would need when parachuting into an enemy territory. I had a rifle strapped to a Bergen which was strapped to my leg. Mortar bombs and extra ammunition were packed into my Bergen, along with army-issue food rations. I had a military parachute on my back and a reserve parachute on my front and a helmet on my head. This phase of training progressed us to be able to make military parachute jumps with all this kit attached to us. Each day was enjoyable, and we had the added bonus of being able to go out in the evenings for socializing. Our platoon's claim to fame at the time was that we drank the Brize Norton bar out of Bass beer!

I suppose it was too much to hope for an incident-free time at Brize Norton. Our Corporals came into our barracks late at night and the worse for wear through intoxication by alcohol. We had to get out of our beds and have bare-knuckle fistfights with each. Two names were called out, one after the other, and we two would have to fight. After fifteen minutes of this, one of the older recruits told the Corporals to lay off and get out of our barracks. I could not believe what I was hearing. Amazingly, they listened and left our barracks. Nothing happened to him the next day; we were shocked. My guess is the older recruit had worked out we had passed everything, and we were now valuable merchandise to our officer. He, our officer, would not want things to go wrong now. The Corporals realised this as well.

With the exception of one guy, we all completed our eight military parachute jumps out of a C-130 Hercules aircraft, and a couple of parachute jumps out of balloons. The C-130 jumps were scary, to begin with, but my thoughts were that I have come this far, and whatever, I will jump out of that big bird! A jump consisted of sitting opposite each other inside the C-130 Hercules with all our kit strapped to us. Nearing the Drop Zone, we would stand up and hook our parachute static lines to a cable running along the length of the Hercules aircraft right above our heads. We would then apply the buddy-buddy system, check each other was hooked up correctly and check each other's kit. One of the dispatchers would then walk along the line of paratroopers and check we were hooked up to the cable. Now facing the exit doors on each side of the plane, the doors were opened allowing the wind to gush in and the noise of the engines to increase dramatically. An RAF dispatcher stood by each exit door, and as soon as the red light by the door came on, the dispatcher shouted, "Red on!"

A few seconds later when the green light came on, the dispatcher would shout, "Green on! Go!"

We followed each other to the doors, waiting for our turn to jump. The dispatchers timed the jumping by tapping us on the shoulder signalling that we were to jump just after the paratrooper at the opposite door jumped out. This stopped us banging into each other underneath the plane and our parachutes becoming tangled up.

When I jumped out, I hit the slipstream of air and I rushed past the Hercules at an incredible speed. My legs were pulled tightly together, and I placed my arms over my reserve parachute and around my rifle. The rushing wind turned my body towards the back of the plane into a horizontal position, and I sailed in the slipstream from the exit door to under the Hercules. I watched the metal bottom of the Hercules speed away from me while my static line unravelled my parachute. A tug pulled me upwards as soon as my parachute filled with air, and I then began my descent. I looked up to see if my parachute was fully inflated. It was. I looked around me to see if any other paratroopers were potentially going to tangle with me, but it was clear. I looked down and I saw the ground rushing towards me. I only had a few seconds because we were dispatched at only eight hundred feet from the ground. This was to enable us to get on the ground as quickly as possible to become ready to fight. I released my Bergen strapped to my left leg with my rifle attached to it, and both Bergen and rifle fell some ten feet below me before stopping as it was attached to a rope which in turn was attached to my parachute harness. The ground was coming towards me now at speed and I braced myself for impact by adopting the Para-roll position. Bang! I hit the ground and did a para roll. I released my parachute, grabbed my rifle and threw my Bergen on my back. Then I ran to the Rendezvous Point to meet up with the rest of my platoon. We were ready for battle, and we were ready to kill.

I passed Brize Norton and with that, the Para Selection process; I was a Paratrooper!

Our passing out parade was conducted with the pomp and circumstance that the British Army is famed for, and I was awarded the coveted Para Wings and Maroon beret.

I was a fully qualified paratrooper and ready to join a battalion.

Berlin, East German

'First Posting'

A few of us who passed Para Selection together joined The Second Battalion of the Parachute Regiment, known as 2 Para. The three battalions had their own specific reputations. 1 Para were known as the sports battalion, 2 Para were known as the proficient soldiers and 3 Para were known as the cowboys. I joined 11 Platoon, D Company in 2 Para.

At the time when I joined 2 Para, they were posted to a two-year tour in Berlin. This posting was at the time when the Berlin Wall was still up, and Berlin was surrounded by East Germany. There were only three ways to travel to Berlin, and these routes to and from Berlin were known as 'corridors'. One corridor was for aircraft to fly from West Germany to Berlin, a road corridor to drive from West Germany to Berlin and one railway line running from West Germany to Berlin. Berlin city at this time was divided up into different sectors and each sector came under the authority of the country in charge of that sector's administration. The sectors were British, French, American and East German.

2 Para's barracks were in the Spandau District, sited opposite Spandau Prison. Spandau Prison held the notorious German Nazi criminal from the 2nd World War, Rudolf Hess. He was the only prisoner in Spandau Prison, and it was rumoured that he was used by the East Germans as a pawn so that they could have access to the West through their involvement in taking their turn to guard Rudolf Hess. Each sector took it in turns to guard Rudolf Hess for one month at a time; the Americans, the French, the British and

117

the East Germans. I was on guard duty a couple of times during the British sector's turn, and during these guard duties, we lived in Spandau Prison and took turns at guard duty in the towers surrounding the prison.

At this time, various terrorist groups wanted to break Rudolf Hess out of prison, so this meant we were always on high alert. One of the instructions we were given whilst on guard duty was to not, for any reason, look at Rudolf Hess when he walked around the grassy grounds for his exercise time. The reason for this was that Rudolf Hess liked to cause sensitive international incidents between the East Germans and the western nations. He would do this in order to raise the perks he had in prison. Once, whilst on guard duty, I watched him from the corner of my eye. He knew I was watching him, but my head was not turned towards him so he could not accuse me. He was dressed in a long Crombie-like coat with long johns underneath. On his feet, he wore black army-like boots, and he had a black armband (for mourning) on the arm of his coat. Spandau Prison had an exceptionally eerie feel to it. This may be because it was rumoured to have been used by the Germans in the Second World War to guillotine hundreds and possibly thousands of people. Death was in the atmosphere at Spandau Prison.

When the French, British or Americans took their turn to guard Rudolf Hess, he was given the basic requirements a prisoner should have. When the East Germans guarded Rudolf Hess, he was given luxury. The East Germans wanted him to live a long time as, this way, the East Germans had a regular foothold in West Berlin.

Other duties in West Berlin consisted of patrolling the Berlin wall and observing the East German guards on the other side of the wall. The East German guards had to do a one-year posting in which they had to guard the wall to stop East German people from escaping. When the East German guards were in their last month of duty, they would hold up a small beaded string with knots in to show us, who were observing them through binoculars, just how many days they had left. This was a small connection between human beings on opposite sides in the Cold War era.

I also took my turn a few times to guard the train that travelled from West Berlin through the train corridor into West Germany. The train made a couple of stops in East Germany. I was armed with a 9mm Browning pistol, and when the train stopped at East German train stations, I had to make sure no-one got on or off the train. I would stand at the train door and look out of the window, scanning up and down the train. Opposite me would be an East German soldier armed with a rifle and standing to attention. He also had the responsibility of making sure no-one got on or off the train. We were enemies and we stood three feet from each other weighing each other up. It was a strange encounter with the enemy, so close to each other, yet both pawns in the polarized ideologies of the cold war era.

'Paki shit!'

"Crow, you're a fucking crow!"

"You piece of shit!"

"Fucking run, you crow, and get me a bacon sandwich!"

This was the normal and expected conduct of an 'old sweat' towards a new guy, a rookie, 'a crow'. An 'old sweat' is the idiom for a member of 2 Para (the 2nd Battalion the Parachute Regiment in the British Army) who had been through the 'crow' system or initiation, and progressed into acceptance by the members of a platoon and company. Not only did I have to pass seven months of Para Selection to earn my much-coveted Maroon Beret and Para Wings, but I also had to endure the process which would lead to me being accepted into the brotherhood of the Parachute Regiment. All newly passed-out Paras who joined their battalions had to go through this rookie assessment and initiation. This process was a way of testing and observing the new rookie by the 'old sweats' to ascertain if this new guy could be trusted in a conflict or war situation; trusted to be loyal, brave, courageous and willing to die for the regiment and brothers-in-arms.

This process could last from months to a couple of years. Unwritten rules meant that I could not speak to any members of my platoon unless I was first spoken to. I was obliged to run degrading errands for anyone who asked, no matter what the errand was. It could be running a couple of miles to get some sky hooks (no such thing existed which I came to realise), or going to the barracks of the battalion's cooks to get them out of bed to cook a meal at 2.00 am after the lads had returned from a boozy night out. The cooks never complained; they were resigned to the fact that they were attached to this crazy, violent regiment. The cooks also knew that, on one occasion, three cooks had refused to get up, and the consequence of their refusal meant that they were escorted in the middle of the night to a bridge, tied up, and hung upside down by ropes until roll call at 8.00 am.

I personally excelled at any task I was given, whether it was one of the tomfoolery tasks given to me by the lads, or professional training tasks with the platoon, like running 15 miles with a heavy Bergen on my back or dismantling and assembling a machine gun in seconds. I needed to impress the platoon paratroopers and my non-commissioned officers as well as my commissioned officers.

Part of the unwritten rookie expectation is to be socially isolated from the other platoon members. I had to wait until I was approached first for anything and that included me speaking or requesting information. I didn't have a problem with this expectation; I could do my time as a rookie, no problem. One 'old sweat', Private *M and his new sidekick, Private *F, gave me a different dilemma. Their entrance into my life turned into a terrifying living nightmare for me, one which inflicted so much suffering and trauma on me, trauma which I have only in the past few years fully dealt with.

Private *F and Private *M hated me; they loathed and despised me. Two depravities in their mind's eye generated the sadistic desire in them to inflict cruelty and pain on me. These were the depravities of racism and jealousy. As time moved forward, their depravities grew into a raging desire to kill me. I am mixed-race, half-Indian and half-White British. At that time, people of colour were few and far between in the British Army. Their internal racism was activated because, to Private *F and Private *M, I looked of Pakistani origin. I was also a very handsome young man (often likened to a young Elvis Presley), to whom women were drawn, and this evoked extreme jealousy in both Private *F and Private *M, both of whom were not particularly good-looking or successful with the ladies!

Private *M was about six foot five and weighed around twenty stone. He was a heavyweight boxer and boxed for the 2 Para boxing team. He had previously been kicked out of the UK police force before he joined the Paras, no doubt for sadistic behaviour. I remember watching him having a fistfight outside the NAAFI, and the thumping of fists on bone sounded like a steak being pounded. Private *M never flinched.

Private *F was about six foot two and of muscular build. Private *F was not too bright and spoke in a rather simplistic monotone, not speaking very often as he never had anything to say. He was absolutely covered in acne all over his face, and his nickname was

'Plooky' (from the Scottish word 'plook' meaning a spot or pimple) because of his acne. Both Private *M and Private *F hated 'Pakis' and neither were lucky with the ladies. This made me their number one target for venting their sadistic hatred, racism and jealousy on.

I endured a year of severe physical, verbal and racist attacks from Private *M and Private *F during my 'crow' initiation period into 11 Platoon, D Coy, 2 Para. I endured these attacks nearly every night. Private *M and Private *F would come into my room each night and begin their sadistic humiliation of me. Their 'enjoyment' almost always began with them spitting at me; spitting onto my face, snarling obscenities from their sneering, leering mouths just a few inches from my face. Many times, pushing me down onto my bed and standing over me, spouting, "You dirty Paki bastard", or "You piece of brown shit."

Increasingly, these attacks escalated into more violent assaults. Slapping, punching, kicking and holding me down on the floor, continually spitting in my face, humiliating me with verbal abuse whilst laughing sadistically. Every time, before leaving me alone and leaving my room, they would pull all my kit out of my locker and throw it around the room, stamping on all my immaculately ironed clothes.

I was in a deep sleep one night, which to be honest I rarely experienced as I usually had to sleep with one eye open, when I woke up to the smell of smoke and burning. Flames were all around my face and head. Jumping out of bed in panic and fear, I realised Private *M and Private *F had placed a large amount of tissue paper around my head whilst I slept and set the tissue paper on fire. Private *M and Private *F stood by my bed in the dark, laughing hysterically with pleasure. I frantically put all the flames out by beating them with a blanket. Thankfully, Private *M and

Private *F left my room, as they had had enough entertainment for that night.

Private *M and Private *F's hate for me began to intensify, progressing from loathing and racist disgust, to severe physical attacks. To add to my anguish, their hate evolved into a yearning to kill me, to murder me. Their abusive language changed; now added to their vicious vocabulary were the words 'kill him'.

"We are going to kill you, you dirty Paki bastard."

"Do you hear us? Kill you! You fucking piece of brown shit."

"Kill you!"

Their hate was now a rage!

Our battalion went on exercise manoeuvres in Sennelager, West Germany. Arriving back at our barracks after a day's training, I was enjoying an evening meal in the cookhouse when a concerned member of my platoon told me that Private *M and Private *F had boasted that they were going to kill me that night. He told me, "When you leave the dinner hall, they are going to kill you in the dark with a shovel. They're going to smash your head in."

I asked him how he knew this, and he told me he had overheard them talking.

I knew that this had a high likelihood of being true; in my heart, I could feel it. Panic and fear immediately filled my whole head and body. My childhood friends, fear, depression and dread, paralysed me. All I wanted to do was sleep after a day's skirmishes and live firing training. "How could I be safe? What could I do?" I had to move quickly and hide. I grabbed a shovel from the side of the door to the cookhouse and ran into the dark, looking for somewhere to hide. I needed somewhere I could have my back to a wall and be able to swing my shovel if found. I found a doorway to a disused building a little way from the main barracks. Terrified and anxious that I would be found soon, I waited and waited in the dark with the army shovel in my hands, ready to defend myself; ready to fight for my life. After some time, I sat down with the shovel tightly gripped in both hands; I was so tired that I eventually fell asleep sat upright. I stayed there all night, and at first light, I made my way back to my barracks to make it in time for the 8.00 am roll call. I knew the resumption of the daylight manoeuvres would protect me, for now.

'Poke his eyes out'

It was early evening and I was in my room on my own. Two looming beasts appeared and stood in the doorway. There was only one way in and one way out for me, and the doorway in which Private *M and Private *F were standing was it. I quickly contemplated jumping out of the window, but it was too high. I was two floors up, and the least injury I could expect from the impact of a jump from two floors up would be a broken leg, probably a compound fracture. I sat on my bed, helpless, and resigned to the beating to come. My head was tilted forward; I was looking at the floor, submissive and too frightened to look up and meet the eyes of Private *M and Private *F. Connecting my eyes with theirs could provoke a rageful attack on me. Sadistically, Private *M and Private *F stood in the doorway and stared at their prey like a couple of cats toying with a mouse before the kill. Their sinister play with me intensified the atmosphere, and they appeared to take great pleasure in blocking my escape route. The menacing self-gratification of their power and control over me puffed them up into smirking monsters with evil intent.

"We're going to kill you, you stinking Paki bastard!" Private *F said in an intimidating tone.

Then silence. They lapped up the pleasure and amusement the long silences gave them. Still standing in the doorway, Private *M growled, "I'm going to poke your eyes out and stuff them down your throat, you piece of shit."

Again, silence was inflicted on me for a few minutes. Private *M pulled a long knife out of his jacket. The blade was glistening silver and narrowed at the end into a tapered point similar to a spear blade. I was so subdued and full of panic and fear that I couldn't move. They rushed towards me and started punching and kicking me. I covered my head and face with my arms as the punches rained down on me. Private *F grabbed one arm and Private *M grabbed the other and they threw me on the floor. I was dazed by the impact of the punches and lay on the floor helpless and completely vulnerable, at the mercy of these animals. Private *M, in a quiet, ominous tone, instructed me to lie flat on my back with my arms down by my side. I was compliant, completely compliant. Private *F knelt beside me and said, "If you move, you fucking Paki bastard, I will kill you."

I began to sense they had a plan.

Private *M lay down with his left arm on my throat and his right hand holding his knife above my face. He smiled at me with a snigger, his lips curled back revealing his teeth. "I'm going to poke your eyes out, shit face."

Private *F sat astride my torso and applied all his weight and strength onto me so I couldn't move. I was petrified, immobilised like a man playing dead with a grizzly bear on top of him waiting for the first flesh-ripping bite.

"Keep your fucking eyes open, cunt."

Private *M held his knife a few inches in front of my face, and an eerie silence filled the room. Private *M's face, with his gloating sadistic smile, was now about six inches away from my face. He held the knife an inch above my left eye, then moved the knife to an inch above my right eye.

"I'm going to cut your eyes out, Paki shit."

Private *M gently lay the flat of the blade of his knife onto my left eyeball. He was revelling at the sight of my eye blinking profusely and seeing terror, pure terror in my stare. He was experimenting to see what happened when he touched my eye. He held the blade an inch away from my eye once again, purposely intensifying my fear and panic. This was it; he was now going to pop my eye out of its socket with the point of the blade on his knife. He held the point of the blade a few centimetres from the corner of my left eye. I couldn't move. If I tried to move, he might just stab me in the eye.

Slowly, very slowly, he was moving the knife towards my eye. Private *M touched my eye with the flat of the knife's blade. My eye blinked profusely, water streaming out, and at that moment, another 'old sweat' came into the room. He quickly sussed out what was happening, and when I say sussed out, he knew exactly what, or more accurately, who he was dealing with; Private *M and Private *F. I recall that the old sweat had exceptionally blond hair, and in a quiet voice, he talked to Private *M saying, "Hold on, you don't want to do this. You will end up in jail."

Private *M ignored the old sweat and continued to hold the point of his knife near my eyeball. The old sweat knew he needed to keep the situation as calm as he could. The old sweat continued gently talking to and coaxing Private *M to realise that this would not end well for him. Thoughts raced through my mind; "Would Private *M and Private *F turn their attention towards the old sweat? Would he gouge my eye out?" About twenty or so minutes after the old sweat entered the room, Private *M got off me, Private *F stood up, and they both calmly walked out of the room.

'Run for your life!'

A guy I did not know very well burst through the double stairwell doors at the far end of the corridor and sprinted towards me.

"Run Paul, run! Quick, you have got to get out of here! Private *M has gone crazy and he is coming to kill you!"

"Shit! Fuck! Where is he?" I said.

"He is coming up the stairwell at the other end of the corridor."

I was standing in the corridor by the double doors which led to the stairwell located at my end of the barrack room's long corridor. Private *M was coming up the staircase at the opposite end of this corridor.

"You've got to be quick, Paul. He has been drinking and he is in a rage to kill you." Incomprehensible terror and dread filled every fibre of my body.

"Fuuuuuck, what shall I do?"

Private *M burst through the stairwell double doors at the far end of the corridor. He saw me standing at the opposite end of the corridor to him and sneered sadistically. I could see his eyes, and they projected pure hate, a desire and need to extinguish me. Private *M began to walk very quickly towards me, his prey. His head and shoulders were leaning forward, and he looked like a crazy man-bull, snorting and snarling as he advanced towards me. It was an incredibly scary moment. I ran through the double doors to my right, pushing the doors with so much force that they smashed into the wall causing an almighty bang. Sprinting down the stairs and jumping four or five steps at a time, I charged through the double doors on the ground floor. These doors led directly out of the barrack block, and once outside, I had no idea where to run to. I knew nobody was going to help me. I was on my own.

Private *M was running down the stairs behind me shouting, "I'm going to kill you, you Paki bastard." He began to sing the words in a high-pitched voice and tone, "I'm going to kill a Paki today."

I turned left and began running towards the 2 Para guardroom which was about half a mile away. Our barracks were enormous and stretched over a huge area of land. I looked back once and saw Private *M jogging after me with the same sneer/smile on his face. He really was a sadist and a racist and enjoyed every moment of the pain and heartache he inflicted on me. I ran with fear and trepidation that I would be caught, and I had no protection. I was alone in this living nightmare. I got to the guardroom and told the Corporal on duty, "Private *M is coming to kill me. Please help me."

He responded only to tell me that he could not help me. I think he feared Private *M; most of the guys did. I begged the Corporal, but he would not help me. We both heard Private *M coming, he was shouting and snarling, "Come here, Paki Parks."

I ignored the Corporal and ran into the guard room, down the corridor and into the end communal prison cell. The lights were off, and I ran to the end bed on the right. This was the fourth bed up from the prison cell door. I could hear Private *M's voice, demanding that the Corporal on the front desk tell him where I was. I dived under the fourth bed on the right and hid. I heard Private *M's footsteps coming down the corridor slowly. He must have been looking into each cell room to see if I was there. I knew he would see me when he came to peer into the room I was hiding in, even though I was under the bed. In my panic and desperation,

I had an idea. I grabbed hold of the springs on the underneath of the bed base and pulled myself up to a position where I was completely flat against the base of the bed. I pushed my feet and legs against the sides of the underneath of the bed with the points of my toes pushing against the metal base, and the inside of my ankles flat against the base springs. The physical position of my whole body from my head to the tips of my toes was completely flat against the underneath of the base of the bed. I effectively became part of the silhouette and shape of the underneath of the bed.

I was extremely fit and my strength to body ratio was exceptional at this time of my life. This physical fitness enabled me to be able to press my whole body into the bed base, camouflaged in the shadow and shape of the bed.

Private *M appeared at the doorway of the communal prison cell I was hiding in. The corridor light was on. The cell light was off. His body shape loomed in the doorway as he scanned the room. I could see him with my right eye. The large outline of his profile stood in the doorway. He reached into the room with his right arm, whilst staying in the doorway, and turned the lights on. He scanned the room again. He cast his eyes over each bed, starting from the left bed closest to him and making his way up each bed on the left of him. He did this slowly and meticulously. He was now looking at the top left bed opposite to me. His eyes moved from the top left bed over to the right row of beds. I was hanging onto the underneath of the top right bed. I could see his eyes scanning the bed I was under. I froze!

Somehow, I made every muscle, nerve and part of my body go into a sort of hibernation state as I hung on. It seemed like a lifetime while he scanned my bed. "Would he see me?" Then, relief, his eyes moved to the bed next to me. Private *M continued to scan the beds and eventually looked up somewhat confused. He stood there for a few minutes; I suppose he was waiting for his prey to appear. He then turned around and walked out of the guardroom. I let myself down onto the floor. I had clenched onto the springs of the bed base for so long that I had lost all feeling in my fingers, and lay there for a while trying to get some feeling back into them. It had worked though! Somehow, I had blended into the bed base silhouette. The Corporal walked down the corridor to the door of the cell I was in. I knew it was not Private *M because of the sound of his walk. He saw me on the floor under the bed and asked if I was ok. I answered him with a, "Yes, but can I sleep here tonight, please?"

The Corporal nodded his agreement and turned the lights off. I slept under the bed on the floor until the morning. I felt safe and ready to pull myself up under the bed in case Private *M came back. In the morning, I made my way back to my barracks to get ready for roll call.

I was 18 years old at the time when this all happened.

'The worm turns'

It was about 10.30 pm and I had just finished my ironing, tidied my locker, cleaned my boots and got my webbing sorted for the next day. This was pretty much my normal routine in preparation for the next day. My bed was directly opposite the entrance door to my room and I was just sitting, not really thinking about much, just sitting. Suddenly, my door swung open and Private *F stood in the doorway, standing still and glaring in my direction. He was on his own. There was no sign of Private *M. It seemed strange to me that he was alone, as I had come to expect the almost nightly ritual of beatings and racial abuse by both Private *M and Private *F. He stepped into my room and closed the door behind him. I could tell he was confident that I would be submissive and subdued as normal. As always, it began!

"You dirty Paki piece of shit. You're going to get such a kicking!" Private *F's smirking sneer seemed even more evil than normal, but I also sensed, just for a second, a clumsy sort of unsureness in Private *F's walk towards me. He was not as confident without his accomplice; this weakness I spotted in a milli-second. Two dynamic undercurrents collided at that moment; Private *F was not as confident as usual and Private *M was not with him. I was at my wit's end with the beatings, torture and racial abuse inflicted on me by these monsters. I'd had enough. I couldn't take any more. I stood up as Private *F walked towards me, and immediately, he swung his right arm and, as I ducked, punched me directly on the right side of my head. This time, though, was different; this time I wasn't just going to stand there and passively take my 'punishment'. For the first time ever, I punched back! I swung my right arm, clenched my fist and connected with the left side of Private *F's head. For a split second, he was totally shocked, gobsmacked; the worm had turned! He responded with, "I'm going to kill you, you fucking Paki Bastard!"

The beginning of the end began.

It was to be the end of Private *F and Private *M beating and torturing me daily, but the beginning of a lifetime for me of flashbacks, night terrors, aggression, hypervigilance, depression and dissociative episodes. This was one more trauma to add to the dozens of other traumas constantly invading my mind, creating confusion and mayhem and resulting many years later in a diagnosis of Complex Post-Traumatic Stress Disorder ('C-PTSD') and PTSD with dissociative subtype.

Mayhem! A brutal bare-knuckle fight began between Private *F and me; we both understood that this was most likely a fight to the death. In me, there was a strange combination of panic and fear mixed with instilled 'Para' aggression and ferocity. Paras were, and still are, trained and programmed to be able to turn into raging violent killers at the flick of a switch, not giving in to anyone or anything until the bitter end. This was the modus operandi for the fight between Private *F and me.

Blow after blow, we punched each other; throw after throw, we threw each other to the ground in this close-contact combat. We were both at the prime of our fitness, fit as an Olympic athlete. This fitness meant that we were able to sustain a twenty-minute ruthless, vicious, and extremely violent fight. We were covered in our own and each other's blood. There was blood everywhere, on the floor, ceiling and walls. I knew that I wouldn't be able, physically, to sustain this intensity for much longer, so, with all the strength I could muster, I swung one final, decisive punch. The fight had ended. My fist had connected directly with Private *F's jaw, and I still see clearly to this day the image of Private *F spinning upwards to his right side and then ending on the floor, heavily dazed, with his jaw evidently out of line with his face.

For a few moments, everything was motionless, quiet and still except for the low muffled moans of Private *F. I wondered for a moment if he was dying. He was breathing heavily; his eyes were open, and he began to try and talk. In some ways, I felt a sense of relief that he wasn't dying, but also complete dread. What if Private *M comes looking for Private *F?

Faced with the scene in my room and the damage done to his sidekick, Private *M would surely kill me instantly! I grabbed a change of clothes and ran out of my room, down the stairs and out of the barracks. On my way out of the guardroom, Corporal made me sign out as per protocol; there was nothing I could do to hide the fact that I had been in the barracks at the time. I was terrified of Private *M and did not know what to do about Private *F. I walked around Spandau area all night, and signed back into barracks about 7.00 am before roll call. I walked slowly to my barracks, not really knowing what to expect. As I reached the top of the stairs, I could see that members of the Military Police were both inside and outside my room.

'Lifting the Lid'

"Are you Paul?" one of the policemen standing duty at my door asked.

"Yes," I answered.

"Do you know what happened in your room to Private *F?"

"Yes," I replied without hesitation; there was no point in trying to avoid the inevitable.

"Ok, we need to talk to you. Go get a brew in the cookhouse and we will come and get you when we're ready."

I walked to the cookhouse, got a cup of tea and sat on my own and waited. All the other Paras dressed in working uniform for the day eventually left the cookhouse and went to their rollcalls and various duties. I sat and waited, still in my civvies, not knowing what had happened to Private *F, and what would happen to me.

At about 10 am, two Military Policemen in uniform came into the cookhouse and arrested me. I was marched in double time to the Welsh Guards' barracks and prison which was situated right next to our barracks. I was put into a prison cell and guarded by the Welsh Guards. I still had no idea what had happened to Private *F, and no idea what might happen to me. All I was told by the Military Policeman was that Private *F was in hospital. I had, as I had thought, broken his jaw, and that someone from the Special Investigation Team was going to come and talk to me at some point.

I was kept in the Welsh Guards' cell for three days before a plain-clothed Military Policeman came to interview me. During those three days, I was collected by 2 Para's Regimental Provost Police each day for an hour and a half of double-quick time square bashing on 2 Para's parade ground. For 1 ½ hours, I was ordered to march in double-quick time. This is like sprinting but walking, taking each step as fast as you can to the beat of the Provost Sergeant's call and timing. My arms had to come up to shoulder height and be completely straight. My steps were extremely fast and non-stop. Added to this I had to carry a forty-pound artillery shell on my right shoulder. "Left-right! Left-right! Left-right!" shouted the Provost Sergeant as fast as he could. Any slacking in speed or not holding the forty-pound shell straight meant a punishment of thirty extremely fast press-ups.

On the third day of my imprisonment, a Military Policeman in plain clothes came to talk to me in my cell. He was a detective, and his demeanour was gentle and patient. My training kicked in, and I immediately went into 'prisoner of war' mode. "Do not say anything. Just give your name, number and rank," I said to myself. To begin with, I did not answer any of his questions or respond to any of his comments. Little did I know that he had already gathered a lot of information from my fellow Paratroopers in my platoon and company. The detective already had a pretty clear picture of the situation I had found myself in with Private *F and Private *M, and he was trying to get me to open up and talk with him. He gave me a scenario to think about; "What if someone had to fight for their life; what would you think would happen to them?" This began a game of cat and mouse between the detective and me. You see,

I didn't know who I could trust. I had told my NCOs about Private
*M and Private *F, and most of the lads knew about the punishing
beatings I got on a regular basis, but no-one had tried to help me
or stop it from happening.

Here I was in jail, and at this point, I did not know what was
going to happen to me. I was completely vulnerable, vulnerable to
the power of the authorities, my senior officers and the police. I was
understandably cautious. So began an afternoon which lasted about
four hours, with me saying things like, "What is your opinion about
a scenario, not about me of course, this is just a story to see what
you think; a scenario in which a guy is brutally beaten up every
night for a year?"

The detective responded by saying, "The Military Police would
look into it, investigate it, and bring the perpetrators to justice".

"What if the perpetrators had held someone down for hours
with a knife on their eyeball, threatening to poke their eye out at
any minute?"

"I would listen to the person who had been tortured and get
them justice."

This façade of a conversation went on for hours. I feared
admitting that I had had the fight with Private *F, as I was scared
I would not be believed. Eventually, I trusted the detective and
shared with him the year of torture I had endured. He formally
arrested me and charged me with breaking Private *F's jaw. He
told me that Private *F was in hospital, and eventually, I learned he
was hospitalised for six weeks and had to be fed through a straw for
much of the time as his jaw was wired up.

I was told that Private *F and Private *M would be facing a
Court Martial for what they had inflicted on me. But so much for
trusting an institution; I was told that I would be facing a Court

Martial as well! I was next visited by a noticeably young lieutenant who told me he was my defence advocate. He was not a lawyer or legally trained, he was a young infantry officer. He informed me that the Commanding Officer wanted me to admit what happened between Private *F and I that night, and if I did so, I would get 28 days hard jail and that would be the end of it for me. Naively, at the age of eighteen, with no formal education and no reliable parent to get advice from, I agreed. It seemed like the quickest way to get me out of jail and back to my platoon.

Before the Court Martial, I was moved to the 2 Para jail and guardroom into the custody of the 2 Para Provost Sergeant and his men. This was absolutely terrifying for me because Private *M was being kept in the same jail. The guardroom consisted of three individual cells situated next to each other on the left side of a corridor which led to a communal cell at the end of the guardroom, housing six prisoners together. Private *M was in cell confinement in the first cell on the left as I walked down to the communal cell at the end. As I was marched past Private *M's cell, he looked out of the bars of his cell and snarled at me, "You're fucking dead!" At least in the communal cell, there were a few guys I knew, and we slept on single beds arranged a bit like a dormitory.

'Court Martial'

At the Court Martial, I was marched into a large room and at the far end of the room was a long thick wooden table with four officers who were seated and watching me being marched in. One single chair was in the middle of the room some ten metres away from the officers sitting at the table. I saluted and sat down. I was then asked by one of the officers to give my name. In an earlier briefing, I was told that when I was asked to give my name I was to stand up, salute, give my number, rank, name, and sit down. This I did. The young officer advocating for me stood up, and recounted to the Court Martial officers something like this:

"Parks is an excellent soldier. He defended himself in a fight with Private *F. Parks had been bullied for a substantial length of time. Parks regrets the injury Private *F received in the fight he had with Private *F."

The four officers leaned over and mumbled amongst themselves for a few seconds. One officer ordered me to stand and said, "Parks, we find you guilty of assault on Private *F, which resulted in Private *F being hospitalised with a broken jaw. You are sentenced to twenty-eight days in jail." The young officer looked at me from where he was standing, just in front of me to my right and winked. The Provost Sergeant shouted at me, "Parks! Salute and double-quick time. Left, right, left, right, left, right!" I was double-quick marched back to the guardroom jail. Private *M was not in his cell. By the end of the day, I was informed that Private *M had been given two years at The Military Corrective Training Centre in Colchester, which is effectively prison for the Military, and kicked out of the army with a dishonourable discharge. It was decided that Private *F would be transferred to 1 Para when he came out of hospital. I began twenty-eight days in the Glasshouse (military jail).

'Glasshouse'

In reality, my time in the Glasshouse would not bother me too much because I was a very fit young man, and the life I had been forced to live up until this point prepared me for whatever 'shit' was thrown at me.

137

My routine in the Glasshouse was the same every day. At 6.00 am every morning, I was woken up with the order, "Get up, you horrible little man; hands off cocks on socks!" I had fifteen minutes to get washed, shaved and on parade. I would then be tasked with shining a large steel bin. It wasn't shining as such; it was what the army calls 'bulling'. With a cloth and brass shiner, I would place the cloth over one of my fingers and go round and round making little circles on the steel bin to shine it. The whole bin looked like glass. If I looked up or took my eyes off the bin, I would be 'beasted', given an extremely physical exercise to do as a punishment, such as 50 sit-ups. I had to do this for over 2 hours until breakfast time at 8.30 am. This was the time most of the soldiers were leaving the cookhouse after their breakfast. I was double-marched to the cookhouse with a forty-pound shell on my shoulder, and a white helmet on my head, then hurried through my breakfast with shouts of 'You waster! You horrible little man!' After being double-marched back to the guardroom, I was given five minutes to go to the loo and then back to 'bulling' the steel bin.

At 10.00 am, I was double-marched to the assault course, and with a forty-pound shell on my back and forty pounds of sand in webbing around my waist and on my back, I had to run around the assault course sixteen times with additional press-ups on the way! After the assault course, it was double-march back to the guardroom and five minutes to get a shower and then back to 'bulling' the bin! Lunch, like breakfast, was a very hurried affair! At 2.00 pm, I was double-marched around the main square for an hour carrying a forty-pound shell on my shoulder, in full view of everyone as the square was in the centre of the barracks. I was determined to not be cracked, and I double-marched straight and strong. Sweat, grit and pure determination were going to get me through this jail time.

More 'bulling', then a hurried dinner followed by yet more 'bulling' until 8.00 pm. I was then given until 10.00 pm to polish, iron and wash my kit. It had to be immaculate for the next day, and I mean immaculate. At 10.00 pm, lights were out, and I was in bed until 6.00 am. This same monotonous routine continued for twenty-eight days.

'R&R (Rest and Recuperation)'

On one of my leaves from Berlin, I decided to buy a motorbike and drive it back. I had never ridden a motorbike before, and at the time, I could drive up to a 250cc on my provisional driving licence. I bought a 250cc Honda Dream and practised driving it around the roads of Essex. I then drove it over to West Germany and up the corridor road through East Germany and into West Berlin. I was given a time limit to get from the beginning of the corridor and arrive in West Berlin. Halfway up the corridor, I had to stop at an East German checkpoint, and the East German guards took their time with me because they admired my brand-new motorbike so much. I arrived safely in West Berlin with my brand-new sparkling motorbike.

On another leave, myself and a couple of my friends ended up in the Rhodesian Embassy in London. It was at a time when members of the British Army and former Army members were being actively recruited to join various mercenary groups throughout Africa, to fight in the many conflicts occurring in different African countries. The pay was always good and attractive. We were young and full of hunger for adventure. When we entered the Rhodesian Embassy, we were quickly led to an extremely attractive lady sitting behind a desk, and she was delighted to see us. We were told about the money we could earn and given the offer of an immediate start. This was the time of white rule in Rhodesia and the uprising of the Black people against white rule which was led by Robert Mugabe.

My friends and I were not political in any way, and we were not racist. We were just young trained paratroopers looking naively for adventure and money. We were ready to sign up and go AWOL from the British army and leave for Africa. The lady told us to go and have a pint, and when we came back, she would have all the paperwork completed and we would be on our way to Rhodesia. The three of us went for a pint and got talking about the consequences of going AWOL and becoming mercenaries. Our conversation went one way and then another, as we debated the pros and cons. In the end, we decided to give it a couple more months in 2 Para, realising there were plenty of mercenary recruiters about at the time. If we wanted to change our mind, we easily could.

West Berlin was a vibrant and lively city, and as young men, we had a lot of fun there. The nightlife was extraordinary, with many discos brimming over with young women. Although none of us were particularly naive with regards to the opposite sex, we did find the Berliner's relaxed attitude to sex somewhat of a culture shock! I remember going to a public sauna for the first time in my life, and sitting in my shorts, when naked women and men came in and sat down next to me with no inhibitions about being naked. This was normal to Berliners.

There was also a park situated in the middle of Berlin's busy shopping region. It was remarkably similar in appearance to a smaller version of Hyde Park in London. In order to enter this park, though, it was expected that you stripped completely naked! There were no fences or screens to give some privacy. The park was a lovely large grassy area, and people would go there during their lunch breaks, strip off, and have their lunch, stark naked!

In the centre of Berlin was a large NAAFI, and drinks were exceptionally cheap there. On a night out, we would first go to the NAAFI for a short while, making the best use of the cheap drinks, and then hit the nightlife. A dark aspect of this exuberant nightlife was the many dangerous fights we would get into. Mixing trained, aggressive paratrooper killers with normal citizens was always going to be a recipe for trouble, especially if you add excessive amounts of alcohol into the mix. Some of the guys would go to the gym before a night out in order to practise a right punch or a kick to the head. Many of the fights we had, and some of the fights I was involved with, were dangerous and extremely violent.

One night, we were in a disco and it was quite late. I got tapped on the shoulder and told I was needed to go with some of the lads to help them. We got outside the disco and a group of five or six of us began following our friend who needed our help. He began running and we ran with him until we came to the top of a flight of stairs. Halfway down the staircase was a gang of German men who obviously hated the British. Our friend told us they had attacked him earlier. As soon as he had told us this, he took a running jump and leapt in the air headfirst, flying down the staircase and colliding with the first member of this gang. We all followed him, running down the stairs to help him. At the bottom of the staircase, some workmen were working with boiling hot tar. One of their gang members picked up a boiling bucket of tar and threw it at us. Some of the tar caught me on the side of my neck, and I had scars from the burns for some years after. Others of my friends were splashed with tar, and this enraged us. A bloody and violent fight broke out, and unfortunately for the German gang members, they ended up covered in boiling hot tar. After the fight, we returned to the disco, patting each other on the back and continued to dance and drink the night away.

On another occasion, four of us went to a beer festival. It was a hot summer's day and the beer tent was full of German people, men and women, who were sat around long tables drinking beer from huge tankards. At the front of the large tent was a stage with a raised platform. We sat at a long table in front of the stage alongside the locals. One of our guys was very drunk, and we were about to grab him and take him back to barracks when he jumped onto the stage and started dancing and singing for everyone. To begin with, the Germans laughed at him. However, the mood changed. Unfortunately, the person trying to convince him to get off the stage grabbed him by the arm, and this flicked his paratrooper aggressive switch. Our friend started calling all the Germans in the large tent highly offensive names, and some more Germans jumped onto the stage to try and push him off. That was it; bedlam broke out. The rest of us British jumped on top of the long beer table and ran to the stage to help him. The whole tent was now baying for our blood. We were fighting Germans jumping on the table to get us, and we were being attacked from all sides. We grabbed our friend and pulled him underneath the table. We had to be quick. We began crawling as fast as we could underneath the tables towards an exit. As there were so many people in the tent, it made it difficult for the Germans to get to us, although we received many kicks! Jumping up from under the table, we punched and fought our way to the exit door, and once free, ran through the packed crowds and out of the front gate. Germans were still running after us! Thankfully, there was a taxi near the entrance, so we just jumped in the taxi and left with Germans in hot pursuit!

Many of our training exercises were held in Sennelager, West Germany. Our battalion would travel down to Sennelager for a few weeks at a time to go on manoeuvres and undertake various training practices. A group of us were on our way back to barracks after a night out, and we noticed, up an alleyway, that a fire door was open giving access to one of the Peep Show venues. We had all had a bit too much to drink and decided to creep up the alleyway and go into the peep show. We were full of arrogance and filled with the bravado of drink. The peep show was set up like a small theatre, and we took our seats on the front row. There was only a couple of other people in there, a male and female couple and a single man, all of whom sat a few rows back from us. In front of us on the stage, a naked attractive woman was performing. We noticed a group of several foreign men gathered at the back of the venue, all carrying hockey sticks. We put two and two together and realised the owner of the red-light venue had phoned his friends to come and help evict us. The owner came and asked us to pay an extortionate fee. We had no money left and told him that we couldn't. When he walked back to his friends, we ran back out of the fire door and down the alleyway out onto the road, pursued by the men with hockey sticks, swinging the sticks at our heels as we ran. Our barracks was only a few hundred yards away, and as I sprinted, I felt and heard the full swing of a hockey stick swooshing through the air. The stick missed my skull by millimetres; I knew this because I felt the hockey stick rush through my short hair. The blow, I have no doubt, could have either killed me or left me brain-damaged. At that moment, I thought about stopping and punching the hell out of this guy. I did not fear him, and the para 'trigger' kicked in. I was invincible in this moment. Instead, for some reason, my sprint nearly doubled in speed, and retreating was, I decided, an option. We ran to our barracks and when we calmed down, we were relieved that we had got out alive.

On another outing, after being on exercise in West Germany for a week or so, I was out with some friends. I had had a few too many drinks, but I was ok. Unfortunately, the Military Police were patrolling the area and a patrol stopped me as I was walking back to barracks. They told me that I had had too much to drink and that they were taking me back with them. I went with them peacefully and did not make a fuss. When they got me to their offices, they started to become difficult with me. I am not sure if they had a dislike for Paras. Anyway, for some reason, they left the interview room with me in it on my own. I looked around and I noticed a window in the interview room was open. I clicked into escape and evasion mode, ran to the window and opened it enough for me to jump out and run back to barracks. I have always wondered if they left the window open as a bet, just to see what I would do.

Once again, we were in a disco in West Germany, one which was frequented by British and American servicemen. A fight broke out between the American and the British military. Again, the fight was brutal and violent with many injuries being incurred. I was not involved at all, but I did see some of our guys who were involved in the fight at the opposite end of the disco. I started to make my way over to help. A very tall Black American serviceman saw me begin to move, and out of his jacket, he pulled out a pistol, cocked it and pointed it at my face. He was standing only about four feet away from me. He was very calm and cool in his manner. He pointed to the exit door of the disco and told me to walk. I considered whether I should rush him, but with the pistol cocked and ready and pointing at my face, I turned and walked towards the exit door. For an instant, I wondered if he was going to shoot me in the back of the head. I went through the doors and down the stairs and as the Police were just arriving, I walked back to barracks.

I drank far too much in Berlin. I drank most nights. It was a problem, but I didn't know it at the time. I remember falling asleep on the side of a dual carriageway when I was walking back to barracks one night, my head only a few feet from the cars zooming past me as I slept. I was woken up by a kind army officer who put me in his car and drove me back to barracks.

The nightlife in Berlin was vast and lively. On one night out, my friend *Pete, a fellow paratrooper, and I found ourselves walking up a stairwell, which was dark and poorly lit, which led up to black double doors. We opened the doors to reveal a vibrant, packed disco in full swing. A live band was playing, and people were energetically dancing in the crowded venue. The disco was large with flashing lights and had a stage on which the band was playing. This was a young German adult's venue, a venue where members of the British Army were not welcome or wanted. We could tell this by the disapproving looks we got, and the sophisticated demeanour of the young men and women dancing. Unfortunately for them, and probably unfortunately for us, this prejudice towards us was an enticement to a couple of young cocky paratroopers. So, what does a couple of young paratroopers do in this situation? Dance their hearts out in front of the stage and the band.

At this point in our lives, we believed we were invincible. We were paratroopers, an elite part of the British Army, and we were not scared of anything or anyone. Indeed, we had been programmed and trained to advance into trouble, not run away. We were having a ball, and to our surprise, many beautiful young German women began to join in and dance with us, exuding joy and energy. The German women, *Pete and I, were dancing together, singing and shouting to the sounds of the band.

This scene proved to be too much for the band, and two of the electric guitar players jumped off the stage in the middle of a song. Out of my left eye, I caught sight of one of the guitar players lift his guitar high above his head and swing it towards mine. I ducked and the guitar smashed into my shoulder and broke in half. Screams and chaos erupted immediately. Women ran away from the dance floor, falling over each other in their desperation to get away. *Pete and I found ourselves back to back, with the band attempting to punch, kick and smash guitars over our heads. We fought back with the ferocity that young paratroopers can muster in an instant. Punches, kicks, chairs and guitars all came at *Pete and me. We managed to stay on our feet, as we knew if we went down, we wouldn't get up again. These people really wanted to hurt us.

More young men in the disco joined the band in fighting us. I threw punch after punch, either knocking each advancing person to the ground or halting them in their tracks. *Pete did the same. We were now side by side, stepping backwards with the tide of people in front of us. Suddenly, we crashed through some large swinging doors that led into a kitchen and landed on our backs. We looked at each other, smiled and then jumped to our feet.

The now angry mob pushed their way through the double doors. Young men and women picked up pots and pans and started hitting us with them. *Pete and I were blocking the blows of pots and pans with our arms and hands. We were still being pushed backwards by the force of the mob, which was baying for our blood. Violence is contagious. Our backsides hit an emergency exit door bar and we fell out of the kitchen, falling backwards onto the iron fire escape platform. The mob stopped at the threshold of the fire exit and looked down at us laying on our backs. *Pete and I looked at each other, laughed, picked ourselves up and ran down the fire escape as fast as we could.

Northern Ireland, UK

'Pathfinder Platoon'

Battalion life began to change once we were informed of our next posting. We were to be posted to Northern Ireland for a two-year tour. In general, myself and the other paras were pleased with this posting and looked forward to it. We were so naïve, considering the terror, blood spilled and loss of life our two-year tour would bring upon us, as well as the mental scars that would ruin some of our lives.

Our training became much more intense. Getting ready for Northern Ireland meant we were always being conditioned to have a serious focus on our mental attitude and to be alert. This attitude we were told, will save lives. I was selected to train to be a sniper. My fieldcraft skills and shooting skills were finely tuned to near perfection on this course. Whilst we were still in Berlin, my platoon Sergeant asked me if I would like to join the Pathfinder Platoon.

This platoon was the elite unit of 2 Para. To join this platoon, you had to be an experienced paratrooper and generally much older than I was at the time. Most of the guys in the Pathfinder platoon were in their thirties or late twenties. I was nineteen years old. Potential members of the Pathfinder platoon had to take part in a selection course and pass it to join them. For some reason, perhaps it was due to my performance as a soldier in D Coy and my performance on the sniper course, my sergeant volunteered me to join the Pathfinder platoon. I only had to do a short selection course which included stripping and assembling unfamiliar rifles, guns and pistols within a time limit. I was only shown how to strip and assemble a weapon once. I also had other mental tests that I had to pass. I passed all the tests and joined this scary-looking bunch of elite older soldiers, still only a teenager myself. Thankfully, they accepted me straight away. There was no 'crow' or rookie treatment; they measured me by my ability to do soldiering well, and to excel at fitness and any task given to me. I enjoyed belonging to this platoon. Being part of this platoon garnered a level of respect from other members of 2 Para and from the officers and NCOs (Non-Commissioned Officers) of the battalion. The role of the Pathfinder platoon in wartime was to parachute behind enemy lines and prepare a Drop Zone for the rest of the Para battalions to be parachuted in. This involved learning to live and hide behind enemy lines. It also involved learning to destroy bridges, railway lines and targets like electric pylons whilst hiding behind enemy lines.

Our Pathfinder Platoon once did an exchange and mini selection course with the French Commandos, who were the Special Operations Force of the French Navy. We had to pass their French Commando Course and earn their French Commando badge. This was a course where we learned and practised how to use magnetic mines to 'take out' a tank. We had to lie in the press-up position while tanks drove straight at us, then when the tank was about to drive over us, we would touch the moving tank's track before we rolled out of the way. It was a great course and it enhanced our explosives training. We learned a lot about making booby traps with explosives in order to blow up buildings and bridges.

Our Pathfinder platoon also did some anti-terrorism training with the American Delta Force while we were in Berlin. As you would expect, this involved working with Bell UH-1 Iroquois helicopters (nicknamed 'Hueys') around Berlin a lot. The Americans love their Hueys!

The role of our Pathfinder platoon in Northern Ireland changed and we became the COP platoon. This stood for Covert Operations Platoon. This new role meant we had to train for covert operations of all kinds; covert ambushes of the IRA, covert work in civilian clothes to gather intelligence, covert photography, and covert support for the Special Air Service (SAS). Eventually, I grew my hair long and wore an earring!

'Ballykinler'

I arrived at Ballykinler Barracks in Northern Ireland in the early summer of 1979. Ballykinler Barracks was our base camp for the operations we undertook throughout Northern Ireland. The barracks also had quarters for the men who were married, which provided accommodation for their families to live in. I was part of an advance party to Ballykinler since I was in the COP platoon.

Drinking heavily had become a big part of my life now, and I developed a difficulty sleeping and I would have a constant fear of not feeling safe. I was not aware at the time, however, that this was a problem. I thought that the bad dreams I had of Private *F and Private *M kicking me, punching me and holding me prisoner with a knife on my eyeball was something I just had to live with and try to put to the back of my mind. It was not a problem for me, I thought. I just got on with things and I drank when I had the chance. This helped to dull my mind and help me sleep. Booze helped me cope. At times, I became very depressed but also aggressive.

On site at Ballykinler Barracks was a kebab shop. While the Advance Party was waiting for the rest of the battalion to arrive, I found it hard to sleep, so I drank a lot of beer one evening and then went down to the kebab shop to buy a kebab. While I was waiting for my kebab, the Light Infantry Provost patrol came into the shop and started 'taking the mickey' out of me. The Light Infantry were still in Ballykinler Barracks waiting to hand the complex over to 2 Para. The handover was taking a couple of months to do. The four Provost Light Infantry guys kept on taking the mickey, calling me a 'wingnut' and making derogatory, disgusting comments about the maroon berets that we so proudly wore. To be honest, I should have walked out and gone back to my barrack room. However, I was full of booze and full of outrage, rage and depression; not outrage, rage or depression from the silly little names I was being called, but outrage, rage and depression resulting from a year of torture by Private *F and Private *M. Something triggered in me, and I told the Provost patrol to, "Fuck off and go away!"

Instantly, they tried to arrest me. I fought them for fifteen minutes. They could not get hold of me or arrest me, so one of them called for reinforcements. In the end, about ten Light Infantry guys wrestled me to the ground and handcuffed me. The next morning, a Light Infantry junior officer came to see me in prison. His jaw dropped and his mouth hung open when he saw me. He expected to see a six-foot five, twenty-stone mad paratrooper, after the information he got about the Provost patrol's struggle to arrest me. Instead, he got me, baby-faced and weighing about twelve stone! He was physically stunned and asked me to confirm my name to check if he had the right person. There isn't much that can stop a paratrooper who has 'switched on' the aggressive, invincible para trigger. I did not really care what would happen to me now; depression had a hold of me.

Later in the morning, I was marched at double-quick time by the Light Infantry Provost sergeant to their Regimental Sergeant Major. I was sentenced to 28 days in jail and held in the Light Infantry's jail. This jail-time was hugely different to the 2-para jail time I had experienced. As prisoners, we merely sat in our cells all day and all night and did nothing. On one of the officer's visits to check if any prisoners had any complaints, I asked for some daily exercise. The other prisoners hated me for this request because they were then roped into taking exercise with me too! Thinking they would make a mockery of me, the para in their jail, the Provost sergeant organised their physical training instructors (PTIs) to take us on lengthy runs each day. I loved the challenge. The PTIs made all the prisoners have beasting exercises on these runs and pitted us against each other. Of course, I had to uphold the Para reputation. My Para arrogance and the rage inside me consistently gave me the willpower to beat all the other Light Infantry prisoners at every physical task we were given. Towards the end of my 28 days, I got called to the Regimental Sergeant Major's office for a chat. He sat me down in a chair in front of him and said to me that he found me to be an enigma, but an enigma who could be trusted. He asked for my help with a matter he had to deal with. A complaint had come from one of the prisoners about a Provost Corporal. The complaint was that the Provost Corporal had been bullying the prisoner.

"What are your thoughts, Parks, and is this true? You would know, Parks."

I told the Sergeant Major, "The prisoner was a bit weird, and the Provost Corporal was an arsehole and an idiot, but not a bully. The Provost Corporal was doing his job within expected boundaries. The prisoner in question, I believe, is weak morally".

The Sergeant Major smiled at me and thanked me.

I was quick to add, "I don't want any privilege for this".

He said, "I know."

A day later, the Corporal's wife and children came into the guardroom. His wife walked down the corridor to my prison cell and simply said, "Thank you for telling the truth."

She was incredibly beautiful, and I thought to myself, "What are you doing with an idiot like that?"

I said nothing to her and just smiled. She turned and walked away. I never had any trouble telling the truth, and I was glad for his children.

'Covert Ops'

We were told the Covert Operations Platoon would have to do a six-week foot soldiers' duty at Newry town's front-line base camp before we would get stuck into the role of covert operations proper. My depression had got really bad by now. I bluffed my way through each day and pretty well isolated myself to my bed space when I was not on patrol. The 'Black Dog' as Churchill called it, was so heavy on me, I was desperate. I found out discreetly, that the Queen could give permission for someone who wanted to leave the army, to leave. In my desperation, I wrote to the Queen to ask for her permission to leave the army. Of course, I was denied my request. I wondered if my seniors knew about my request to the Queen. If they did, no-one let on. I now hated being in the army.

When I joined the army, I had hope that my companion, fear, and my buddy depression would leave me, but they never did; they just got worse. I was the expert at getting on with each day and hiding how I was truly feeling.

'English Pigs! Riot!'

Before engaging in our covert missions in Northern Ireland, we were posted to Newry to get some foot patrol experience. The company we were attached to was the 2 Para Support Company, C Bruneval Company. This company consisted of the specialised Machine Gun Platoon, Mortars Platoon and us, the COP Platoon. This company was thought to be the cream of 2 Para. We were based at Newry during the marching and riot season in the summer of 1979.

I was part of a four-man open Land Rover patrol driving around Newry, showing a presence to the public, and having the capacity to be a Quick Reaction Response Patrol to a riot situation. The open Land Rover had no sides to it, just seats on each side. This was to enable us to quickly and instantly jump out of the Land Rover and be ready for whatever confronted us.

On this particular day, a call came over the radio telling our patrol to go and help an RUC (Royal Ulster Constabulary) foot patrol who had been surrounded by a large mob of rioters. We raced to the co-ordinates that we had been given, hanging onto anything we could on the Land Rover as we zoomed in and out of various streets. We soon turned the corner into the road of the incident, and we were confronted by a mob of about two to three hundred rioters who had surrounded four RUC policemen on foot. The four-man RUC patrol had their backs to the wall of a building, and the look in their eyes and their body language revealed they were terrified and had succumbed to the inevitable. Terror and fear filled their eyes, mixed with the recognition that this was potentially how they would meet their death at the hands of this mob. We got there just in time because the RUC policemen were starting to fall under the pressure of the rioters punching and kicking them. The RUC guys saw us, and they must have thought we were about to abandon them when we began backing up our Land Rover out of their sight and the sight of the rioters. We needed to secure the Land Rover away from the rioting mob. We found a secluded little alleyway and parked the Land Rover there. We left one of our patrol with the vehicle; he was fully armed.

The other three of us ran towards the rioting mob with our rifles in hand. We had no riot protection equipment with us, just our rifles and army smock jackets on. The rioters were facing the RUC policemen, so we were able to get close quickly. There were no other patrols we could call on for help, as every patrol was stretched and engaged in other riots and incidents. It was just the three of us. The only options we had were to either start shooting, under the justifiable reason that the RUC policemen's lives were about to be lost, or battle our way through the crowd to form a small wall around the RUC patrol. We decided to just keep running and violently fight our way through the mob. Punches rained down on us from all sides, along with kicks to our shins and thighs. I saw the blades of knives, in the hands of some of the rioters, flash in the sunlight. We had to swing our SLRs (Self-Loading Rifle) viciously from side to side, occasionally smashing into someone's head or face with the butt of our rifles, causing blood to spurt out of the smashed noses and cracked heads of the rioters. It almost didn't feel real; it felt like I was in a slow-motion scene of a movie. Finally, the three of us made it to the RUC foot patrol. Now our backs were against the wall with them.

This opened up another form of attack from the rioters; it meant that they could throw bricks and stones at us because it was just us against a wall. I found myself ducking bricks, whilst, at the same time, fighting off women who were trying to scratch my eyes out, punch me and scream, with twisted up snarling faces, threats like, "You fucking British shits! We're going to pull your fucking eyes out. We're going to rip your fucking heads off."

The three of us in our patrol looked at each other; the mob were trying to rip the rifles out of our hands, and we were completely outnumbered by two or three hundred. We knew we too would go down with the RUC patrol and probably be kicked to death, so we cocked our weapons ready to fire. Just then, the rioting mob began to split in the middle, half beginning to move to the left and half moving to the right. We knew that once the rioting mob had split, IRA gunmen would shoot at us from the back of the mob. We were pinned in like ducks in a row on a fairground stall. I do not know why or how, but an instant need to survive came over us all at once. A paratrooper's pride and rage. We did not want to start shooting women and children, so we shouted at the RUC patrolmen, "Get a fucking grip and follow us."

The mob splitting weakened their relentless attack on us, and as we began our attempt to reach safety and freedom, we shouted, "Airborne all the way!" It was corny, but it worked!

We smashed, kicked, hit, swung and head-butted our way through the weakened mob. We eventually managed to break away from the clutches of the mob and ran to our hidden Land Rover. By now, another RUC Land Rover had arrived and picked up the RUC patrol. The three of us were running to our Land Rover with the rioting mob chasing us. I was the last one to reach the Land Rover just as it was pulling away to get some momentum going forward to escape the mob. I had to run and throw myself at, and into the Land Rover. I knew that if I tripped or fell, I would have been caught by the mob. Launching myself towards the Land Rover, and at the same time throwing my rifle to one of the guys, I landed safely. We sped away.

'Warrenpoint'

It was early afternoon in Newry base camp. We had had lunch, and I was off duty so decided to go for a sauna. A Senior NCO and I were the only two in the sauna. We chatted together, irrespective of our differing ranks, and he talked to me rather like I would have expected a father to his son. I really enjoyed this talk. I had never seen my father, nor had a father-like role model in my life. I sensed he really cared for me. He shared many thoughts, and I listened intently. I clearly remember him saying to me, "Remember this, Parks; when you leave the army the only thing you will take with you is an army suitcase. Remember, the most important thing in life is your family."

It was a profound moment between us. He knew I was listening to him and he knew there was a connection between us. He asked me to do him a favour, to do sanger duty for him. He was in a very reflective and sort of contemplative mood, and this encounter with him touched me deeply. Little did I know at that moment, when I agreed to do sanger duty for him, later that day he would be blown to bits by an IRA bomb.

I began my sanger duty in the sanger that covered the back of Newry base camp. This sanger had a view of anybody who might try and sneak up and leave an improvised explosive device on the back wall. There was a strip of waste ground running along the back of the Newry barracks which separated it from a housing estate. My sanger's view had sight over the full left and right walls of our base. Sanger duty was usually only for a couple of hours. Two hours came and went, then three hours and still no-one to relieve me. I radioed in to find out when I would be relieved, but there was no answer. I stayed put, knowing that I could not leave my post. It would only take a few seconds for the IRA to plant a bomb on the back wall, or for an IRA sniper to get into a shooting position. Four hours went by, then halfway into my fifth hour, the sanger door opened, and I was relieved. I walked out of the sanger, and in front of me sitting on a little long brick wall were several of my cohort. I walked up to them and casually said, "Hi! How are you doing?"

There was complete silence.

I tried again, "You ok, lads?"

They turned to me and said, "Where have you been? Don't you know?"

I told them that I had been on sanger duty for nearly five hours and nobody in the ops room would talk to me when I radioed in. Then they told me the devastating news.

"There have been two massive bombs. Many of our guys have been blown to bits."

I was stunned.

"What? You're kidding! You're fucking kidding!" I screamed.

"No, I wish we were," one of the guys replied. He was someone that would not kid around. "How many? Who?" I asked.

"Not sure yet," came the answer.

Shock, disbelief and an ache in my stomach consumed me.

"Shit!" I said to myself. "All this, and I was stuck in a sanger."

The guilt hit me hard at this point. I was due to be on one of the quick reaction forces before I said yes to sanger duty.

"What the fuck was I doing stuck in a sanger while my mates were getting blown to bits?"

I slowly walked past them and towards the front gate. As I got closer and closer, the scene began to unfold in front of me. The front gates were two twenty-foot-high corrugated steel doors. Many of my platoon, the COP platoon, were at the front gate. These guys were experienced but crazy guys. Their bayonets were in their hands. Their eyes were popping out of their heads with rage and a lust for blood and revenge. They were swearing and shouting, "Open the fucking gates! We are going to spill some guts and kill some Fenian fucking bastards!"

Standing in front of the gates were some soldiers from another regiment with rifles and orders to stop us getting out. This was a dangerous situation. It could have gone any way. I took my bayonet out and I too held it up. At this point, I did not feel the rage they felt. I just felt guilt. I thought I was a coward.

We looked like an African tribe bunched up with their spears full of lust to kill, shouting and snarling. Then we all stopped. Professionalism seemed to be caught by us all, and it spread through our group at the gates like wildfire. Calmness returned. Rage was present but controlled.

The task then was securing the bomb sites, which carried on late into the evening and through the night. I am choosing not to describe in this book what I saw and witnessed that day, out of respect for the widows and children who are still alive today and who lost their loved ones in what has been described as the deadliest attack on the British Army during the Troubles, and the Parachute Regiment's biggest loss since World War II. Eighteen soldiers were killed and six were seriously injured. Six members of A Company from my battalion, who were on their way to relieve us, were killed in the first roadside bomb. Ten paras from my company, C Support Company, were killed in the second bomb. Two soldiers from the Highlanders and an English and Irish civilian were also killed. The attack happened on the same day that the IRA assassinated Lord Louis Mountbatten, a member of the British Royal Family.

The next day, I was tasked to go out to the bomb site with some others for a photoshoot for the BBC. We stood in three ranks with the smell of death and the scene of mangled lorries and Land Rovers along the road. I felt an overbearing sense of death weighing down on me. It was like a black blanket smothering me. The last post was sounded, and the BBC photographer took his pictures. That night, a group of us were driven back to Ballykinler barracks. I personally was petrified on this journey because we were in four-ton lorries again.

Would we be hit?

I clenched my body tight and squeezed my shoulders together. Silly really, because this contortion of my body would not stop me being blown to bits if we were bombed.

It was dark on our approach to Ballykinler barracks; then it began.

In the distance, we could hear a howling, an eerie, out-of-this-world sound of howling. It increased the nearer we got to the barracks. We drove through the gates and stopped when we were safely inside the barracks. The howling, screaming, sobbing was piercing. Women and children of all ages ran to the back of the lorries we were sat in, hoping against hope that a mix-up had been made and their loved one was in the back of the lorry. Women and children stared into the dark of the lorry at my face. I was sitting on the end seat nearest the tailgate. Our eyes met, and I could see the despair and disappointment in the eyes of the wives and children. I was not their daddy; I was not their husband. At that moment, I really wished I could have been the one they were looking for.

My guilt, shame and depression escalated from that moment. I was plagued by the images of what I had seen on the roadside. However, we went straight back into duties. We had no time off and no pastoral support. We were just told to get on with things, that that was the best way.

A few days later, COP platoon were standing outside our special intelligence briefing room when coffins were being loaded onto lorries. We stood and watched. My colleague told me that the coffins had sandbags in them to give them weight, as not much of the bodies had been found. It was at this moment he told me they only found an ear of my Senior NCO. I was devastated and this horror stayed with me until I was sixty-one years old. This was the only connection I had with the dead of the Warrenpoint Massacre after the bombings; seeing some of the coffins being put on the back of four-tonners. I never attended any funerals or gatherings.

It was only this year (2020), through expert therapy, that I have been able to truly process what happened over those few days and deal with the devastating effects of the trauma.

'Seek and destroy'

Aggressive seek and destroy training began for us, the COP platoon, in Ballykinler during our two-year Northern Ireland tour. Our role was primarily covert operations and covert ambushes. One of the roles, that of covert ambushes, developed into tactics to covertly seek and destroy the IRA, the enemy. The IRA would demonstrate their free movement and influence over the Northern Ireland population by establishing armed roadblocks in various locations along the border with the Republic of Ireland, or wherever they thought they could exert their power. Our role was to drive around the border and find these roadblocks and engage the IRA with firepower with the aim of killing or capturing them.

We trained and trained until our ambushes were perfect. Our weapons were varied and unconventional; pump-action shotguns, American ArmaLites, 9mm Brownings and grenade launchers. We were armed to the teeth and used unmarked vans to travel in for covert cover and to seek and destroy the enemy. Driving around bandit country on the border between Northern Ireland and the Republic of Ireland, our van driver was armed with a 9mm Browning and had a pump-action shotgun by his side. In the front of the van, the person in the passenger seat was armed with a pump-action shotgun. In the back of the unmarked van were eight of us, four on each side. We were armed with ArmaLites, SMGs (submachine guns), shotguns and 9mm Brownings. We drove around the border hoping to bump into an IRA armed patrol or roadblock.

If we were to come upon a roadblock, the SOP (Standard Operational Procedure) we had developed and practised was for our driver to give those of us in the back of the van a running commentary of what he could see, and the distances that we were from the roadblock as we approached it. This would go something like this;

"IRA armed roadblock one hundred metres in front of the van. Two IRA manning the stop point, one armed with a pistol, one armed with a shotgun. Looks like two IRA ambush cut-offs. One cut-off twenty metres this side of stop point. One cut-off twenty metres other side of stop point. Fifty metres away, forty metres, thirty metres, stand by, ten metres."

All of us in the rear of the van at this point would remove the safety catches on our weapons. We were now ready, pumped up, professional, prepared to engage the enemy, and fully trusting our cohorts. The SOP for the driver would be to pull up slowly to the IRA member facilitating the roadblock and stop. As soon as the IRA member came to the window of the driver's side door, our driver's instructions were to shoot him in the head. Immediately, the front seat passenger was to jump out of the van and shoot the other standing member with his shotgun. As soon as we heard the first shot, this was our signal to burst into action by leaping out of the rear of the van, four on the left and four on the right. Two of us were to skirmish forward covering each other, killing any IRA member we saw, and working our way up to the IRA cut-off. This IRA cut-off would inevitably have machine guns, so we were to kill anyone in this cut-off to immobilise the ambush. Two of us were to skirmish to the rear of the IRA roadblock, working our way to the rear ambush cut-off and killing them also. This was our job; this is what we were trained to do. War, and believe me the Northern Ireland 'Troubles' was a war, is not pleasant, is not something most of us would choose to take part in, but sadly, in a diverse world, it is inevitable.

Once, I recalled when we were training in secret in the fields near to Ballykinler Barracks, a helicopter flew in and landed right by us, the COP platoon in training. To our complete surprise, some top brass generals exited the helicopter. Apparently, they had come to thank us and encourage us. The top brass stood in a line and watched us demonstrate our finely-tuned seek and destroy counter-ambush technique using an unmarked van. They all seemed extremely impressed, clapped us, then got back in the helicopter and took off. It was rather weird!

After patrolling bandit country all night trying to find IRA roadblocks, I was sitting in complete darkness in the back of our unmarked van, tired and ready for bed. Suddenly, there was a loud bang. A shot had been fired from inside the van. We were in complete darkness and had no idea of what had just happened. Everyone waited to see if anyone had been hit. After some debate in the dark, we realised that one of the guys had accidentally cocked his sub-machine gun (SMG) and it had fired a single shot. There were no signs of any one of us being injured, so we carried on our journey back to base camp. On the drive back to camp, dawn began to break, and the morning light began to shine into the back of our van. A beam of light shone through a 9mm bullet hole two inches from the right side of my head. The 9mm bullet had missed my head by two inches! Two inches from potentially being shot in the head by one of my own guys! I would have died instantly.

After another long night looking for IRA roadblocks, we were all tired and, quite frankly, pissed off. We had spent all night driving around the border, and we needed some light relief. So, our driver, for a laugh, and to cheer us all up, drove around roundabouts the wrong way and along main roads on the wrong side of the road. We laughed, shouting, "Get back in lane, you fucking idiot!"

"Watch out!"

"You're going to kill us!"

We laughed and laughed and laughed. Looking back, not really a smart thing to do, but it did relieve the tension!

'Protection Duty'

We began the work of our covert operations role straight away after returning to Ballykinler Barracks following the Warrenpoint Massacre. Some of this secret covert work consisted of gathering information about the IRA movements. We set up observation points. For example, we would camouflage ourselves well and live in a bush for a week or two making sure we had a direct line of sight to the entries and exits of a farmhouse building. Key to this was our ability to hide and function without being seen. Other missions meant we applied the same tactics with various IRA accommodation and IRA members who were our targets. We were trained in photography and we built a log of intelligence by photographing and logging IRA member's movements. I do remember we thought we were compromised once.

The IRA meeting place in a farmhouse was about two hundred metres from our observation post. We were very well-camouflaged, and we had been living in this observation post for about a week. Previously, at this very area, the IRA had attacked an observation post with automatic rifles and took the observation post members by surprise, and some British soldiers got killed. The reason we thought we had been compromised is because the IRA members came out of the front door of the farm they were meeting in and looked up the hill in our direction. They then sent three of their dogs to scan the hill. We saw the dogs running up and down the hedgerows in front of us. The dogs ran from left to right along the hedgerows and then they ran up the hill to the next hedgerow. Each hedge the dogs completed brought them closer to the hedgerow we were hiding in. This could have been a trap. They could have been keeping our attention so that we were focused on the front whilst an IRA patrol potentially came over the hill behind us to engage in a firefight. We kept our cool as the dogs began to scan the hedgerow which we were in. I turned around to keep watch of the brow of the hill behind us. The dogs were sniffing the hedgerow and came closer and closer to us. We were not sure if the dogs indicated to the IRA, now standing in the courtyard of the farm, if they had found us. The dogs kept going along to the end of the hedgerow we were in, then ran back to the farm courtyard and the IRA members. We never left our position, but we remained on high alert for the next few days and not sleeping much. We took it in turns to keep an eye on the hilltop behind us.

We were also tasked with setting up high-quality ambushes. These were ambushes where the aim was to capture or kill IRA members. The intelligence we had for these missions was that the IRA were going on a killing mission, and we needed to intercept their mission to save lives. I was part of ambushes where there was gunfire and people died.

We were protecting a police officer and his family once. The IRA had him on a list, and there was high-grade intelligence that the IRA were going to go to his farmhouse and assassinate him and possibly his wife and children. We hid in one of his barns. The view from his barn covered the long approach road and his house. We had new Night Heat Detectors to use and we were to report back on their usefulness. We were one of, if not the first, patrol to experiment with this new equipment. On the side of this Heat Detector was written a warning in large letters, advising careful use of the equipment as there was radioactive material inside. I was the leader for this protection mission, so I told the guys they could use the equipment if they wanted to, but I would not make them. It was scary for us all knowing we could be being used as guinea pigs to assess this new bit of equipment.

It was, though, an amazing bit of kit. We could see rabbits, cows and anything moving that gave off heat. If an IRA assassination hit squad approached, we would see them. The policemen did tell us we could help ourselves to the milk he stored in a big open tank ready for processing. He told us that it would be the best milk we had ever tasted because it had not been processed.

"But," he said, "watch out for the bull because he's mean and sneaky!"

In the middle of the night, I climbed down from the top floor of the barn, put the ladder in place so I could get to the next floor down, which then led to a five-foot jump down onto the farm courtyard. I jumped into the courtyard and went and retrieved a bucket of milk for our patrol. On my way back, I sensed I was being watched. I reached up and put the bucket of milk up onto the ledge, along with my rifle. I then began to heave myself up onto the ledge and had just lifted myself up when 'Bang!', the whole barn shook. The bull had tried to ram me and crush me. He had charged my back but thankfully missed crushing me. I had one hand holding onto one side of the barn hatch, and one hand holding onto the other side of the barn hatch. The force of the bull's attack made me nearly lose my grip and fall backwards into its path! A split second saved my life.

Sadly, I heard a few years later, that the policeman was eventually assassinated by the IRA.

'Set-up'

I was beginning to get a reputation for being 'lucky' during our Northern Ireland tour. I seemed to miss death on more than one occasion.

One such occasion was when I was on a mission with a patrol to relieve another patrol who had been lying in wait in an ambush. The IRA had filled a car with explosives and parked the car on a road. A derelict building in a field had a line of sight to this vehicle. For a couple of weeks, 2 Para had been lying in wait in the derelict building, waiting to ambush the IRA when they came to collect the car with the bomb in and drive it to their intended target. The mission of this ambush was to capture or kill the IRA. The ambush patrols lived and slept in the derelict building while observing the car.

Myself and my patrol had just landed and exited our helicopter. The helicopter took off. I was the radio operator. I began to set up communication with base camp. We had a twenty-five-minute walk in the dark across fields to the derelict building to relieve the guys, and for us to continue the ambush. I set up communication with base camp and we were about five minutes into our night patrol to the derelict building; then it happened. The unmistakable sound of a bomb being detonated in the silence of the night. My radio went crazy with the urgency of contact and the response to the incident. We knelt and waited for new orders. At this point, we did not know what had happened; we just knew we had heard a bomb go off close by. Eventually, we were ordered back to base camp and we were picked up. The next day we found out the IRA had tricked our intelligence. The bomb in the car was a decoy and trap; the real bomb was in the derelict building. We knew nothing about that one. The IRA had concreted explosives into the floor of the derelict building, in the room that they guessed an army patrol would set up in and sleep in to observe their decoy car. Every now and then, the IRA would check to see if the British army had taken the bait. Unfortunately, for one of our group, we did.

He was making a cup of tea in the middle of the concrete floor on his small Bunsen burner, when the IRA detonated the bomb hidden under the concrete just where he was sitting. The explosion killed him and catapulted a friend of mine out of the window through which he was observing the car. Remarkably, my friend survived. I felt so guilty, sad and angry for the guy who died. I remember him as a small, kind guy with the heart of a lion. Only twenty minutes later and I would have been killed by the bomb under the concrete.

'Ambush gone wrong'

Sadly, accidents happened which also cost lives on our Northern Ireland tour. A high intelligence ambush was ordered to take place on the border, known as bandit country. The ambush was to continue over Christmas Eve and Christmas day and into New Year's Eve and New Year's Day. To help the married men be at home with their families, we, the single men, volunteered to be part of the ambush during the Christmas period, and the married men covered the New Year period of the ambush. I spent many freezing nights waiting in the pitch darkness for an IRA patrol to walk into our ambush and its killing field of fire.

'Utrinque Paratus' – Ready for anything!

I was off duty for New Year's Eve when word came back to us that there had been a terrible accident, and one of our junior officers had been killed by his own ambush patrol. The young officer had set the ambush. He had set the main killing field body of men behind a bank overlooking a bridleway. The intelligence was that an IRA patrol was due to use this bridleway for an IRA foot patrol. The officer set, some thirty metres down the bridleway on each side of the main killing field, to the left and right, two cut-offs, with the purpose of killing with machine guns. The cut-offs' aim was to cut down with machine-gun fire any IRA members who had managed to escape from the main body of firepower. Also, the cut-offs alerted the main killing field group of approaching enemies. It was New Year's Eve. The night was freezing. The ambush was set with orders to shoot and kill any IRA men walking into the killing field with rifles. The young officer had put a balaclava over his head to help fight the freezing weather and he laid down on the edge of the main killing field group. Wanting to be a good officer and give support for his men, he lost common sense for a moment. He wanted to say 'Happy New Year' to his men. He stood up in the pitch-black night, and forgetting he had a balaclava on his head and that he was carrying his rifle, he walked into the front of the main killing field on the bridleway, to say Happy New Year to his men. The paras lying in wait to shoot and kill an IRA patrol saw a person walk in front of them with a balaclava on and a rifle in their hand. Hundreds of pictures and photographs of this profile were etched into their minds. Hungry for a kill, the main killing field opened fire and killed the young officer and his radio operator instantly, mistaking them for part of an IRA patrol. For many of the men in this ambush patrol, moral injury has followed them for the rest of their lives. I found it extremely hard to come to terms with this accident. It was a total tragedy. What a waste of a young life.

'Lucky escape'

Oddly enough, because we were on a long two-year posting in Northern Ireland, we could go to so-called 'safe areas' to socialise. These areas were the protestant areas such as Bangor. A group of four of us were on our way back to barracks in one of the lad's car. The country roads in Northern Ireland are beautiful but also dangerous. Straight country roads suddenly turn right or left without much notice. In the middle of the night, we were driving back to Ballykinler from Bangor along the country roads. I was sitting behind the driver. My eyes were closed, and I was drifting in and out of sleep. Unexpectedly, a slow-motion scene unfolded before my eyes. Now open, my eyes saw a bridge in front of the car. Our car tyres were skidding and screeching closer and closer towards the bridge. I thought if we smash through the bridge wall, we would fall into the river below and drown. Closer and closer the bridge drew near until we hit the bridge and smashed through the bridge wall. Part of the front of our car was hanging over the bridge and river, and smoke was billowing out from the front of the engine. I hit the back of the driver's seat with my right knee and the impact of this catapulted me upwards, smashing my head into the roof of the car above where I was seated. I must have been knocked out momentarily, and when I opened my eyes, I started to take the scene in.

The other two passengers and the driver were badly hurt, with obvious broken bones. They wouldn't be able to get out of the car. "Shit!" I thought, "We are in a Catholic area of Downpatrick. We have no weapons, no radio; this is dangerous."

Still dizzy from being knocked out, I was trying to think what I could do. If we were discovered by the IRA, we were trapped and could not escape. The lads were moaning and groaning from their injuries. I was standing in the road next to our car when a car drove towards us from the opposite direction with its headlights beaming. My first thought was that this potentially could be the IRA, and we could be in serious trouble.

Instead, the first car to come down the road was an RUC Land Rover patrol. It was a miracle. They called an ambulance and we were all taken to hospital, with guards from Ballykinler being sent out to protect us. A friend of mine, who had been sent to protect us in hospital, said to me when he saw me, "Paul, for some reason, on my way here, I knew you would be ok."

'Four young ladies'

A rather enjoyable part of belonging to the Covert Operations Platoon was driving around in civilian cars, wearing civilian clothes. I did, however, have a shotgun by my side and a 9mm pistol in a holster under my jacket! It was the John Wayne side of operations!

I had long hair and a gold earring in my ear! I'm not sure that this look really disguised me from looking like a British soldier, but I am still here!

These covert operations varied in the aim of their tasks. Sometimes these covert movements were used to see what activity was going on in certain areas of Northern Ireland. Sometimes they were used to 'recce' a potential ambush position. Sometimes they were used to check out a gathering of people. We once recce'd a potential ambush location in the town of Downpatrick. Eventually, we took up positions underneath a Portacabin for an Observation post in the middle of the town late at night. We snuck from this position to the town's Market Place and hid in the shadows of some cow sheds by the main road that ran through Downpatrick.

Four of us were hiding in the shadows of the cow sheds when four young, very attractive women walked from the main road and lined up in front of us. They were only about four feet in front of us and had their backs to us. Next thing we knew, they pulled their skirts up around their hips and pulled their knickers down. Then all four ladies crouched down and began to pee. They carried on gossiping and putting the world to rights whilst they crouched down and relieved themselves! This went on for a long time! Our night vision was attuned to the darkness, so we could see each other and the young ladies. With big grins on our faces and mustering all our strength not to laugh, we waited and waited. We knew if they turned around and saw us, they would scream and run and our cover would be blown. Goodness knows what the headlines would have been, but I'm sure we would have been labelled as 'peeping Toms'! In the same matter of fact way that these young ladies took their knickers down, they pulled them up, straightened their skirts, and went on their way still gossiping and chatting. Once they were clearly out of earshot, we cried with laughter! I've never forgotten that scene and I still chuckle when I think about it.

'Kangaroo Car!'

Northern Ireland was full of contradictions, and I found myself in many bizarre situations. I had not long passed my driving test and a group of us were heading to Bangor for a night out in my green Vauxhall Viva car. I was behind a young Irish girl who was driving the car in front of me. She stopped at some traffic lights that had turned red. I began to kangaroo my car from about ten feet behind her, and there was a lot of spring in the suspension of my car, so it really leapt up and down. I just couldn't stop it from kangarooing forward. I could see the young girls' eyes in her central rear-view mirror. Her eyes were getting bigger and bigger as my car jumped up and down getting closer and closer to the back of her car. Suddenly, I kangarooed into the back of her car with a bang and broke one of her rear-view lights. I got out of my car and went to see if she was ok. The young lady wound the window down a little and she had fear in her eyes. She could see I was a British soldier in civilian clothes. I offered my apologies and assured her I would pay to get it fixed. Reluctantly, she gave me her address to drop some money off to her. Her fear was not towards me personally, it was because if she was seen talking to me, she could be tarred and feathered by her community.

A few days later I made my way to her house and parked up the road so I did not compromise her. She lived in a Catholic area, which was dangerous for British Army soldiers. I sensed I could trust her, and I sensed she knew she could trust me. I made my way to her house and knocked on the door. Her hand and an outstretched arm poked through the small gap in the front door where she had opened it slightly. She never showed her face. I put the envelope with £80 in it into her hand and she closed the door. I made my way back to my car, checked underneath it for any potential IEDs, and drove back to barracks. I felt sad for her living in that situation and I hoped I did not compromise her. Tar and feathering was a terrible thing, and not everyone survived it.

'Papier-mâché and chicken wire'

Another funny car situation some of my friends and I got into was at a car auction on a farm in Northern Ireland. We decided to chip in together to buy a car. We went to this car auction and a lovely

Mini was on sale. We bought it for £50. We were very pleased with ourselves because it was so cheap. We drove down the farm path to the main road to drive back to barracks. It was late evening now and beginning to get dark. We turned right onto the main road and began the journey back to barracks. Fifty metres into our drive, the back end of the Mini collapsed and hit the road. Sparks and fire were flying all over the place, where the metal scraped along the road. We came to a stop and looked up the hill to the farm. We could see them from the road; they were laughing their heads off and waving at us.

We soon discovered that the farmers had constructed the underside of the Mini out of papier-mâché and chicken wire, to give it enough strength to enable it to be driven down the farm road and onto the main road. They saw us coming! We had been completely suckered!

They knew we could do nothing about it; our officers would discipline us for being at the farm, and the Mini had not been taxed or insured. Our plan had been to sort out the tax and insurance once we got the Mini back to barracks. We laughed our heads off, gave the farmers the thumbs up, and walked to town and got taxis back to barracks. The following day we arranged for the Mini to be picked up and taken to a scrapyard.

Aldershot, Hampshire, UK

'Leaving the army'

Our tour of Northern Ireland had come to an end and our battalion returned to Aldershot. I know now that I was depressed, and that I lugged a deep internal anger around with me; this depression and anger were, however, hidden from the world. I was disillusioned with army life. I did not realise or understand at the time, how my experiences in the army, as recounted in this book, would affect me for the rest of my life.

These army traumas, merged with my childhood traumas, meant a double whammy for me and my wellbeing, which sadly would come to have serious consequences for me and, more importantly, the people I love.

I had had enough of the army. I had had enough of the macho, arrogant, soul-destroying culture. I realise now, aged sixty-one, that at sixteen I left one extremely dysfunctional family and joined another extremely dysfunctional family, both dysfunctional in different ways.

What I did get from the army, though, was an experience of friendship with my cohorts, at the most loyal level of benevolence.

PART THREE

'Awake my Soul'

1981 – 1998
Age: 22 – 39

"The Spirit of the Sovereign Lord is on me...to bestow on them a crown of beauty instead of ashes, the oil of joy instead of mourning..."

Isaiah 61: 1 & 3

Australia

'Civvy Street'

I left the army in August 1981 and began trying to adapt to civilian life. I had no 'trade' as such; jumping out of aeroplanes for a living doesn't transfer well to Civvy Street! It took me a while to build up my courage, and also deal with my pride, to go and sign on the dole and work out what to do with the rest of my life. Employment options were not wonderful for someone with very little formal education, no recognised qualifications and skills such as parachuting, long-distance running with weights on my back, and the knowledge of how to intimidate and kill people.

One of the options I considered was joining the Canadian Fire-fighters. My parachuting skills would be useful to them as they parachuted into regions to deal with fires started in remote parts of the vast wilderness of Canada. I decided that this wasn't an option, as I wasn't sure if I would be allowed back into Canada, having been deported with my family as a child.

I also consider the oil rigs in the North Sea, as well as following the path that many ex-service personnel follow - undertaking mercenary work to accumulate money. In the end, I sold my sports car and bought a ticket to Australia with a one-year working visa!

I was living with my mum at the time and it was she who suggested I go to Australia, as she wanted me to help her move there. Even at the age of 22, having witnessed and experienced things that most 22-year-olds don't do, I was still allowing my mum to manipulate me. I flew into Melbourne, and began to make my way around the coast to Sydney and then on up to Brisbane in Queensland. I made my way by coach, but I was not right mentally.

On the coach ride, I just sat, depressed, and I did not bother to take in the view. My best friends, loneliness, anger, depression and feeling lost, appeared again.

I eventually arrived in Brisbane, got off the coach and began walking through the city streets. The day was hot and humid with a blue sky. I noticed businessmen carrying briefcases and wearing shorts and T-shirts, hurrying up and down the immaculately clean city. I saw Aborigines, both men and women, drunk and wearing filthy and soiled clothes. They laid around in the beautiful Brisbane parks on benches and the grass. The contrast between the Aborigines and the white businessmen was sad to grasp.

After walking for some time, I found myself standing at the bottom of an enormous and vast flight of steps leading up to an office building. The steps were incredibly wide, I would guess about twenty-five metres, and there were about forty rows leading up to the office block. I could not see the whole of the entrance doors, because the top of the steps led to a flat area which, in turn, led to another flight of stairs leading to the entrance doors of the building.

I climbed up the steps and sat down about halfway up. I sat there for a while feeling lost and depressed, and watching the people busily rush here and there. I looked to the left of me, I looked to the right of me, and I looked behind me. There was no-one in sight. I then looked forward, and a man came out of nowhere and sat beside me to my left. We were both facing the busy street in front of us. I turned my head to look at him, and he looked me in the eyes, and said to me, "People are looking for something and searching for the answers all their lives, but the answer is right in front of them."

I glanced down at the step in front of me, and then turned my head towards him again to look at him. He was gone. I looked to my left and I looked to my right. I looked behind me to see where he was. There was no-one to be seen. There was absolutely no way anyone could have walked or run fast enough to get off the steps, and not be seen by me.

I looked down and up and all around me again. He had gone. Years later, I came to understand, after I came to faith, that the man who spoke to me on the steps in Brisbane was certainly an angel steering me. I do believe it was an encounter with God and an angel. God was breathing his breath on me and in me; He was gently and lovingly calling me. I was lost and I was ill. I never knew it at the time, as I sat on those steps in Brisbane, as I had no faith and I was not spiritually 'awake'. I knew the words the angel said to me were profound and fed into my soul-searching for meaning and purpose. It was not my time, however, whilst in Brisbane, to become spiritually awake. There was much more sculpting of me needing to be done by the experience of life before I was ready to kneel and surrender in faith to Christ.

Straightaway, after my encounter with this man, and at the time I only knew this experience to be an encounter with a man, I found a cheap hotel, booked in, and laid on the bed in my room. I remained there for several days, depressed and unable to function. Eventually, I ran out of money and so I approached the British Consulate in Brisbane to see if they could fly me back to England. It did not seem to be a problem for them as I was ex-military. I went back to my hotel and I continued to lay on the bed, depressed, whilst I waited for the airline tickets to be dropped off.

Four days later, I received the airline tickets and flew back to England. I went back to my mum's house. She did her best to make me feel like a failure, that I had let her down.

Peterborough, Cambridgeshire, UK

'Can a crab get out of a bucket?'

I soon realised I was in the clutches of my mum again when she asked me to beat her latest husband up at his workplace. She concocted a story about him and tried to make it as convincing as possible so that I could reasonably contemplate doing this. I was trapped; I had nowhere else to live, and Mum's mind games were getting to me. When I refused to do as she asked, the emotional blackmail started, as she told me that I obviously did not care enough about her to help her. The terrible thing was that I knew the guy; he was living in the same house as us, and I thought he treated her well and provided for her.

While I was living in this rather bizarre situation with my mum, I became more aware that my reading skills and maths skills were at the level of a primary-aged child. Realistically, I probably had the reading capability of a child just out of Primary School. I decided that I needed to do something about it, so I bought some children's spelling and grammar books and set about teaching myself how to read and write. I set myself a target of learning to spell five words a day. I carried this desire of wanting to constantly improve my literacy skills throughout my life. Interestingly, I found a place of refuge in these children's books, but I had always somehow learned how to expertly hide my inadequacy in reading and writing. Avoiding as much as possible the moments when life required me to apply these skills, excuses were always at hand.

Feltham, Middlesex, UK

'The Freudian thing'

My life soon began another difficult phase. I did the 'Freudian' thing and re-engaged in a relationship which was catastrophic for both of us. The beautiful gifts that came out of this relationship, however, were the children born from it. We never had a chance of a successful relationship because we were both seriously damaged people, although we never knew this at the time. In both of our childhoods we had experienced severe childhood abuse of many different kinds. This developmental trauma and the consequences of it, for both of us, manifested themselves in our relationship with each other.

Although I was in a difficult relationship, I wanted to provide well for my family. I retrained and became a bricklayer and progressed this skill into becoming a building contractor. At times, I had twenty men in my employ. Some winters were hard for the building industry, so I branched out into different jobs to get us through the winter.

At one stage, I was a Private Detective, however, I soon gave this work up as the majority of the work was to do with infidelity, and I could not tolerate spending my days mostly digging up dirt on partners, husbands and wives.

I worked at Heathrow Airport delivering all sorts of cars, and I even sold the famous Kirby Vacuum Cleaners one particularly bad winter. My lowest point was working in a factory; that job only lasted three months.

Hereford, Herefordshire, UK

'21 SAS Selection – Territorial Army'

Life was pretty much unbearable during my first marriage for various reasons. I always wondered about earning the coveted SAS beret, and I decided to have some sort of outlet and attempt to earn and pass the SAS (TA) selection course. Bizarrely, I needed adventure in my life even with my mental health and relationship difficulties.

I began the 21 SAS selection process and I also wondered about re-joining the Army full-time.

In 2020, when the Church of England cruelly and publicly humiliated myself and Lois in the national newspapers, the newspapers sensationalized the fact that I had served three years in 21 SAS. Much of my time in 21 SAS was progressing through the selection process. I spent time with C squadron after passing selection, but life at home began to fall apart, which meant that I had to give up my membership of 21 SAS. I do, however, recall some of the challenges of selection.

'The Fan Dance'

'The Fan Dance' consisted of a 15-mile climb up the Pen y Fan mountain, the highest mountain in the Brecon Beacons, with a weighted Bergen, down the other side and a run along a path to some woods. At that point, we were turned around and had to run back and climb back up Pen y Fan on the side we had just come down, back over the top of the mountain and down to the starting/ finish line. This had to be done in a time limit. The only way to make the time limit was to go as fast as you could, and this meant being exhausted all the way from the start to the finish.

The day I was on the Fan Dance, the weather was appalling, with a severe storm. When I got to the top of Pen y Fan on the return leg, the Corporal stationed at the checkpoint was holding onto his tent with all his might as it blew horizontally in the air by the ferocity of the wind. He beckoned me forward for me to check in and give him my name. I shouted my name from a few feet away from him, but he could not hear me over the noise of the wind whistling past us. I had to put my mouth over his ear and shout my name, 'Parks', three times before he nodded his head. I then carried on back to the finish line for completion of this gruelling test within the time limit required.

'SAS Interrogation'

"You're Australian, aren't you?" He repeated this to me about twenty times; "You're Australian, aren't you?" His voice was menacing, and he spoke in a slow monotone.

I knew the wrong response from me would be a fail; I would fail my Special Air Service selection. After two years on the process of selection for 21 Special Air Service, C Squadron, TA., I could fail at the final hurdle, but failure for me was not an option.

I had endured hikes over the Brecon Beacons in rain, snow and heatwaves. I'd had to make cut-off times over vast distances by minutes, and the only way to make those cut-off times was by pushing myself beyond my limits, keeping going even when I felt I had nothing left in the tank. I completed assault courses, underground tunnels with only room to inch forward to find a way out, treacherous chimney climbs where one slip and the very least injury would be a compound fracture, swimming in freezing water, and days of running around the Brecon Beacons with extreme weight on my back. All this could now be lost during my interrogation by the NATO interrogation team. They got to practise their interrogation skills on us; only on us.

I was so incredibly tired. I'd had no sleep and little food for days, running from checkpoint to checkpoint over mountains, hills and forests with no opportunity to sleep. I did this for three days. I knew that at any point I would be grabbed by a snatch squad at one of the checkpoints I had to rendezvous with. I had to meet spies who would give me co-ordinates to the next checkpoint. I needed to avoid being caught or seen, running from one checkpoint to another, as hunting squads were looking for me. I had to keep hidden until the end, the final checkpoint where I would be caught.

Then it happened! Just before the checkpoint, I was jumped by a snatch team. I was roughed up; my hands were tied behind my back and an opaque hood put over my head. I sensed I might be ambushed just before it happened, so I had buried anything that was on me that could help the interrogators break me. I thought I had got rid of everything, but I was wrong.

I was bundled into the back of a lorry and driven to an interrogation place somewhere in Hereford. I was bundled into a dark room and sat on a chair. The hood was taken off my head and I found myself sitting in front of two NATO interrogators and an SAS umpire.

"Sign this," they said.

Not sure what to do, I looked at the umpire and he nodded his head. The form I signed was a disclaimer, stating that if I lost my mind or I was psychologically damaged, it was not the Ministry of Defence's fault. I signed the form, then the hood was quickly put over my head again, and I was bundled out into the interrogation centre and rooms which I could only describe as 'torture rooms'.

Thrust up against a wall with my legs spread open and my hands against the wall above my head, I was made to lean against the wall, draining the strength from my legs and arms. I could not see anything. The floor was covered in shingle so that when I heard the guards walking towards me the sound became louder and louder. This made me cringe with fear, anticipating that the guards were going to grab me. Every few minutes, the guards would crunch towards me, get hold of me and move me into stress positions to continually attempt to wear me down. This went on for hours and hours. I was exhausted and weak.

Suddenly, I was grabbed by the arms and dragged into a room and sat on a chair. The hood was taken off my head and before me was an interrogator looking straight into my eyes with a steely stare. Behind him, on his right, was a large man, and to his right was a woman. All three just stared at me. Their looks were penetrating. I stared down at the floor because I didn't want to succumb to the power of their will. After an hour or so, the main interrogator just said, "You're Australian, aren't you?" Repeating this same question twenty times or more.

I responded with my rank, my army number and my name as I had been taught. I was then hooded up and dragged out of the interrogation room and marched to the room of pain once again. I was put into stress positions until I could not stand up anymore. I thought that I had failed because I was unable to remain standing. I was shattered. I was lifted up and marched into the interrogation room once again. The woman interrogator started to belittle me repeatedly, then the male interrogator pulled out a box of matches that I must have left in my smock. They were made in

Australia. I then thought, "You stupid dicks! The box of matches had completely thrown them; they think I'm from Australia!"

I still to this day have the steely look of the male interrogator in my head. He had a way of wearing me down, but I suppose that was his job! After a few hours, I was dragged back into the torture room with the hood back on. I was screamed at, put in stress positions and worn down some more. It was hell. I never knew how long this would go on for. I never knew if I would crack and ask for it to stop. Of course, this was the whole aim of interrogation; to crack you.

After what I think was a day or so (I had no concept of time at this point), I was suddenly marched out of the interrogation area and taken to some barracks, thrown some towels and told to take a bath, go to bed and get some sleep. I didn't know if I had passed the final hurdle or failed. I fell asleep.

Other guys on the selection course began to come in and do the same as me. I realised I was the first one to get through the interrogation and come out the other side, although we still did not know who had cracked, talked, given up or passed.

The next day we were told. We were told that 1,200 fit and healthy men had applied for this selection, that some 500 had started the selection process and that 8 had passed. Two people from each squadron had passed. I and one other had passed 21 SAS, C squadron selection. Just two of us.

In total, I spent three years with C squadron.

Feltham, Middlesex, UK

'Death Stench'

My adventure ended, and I returned to full-time family life. My marriage was unbearable, and there were many times either one of us would finish the relationship only to find that our insecurities brought us back together in a toxic association. The situation was painful for each other and for our children.

On one occasion, after yet another display of our cruel and deep childhood trauma manifesting itself towards each other, blind to it as we were, I attempted to commit suicide. I had had enough of life. Mixed up with a deep love for my children but a crushing and over-powering sense of lostness, anger and depression, I swallowed countless aspirin tablets. The next thing I knew I woke up in hospital with a tube down my throat and needles stuck in my arm connected to drips. I was violently sick repeatedly. I discovered that some neighbours had called an ambulance for me after they found me in the front garden, unresponsive. Sadly, the army mentality soon kicked in; "I must not show weakness. I'm invincible!"

The first opportunity I had, I got myself dressed and left the hospital, undetected.

I found myself on my own during the Christmas period of 1989 after a prolonged downward turn in our relationship. On Christmas day, I waited at home on my own for a Christmas phone call from my children. The phone call never came. Deep, deep depression enveloped me like a black blanket. At the time, my mum only lived about a 20-minute drive from me, and she knew that I was spending Christmas alone, however, she made it quite clear that she did not want her Christmas to be spoiled. She had a new man living with her and told me to stay away.

I went upstairs and lay on my bed. I lay on my bed for days, maybe as many as ten days. I crawled to the toilet when I needed it. I did not eat at all during this time. I sipped a glass of water during the first few days until it ran out. I did not refill the glass; I just lay there. My toilet need was less and less as time went on, and I could feel death coming. I could literally smell my body dying, the distinctive stench of death, and this death odour was coming from me. I could not move now. I was, in a way, peaceful about dying and I just wanted to sink into death. My heart was broken. I had lost my children. I loved them so much. I was falling in and out of consciousness. No one came to visit me or see if I was ok.

I'm not really sure how or why, but out of the blue, a yearning came over me to fight my depression and get strong so I could help my children. I had an inclination growing in me that my children were in danger. The only explanation I have for this sudden urge to live is this: I found out a few months later that one of my daughters, at the age of four, had been praying every night under her blanket, "God please ask my daddy to come and rescue me and my brother and sisters".

After I came to faith some years later and began to understand the nature and character of God, I really do believe that God answered her prayers, saved my life, and enabled me to get well enough to help my children.

After I got stronger, I started to make enquiries as to the whereabouts of my four children, and I was told that they were living in a large house which was a renowned drug den. In this house lived a dozen or so adults. I later learnt that on the coffee table of this house was a large car, a car carved out of a huge piece of cannabis. All sorts of drug dealing went on from this house, hard and soft drugs. I was going crazy with worry for my children. With the help of a friend and my military skills, I freed my children from this drug den. It turned out my 'freeing' them was only for a short period. Sometimes the law is an ass. I had to go to court to help them. After an uncomfortable and acrimonious court battle, I was given custody of the four children and I, we, began life as a lone-parent family.

'Lone Parent'

As a lone parent, I now had four children in my sole care. My youngest, a girl, was only 18 months old at the time, followed by a four-year-old girl, a nine-year-old girl and an eleven-year-old boy. The five of us together made up our lone-parent family unit.

Today, aged 61 and writing this book, I know I did absolutely the right thing taking on the four children on my own. I also know, with the benefit of hindsight and three years of therapy, that I did not, at the time, have the skills and mental well-being I needed for the task, even though my intention was the right one.

At the beginning of the Lone Parent chapter in my life, I wanted to do my best for the children, so I continued to work full-time as a building contractor and earned good money. I needed a good income to support four children. I employed nannies to look after the children while I was at work, however, it soon became apparent to me that this was not in the best interests of the children. All four of the children needed a parent at home. While I was working full-time, I was out of the house early in the morning and didn't get home until late in the evening. The younger children especially were not happy with me being away all day. After much soul-searching, I decided to give up work and become an at-home Dad, (and Mum as well), to the children. I received Income Support and became what was regarded at the time by the media and government as a 'scourge' on the nation, a Lone Parent on Income Support. The financial struggle of giving up paid work was extremely difficult, but the emotional benefit for the children was obvious, as I could see my presence made them happier.

Financially, no one can survive on Income Support with four children in their care. Bills began to get out of control and negotiating minimum payment terms for bills became a daily way of life. This way of life is extremely disheartening and causes overwhelming anxiety and stress. I was now living below the poverty line, and I had three girls and one boy in my care. I felt very vulnerable and at times helpless and hopeless whilst trying to do my best for them. I had no extended family who would be prepared or able to help practically or financially. It was just me and the children.

'Hide and seek'

Bang! Bang! Bang! It sounded like the front door of our house was going to be broken down. "I know you're in there!" shouted an unfamiliar voice. "Open the door!"

Bang! Bang! Bang! "Open up! Now!"

The shouts came from one of three large men whose shadows we could see through the glass of our front door.

My four young children froze with fear and shock, looking up to my face and eyes for comfort, reassurance and protection. My heart sank and the pain of grief filled me as I saw my children's faces filled with fright. It's not pleasant to see fear in your children's eyes. "Come on, let's play hide-and-seek," I said. "These men are just playing. Let's hide!"

We hid behind the couch in the living room and the children began giggling at this new game. I had a line of vision from behind the couch to the front door. My feelings? Well, I did not know what to do. I had no money, nothing to give these bailiffs. Feelings of desperation and helplessness are perhaps some of the worst human feelings we can have. Being poor, with four children, is overwhelmingly devastating.

Although we were poor, extremely poor, the children were happy. They had that council estate freedom of running around outside and in and out of other people's houses. They played most of the day, but for me, survival was punishing. I was always behind in paying bills. I just did not have the income to cover life's most basic needs. Much of my time was spent on the phone, begging utilities and other creditors to give me time to pay. This was always to buy just a little more time. Food was always the cheapest non-brand available, and many times I was not able to eat, telling the children that I needed to watch my weight. There were no food banks or agencies to help at that time.

I made meals out of Pot Noodles, pouring them onto a plate to make it look like a cooked meal. Constantly fighting the council, going to court for TV and council tax arrears was par for the course of being a single parent on Income Support; it was misery for me all the time.

Despite all this, my children brought much happiness and purpose in my life, and I was determined to break the dysfunctional social cycle that I grew up in and get them all educated to a level which would give them the opportunity to have the positive life that I never had. I didn't want my children to suffer as I had suffered. Stress was my bedfellow; constant stress. all the time, night and day.

'Little Black Book'

An added pressure on me at this time and something which was missing in the children's lives, was the reality that I had no extended family to help me with or support the children. I also had no friends to help me. The five of us, however, learned to become a team, to get through and manage.

Occasionally, and over many years, about every two or three weeks, my mum would appear with a can of soup or a loaf of bread. At the time I thought that she was just trying to be a mum and grandmother, and it was her way of showing care for us. How foolish was I!

One day, she came round to the house, reached into her handbag and produced a little black book and showed it to me. In the book was listed every tin of soup, every loaf of bread, in fact, every item that she had ever given to me. Next to the list of items was very clearly recorded the cost of each item and the date on which she had brought the item to my house. Added to this was another column which detailed an interest charge at an extortionate rate of interest!

Added to this, she also included a charge for the occasional babysitting that she had done for me to enable me to keep an appointment, and I had had no other choice than to ask her. Her rate was not cheap!

According to Mum's little black book, I now owed her thousands of pounds, and she demanded the money straight away. I was still on Income Support, and that was not enough to meet my family's basic living costs. She threatened me with legal action if I did not pay her what she said I owed her. I had never asked her to buy me anything. I had occasionally asked her to babysit, but never dreamt I would be required to pay for her services! This threat she now held over me was dreadful. When I told her that I had no money and that it was atrocious for her to do this to me, she stopped coming to see us. The only reason that I tolerated her visits was that I wanted the children to have an extended family, and I stupidly (or out of my dysfunction) thought her visits gave them a little normality. This was such a mistake because it became evident that she played mind games, not just with me, but also with the children.

I was not a member of a church at the time, and I had no faith or belief system at this point in my life. She had a lawyer's letter sent to me demanding payment be made, and to put pressure on me, got various Pastors to send letters to me, telling me that I should pay her back what I owed her as I was not behaving like a son should.

Years later, when we, my wife Lois and I, didn't send her flowers for Mother's Day on time, my mum got herself admitted to hospital, asked to see the hospital chaplain who was a Church of England priest, and tried to make a formal complaint against me as a member of the clergy! Such was her vitriol.

What I had witnessed in my childhood and adulthood, the way my mum treated her many husbands and partners, she was now applying that same behaviour to me. This was not the first time that she had tried to extort money from me. When I was in the army, she wrote to my senior officer and told him that he was to make me send some of my pay to her! Thankfully, my officer was not easily manipulated!

To get my mum off my back, I stupidly sent her either five pounds or ten pounds from my Income Support every few weeks. Why did I do this? Consciously or maybe subconsciously, I believe I was aware of just how much harm she could do to someone when she wanted to. I still, as an adult in my thirties with four children, lived in fear of her violence and what I now know to be psychopathic mental manipulation of me. I tried to ignore her while I threw myself into trying to provide love, stability and a happy home life for my children.

'Social Cycle'

At the time, we lived in a four-bedroom council house which I had managed to buy when I was working. I eventually gave up my bedroom to a lodger to help me financially, which meant that I had to sleep on the couch in the living room. I battled with the 'Black Dog' daily. I did, however, have the determination and willpower of a paratrooper to keep going forward and trying. This, though, was not the most helpful survival skill, as unaware to me, I was battling to deal with an undiagnosed mental illness.

In the evenings, after I had got the children bathed and into bed, I sat and drank whisky, on my own, except for the company of the 'Black Dog' and anger. Eventually, I found it difficult to listen to music and I avoided it. I forced myself to be cheery for the children and get them off to school. Board games became something I avoided, as noise was a big problem for me. However, I gave the children love and encouragement. With hindsight, I know that they would have also experienced my depression and suppressed anger. This mixed manifestation of me would not have been easy for them. A saying the children would say to me, and it cuts me to the heart to recall this, is "There's Dad's angry eyes".

I know, though, that they knew I was trying my best, and this gives me a little comfort. Today, my 'older' children are in their 30s and 40s and have told me that they do have some very happy memories of the time when we were a five-person Lone Parent unit.

I was determined that I did not want the children to end up like me or their mother, but I was not sure how I was going to stop the social cycle repeating itself. I determined to try and stop it. I wanted it to stop with me.

One way I decided would be helpful for the children was for them to not have lots of different adults come in and out of their lives. What I mean by that is partners for me, potential stepmothers for them. I knew how devastating that experience was for me as a child, and I wanted to give them stability even though I struggled to do this. So, I made the decision to stay single. This decision to stay single evolved into a decision to be celibate, when, a little while later in my life, I had a spiritual awakening. My celibacy lasted thirteen years until I received into my life what I believe was, and still is, a gift from God, my wife Lois.

Did I manage to break the social cycle? Well, my son has a family of his own and an excellent job. Two of my daughters have graduated university with honours degrees, one is married and runs her own very successful business, and the other is raising a child whilst continuing to advance her career choice. My step-daughter too has graduated university with an honours degree, is married and studying for a Masters. Sadly, my other daughter was tragically killed in a road accident, aged 25, just months away from completing a nursing diploma at Nottingham University which she had been studying for whilst raising her daughter on her own. I do believe that the cycle was broken, and although the journey was difficult, it was so worth it!

'Faith awakening'

In January 1991, I opened one of the drawers in my kitchen, the drawer that everyone has where 'bits and bobs' are stored and lying on the top was a Christmas flyer from the local Church of England church. The flyers were inviting people to the Christmas services.

As it was now January, we had missed the services, but something intrigued me about the invite to church. Although I knew very little about church, and had only ever stepped foot inside a church for my mum's weddings, I decided that Sunday School would be a good idea for the children. I phoned the number on the flyer and arranged for someone to come and see me and talk to me and the children about Sunday School. A lovely elderly lady came and met with us in our house, and we arranged for us to attend the church on the next Sunday.

The church was St. Dunstan's, in Feltham, Middlesex. When we arrived at the service, we received a warm welcome. I was conscious of being a lone parent amongst a very well-dressed and well-presented congregation. I sat on the back pew with my four young children. The children happily went out to Sunday School and left me sitting on my own. I sensed something but I did not know what it was I was sensing. Years later, I came to realise that the sense I was feeling, whilst I was sitting on the pew at the back of St. Dunstan's Church, was the same feeling I felt when I was a little boy and turned to hear John Wimber talk on the TV. It was the sense of God's presence.

I listened to the vicar in his sermon, I listened to the Bible readings being read and I listened to the hymns being sung. I quickly wiped away a tear that trickled down my cheek. What beauty this was! I had never, ever, sensed a peaceful beauty in my soul like this before in my life. The contrast of my experience of life was completely at odds with this feeling. I asked myself, "What was this? What is it?"

That week at home, I tried to fathom out what it was I felt in the church service. The five of us went to church the following Sunday, and the same experience happened to me. On that Sunday, my mum had come over on one of her few visits to join us for Sunday dinner. I hated my mum but also loved her at the same time. I had no idea why. Maybe it was that fear had overcome common sense. Even though she treated me and my children the way she did, I had asked her over for Sunday dinner on that particular day. When we got home from church, I asked my mum if she would watch the children for a couple of minutes while I went for a short walk, and she reluctantly agreed. I had an overwhelming desire to go for a walk. My mind was full of questions, questions about what exactly was going on with me deep inside.

I began walking, and I walked and walked for much longer than I had originally planned! Before I knew it, I had been walking for about three hours. For some reason, I was not concerned to get back for my mum. I found myself walking across a large and long field back to my house, and just near a crop of trees to my left, a vision, a picture, one that was solid and real to me, appeared upwards and in front of me. This vision appeared for a few seconds, maybe three to five seconds, then disappeared.

The vision was this: one of my daughters was nailed to the Cross and then instantly, within a millisecond, Christ replaced her on the Cross in my vision, my picture. He was nailed to the Cross with the Crown of thorns on His head. This vision was perfectly clear. Instantly, I was filled with something, and I had an overpowering sense of love and joy. I fell to my knees and stared at the Cross of Christ.

When the vision disappeared, I ran home full of indescribable love and joy. As soon as I got home, I told my mum what had happened to me, and she thought I had gone crazy! I was in a state of bliss. If anybody had come into my house at that moment, I would have given them anything they asked for. If they wanted my

TV, I would have given it to them. If they wanted money and I had it, I would have given them all my money. I was full to overflowing with the Holy Spirit, but at the time, I did not know who the Holy Spirit was. I did not know what was happening to me. I felt like a baby; everything, every experience was new. This was a new way of being and I was a baby needing food and nourishment.

After a few hours of what I now call my 'Road to Damascus spiritual awakening', my mum attempted to phone the local vicar at St. Dunstan's Church. She thought I had completely lost my marbles! She contacted the wrong St. Dunstan's Church in the area, but the vicar that she spoke with asked me to go and see him. I spent three hours spilling my heart out to him and sharing with him what I had experienced. This was my 'Road to Damascus' conversion experience. I have come to learn that my experience of being filled with what I now know to be the Holy Spirit, was me being baptised by and in the Holy Spirit.

The vicar gave me the Gospel of Mark to read and he became my spiritual director. I went home and devoured every word of Mark's Gospel. Each word came alive for me as I read it. I wanted more of God. I wanted to know Him and be close to Him. A passion for life and the activation of my spirit gave me hope and a love for people and a compassionate heart for their pain.

My children and I became part of St. Dunstan's Church community. We attended church each Sunday and joined in the picnics and social events. Three months or so after my baptism of the Holy Spirit, and having experienced, on an ongoing daily basis, flashes of 'electric' like sensations of the Holy Spirit running through my body, I began a phase of what I call a 'dark night of the soul'. It's hard for me to describe accurately this period in my life, which lasted for six months or so, but I had nightly struggles where

I just walked up and down battling what I would call 'dark spirits'. When this 'dark night of the soul' time ended, I had a longing to complete a pilgrimage, completely on my own to give me time to be alone with God.

'Pilgrimage'

A Bible passage I read jumped out at me and came alive to me, and I wanted to walk in the way of this passage. The verse was:

> Luke Chapter 9 Verse 3: "He told them: 'Take nothing for the journey – no staff, no bag, no bread, no money, no extra shirt.'" [copyright: THE HOLY BIBLE, NEW INTERNATIONAL VERSION®, NIV® Copyright © 1973, 1978, 1984, 2011 by Biblica, Inc.™ Used by permission. All rights reserved worldwide.]

I had a deep desire to follow and live according to the teaching of the above scripture. The desire became stronger and stronger until I decided to go on a walking pilgrimage from St. Dunstan's Church in Feltham to Norwich Cathedral. I managed to enlist the help of some of my new-found church community to look after my children while I ventured on my pilgrimage. I would take nothing with me. No money, no coat, no tent, no planning of stops and no food. I decided I would not ask for money or food on my way and I would walk all the way. The following is a word for word transcript of the diary I kept each day on my walk from Feltham to Norwich Cathedral. I have not corrected the spelling or grammar in my diary. At the time when I wrote this diary, I had mostly taught myself to read and write as I had had little formal education at this point in my life.

Diary of pilgramige.

Saturday 4th April 1992

'He hath borne our griefs and carried our sorrow' - Isaiah Chapter 53, Verse 4

Should I go, is it silly, M* cries for me, I miss my children before I leave my house, I cry for Christ in St Dunstan's. Every where seems locked, people don't trust anyone.

I get a drink at Gellette corner at a furniture shop toilets. As I walk through Ealing I start to look for money on the floor, I notice people at cash points. In only a few hours I am tempted. Imagine what it must be like for third world countries. Perhaps I will have more compassion for criminals.

St Marys Ealing is locked up. Christ Church Ealing I get a drink from an outside fountin. Its hard to let go and not worry about food.

Sometimes I manage to and things are easier. Tescos on the way to Hendon I find a baked potato and a cup of tea in the caffee, half eaten.

Maybe I should have took money.

I hope God is with me. God is with me. I'll rest for half an hour. (12.30)

I was looking for money on the road feeling sorry for myself when a man asked me for 20p. How many thousands live like this.

I was angry at seeing a smashed box of eggs on the path, what a waste, I was so hungry.

Two old people had a flat tyre, they were holding the traffic up. I wanted to help, but then I wanted to help because they might give me a couple of pounds. Temptation comes quick to the wanten. I was angry again when two men beat me to it. This is not like me.

Im silly Im hungry tired and have no money. I tell myself I didn't trust on the way to Canterbury [I had previously led a walking group pilgrimage to Canterbury] I must trust on this walk. Just let go and trust. 4.00 and Ive had enough I see a man standing outside a Penicostal church. I asked for a glass of water and he takes me in the church and gets me a drink. I ask for some shelter and he says he has no authority but sends me up the road to a Christian centre.

I meet Adrian about 26 years old. He takes me to his flat gives me coffee and three huge cheese sandwiches, We talk about God and I realize Adrian has strong faith.

Adrean gives me £10.00 and some more sandwiches. We say a very sincere goodbye I walk to the next street and go into a Methodist church. A young coloured lady about 30 years old phones the reverend to ask if I can stay the night. He comes down and meets me but is unable to help me. The lady phones the salvation Army who bring me round a sleeping bag, and two days food. An hour and a half ago I was without food water, money or shelter.

I was praying to find a loaf of bread or a pound. I was tired fed up and worried. I now have £10.00 pounds, three days food and a sleeping bag.

Today I am able to say not just that I feel sorry for down and outs or criminals or the hungry. I am able to say that I have felt like them and that I was easily made vunearable. I should say that I and all people are the same as them. May Christ forgive me.

The lady in the Methodist church who helped me said that she was supposed to be in Church in the morning but for some reason she changed to the afternoon.

I am about 3 miles from Enfield. I will find some where to sleep. There are a lot of derelict buildings around, but I will stay away from them.

I feel I have enough food and money to get me to Norwich. Maybe I will be able to let go better now.

(April 5 – 2nd day)

Last night I found a small cops next to the A40 to sleep in. I was frieghtend and felt insecure, To many pubs around. It began to sink in how lucky I was to get a sleeping bag. It was a clear sky and I could see the big dipper. I was thinking of Jesus in the desert for forty days. How he must have been tempted to the limit. But I see now how he understood us and lived our temptations. I stick my head out of my sleeping bag 5.30AM and the first thing I see is a church sphire. The sky is clear, Above me is a tree just budding.

With the trunk as the (Church and faith) in it branches out to very thin ends twigs. Then I see that the thin ends need to flow back into the trunk as well as out.

Like the blood flowing from your heart it returns rejuvenated ready to feed the body. A circle of faith from the trunk as blood in the heart.

People look at me with curiosity, perhaps with caution, I have a black rubbish bag with my sleeping bag and food in. Its carried over my shoulder, I suppose I look like a drifter.

Today I feel so much calmer and less worried. Because I have food money and a drink. (Shelter and necessities).

Yet yesterday I was near terror with out these necessities to hand. How many people live day to day in this terror. How God must suffer and hurt with them.

We must share our riches with the poor, for the poors sake and most of all for Gods sake.

I keep thinking of something Adrian said, how God speaks to you through the bible.

When the bible becomes alive. As it does, but most of all I recall my first reading of (The Acts).

Why should I or did I doubt if I should begin this pilgrimage without money or food or shelter. We should accept suffering in God as well as joy.

I would have not made this second day without God providing at the right time.

My feet are in a bad way, I have my food and drink but now im worried about my feet. 4.00 I can't take another step and go into some bushes and get straight into my sleeping bag.

While things were good today I didn't think much about God. Now im in my sleeping bag with no shelter and bad feet I get my new testament out and try to find some encouraging words. I pray that it doesn't rain or that would be me finished,

When things are hard we pray for help. We need to discipline our selves to love and thank Jesus when things are good as well. This would help to make our relationship with God unselfish.

St Paul must have been carried by the Lord on all his travels, because no man on his own could do this day after day, month after month year after year without Jesus Christ the Holy Spirit, God.

(April 6th - 3rd day Monday)

It never rained, my feet feel ok after a bit of patching up. Im very stiff. The weather looks glum. I say thank you to Christ for the peaceful night and Im off.

I go through some very lovely villages. Very middle class. It seems if something is missing in these villages. A sort of hollow empty feeling. Are they in the real world with Christ. Do they carry their cross?

Its been raining since 10.00 o clock. My feet are killing me Im tired and wet 3.00pm.

I come to a road I want, I don't know which way to go. There is no one to ask for directions Im in the country. Ive decided to go right, but before I do I will go into the trees for a toilet.

When I come out of the trees a man about thirty asks if he can help me by lifting my bag over the fence.

I asked him if I was going the right way by going right, he said no you have to go left. He told me he knows Feltham remand centre and he did some time in Norwich. He left and I wondered if I should trust him. I did and saved myself walking in the wrong direction.

Again I had enough, please Lord let me get some shelter and food tonight. A very hard two miles to a church with a tower. David the vicar and his wife give me coffee sandwiches a hot bath. Im sleeping in the Vestry on cushions, I have a hot flask of coffee.

Also a lovely beautiful wonderful fantastic Fan heater, (6.00PM). thank you lord.

Going back to today I thought how Ezekiel must have doubted Gods commands, but at the end of each crazy thing he did, he new how he has failed again by doubting, but that God talks and gives just at the right moment. Let go and trust,

(April 7 - 4th day Thursday)

David gives me some coffee and cornflakes before I set off. While im waiting David gives me a Julian of Norwich book to read. Julian talks about hope and explains that hope is also handing over trusting something (God). Hope is very important to our relationship with God.

If evil can destroy hope, evil can destroy trust and faith.

A couple of miles into the days walk I have the urge to get to Norwich to pray. I feel it is God speaking, Or is it God.

I wonder if deep down its an excuse to stop walking. And to hitch hike so that I may have 3 or 4 days in prayer, in the Cathedral or the Julian cell.

I wrestle with this all day until around 3pm. I know if I walk God will provide, I have no doubt. I also have enough food and four pounds which will provide my food anyway.

My feet are sore but I know I can hack it. I feel perhaps four days prayer is what God wants.

Then I think what will people think, will they understand. Then I think what people think does not matter.

Obeying God first is what matters, even if I am seen to fail. God and I know the truth.

Im having a rest on a bench in a green and two Jahovass witnesses come to speak to me. I tell them about my faith in Christ and of hope. From what they say I see how evil has destroyed there hope. So there by destroying there faith in Jesus Christ the saviour. They do not know we have already been saved.

Im seven miles from Haverhill what should I do. What does God want me to do. Is it my evil pride not letting me hitch a ride. Is it the fact that I want to tell people I walked all the way.

Does God want me to hand over more and accept humiliation. Do I need to submit to Gods will more. Failure Failure Failure is haunting me with this decision.

But im only thinking of my personal feelings when I think of failure. If I put pride, failure and humiliation out of my mind, I have no doubt that I should get to Norwich as quick as possible.

I stick my thumbs up, a car stops I get in.

Im in Haverhill in a Wimpey bar having a cup of tea. What shall I do next.

Have I failed myself. Have I failed God. Or have I served God. What shall I do next.

When I go to the toilet im walking back to my table and a tremendous calm comes over me. I realize it does not matter what I do, Just rest in Christ, Just be peaceful in Christ. Just hand over and live for this moment. Christ will lead me. Whats going to happen will happen.

Christ is close I shall sit here for a few hours with the peace of Christ.

Its going to rain. Four churches have no life about them the last one I meet a very nice lady called eve. She phones the minister and then settles me into the vestry of a United Reform Church.

I have electric fires and tea and schones. Not a bad nights sleep. Eve gives me her address because she would like me to send her what I write.

She also gives me some sandwiches for the day. She has a lot of faith in me finishing the walk, so I decide I will walk all the way. It's a nice sunny day.

(5th Day).

Ive rested in the body of Christ again when I needed it (the Church)

Ive been provided for by different Christian churches, yet they all love and serve Christ in love.

I understand why Mother Teresa never has any belongings and travels only in faith. By letting go of everything there is just Christ to provide.

My legs are red raw where my jeans keep rubbing. The journey is making me tired now and my feet are sore after a few minutes. I would like to make Bury St Edmunds 6.00pm.

People are doing Kung Foo. They give me a number to ring. Im reluctant to spend the money on the phone as I only have £1.10 left out of the £10.00 Adrian gave me.

Simon the vicar about 30 comes to see me. He takes me to a homeless hostel. I can stay in the church hall if I want but I chose the hostel. There are 10 bunk beds some chairs and a T.V. A lady gives me a meal of sphagetti bolongse. There is a shower and toilets. The atmosphere is very good. A mixture of all people. Below me in the bottom bunk is a 17 year old girl who is 6 months pregnant. About 4 young people who cannot go home because of violence. Two ex-army men who have done 22 years and receive an army pension but no where to live. A couple of devorced men who now have nothing and no home.

A young man and women who look very much in love. And various other people. We are all in a room the size of our ground floor of the Feltham centre.

1.00am in the morning and we are all woken up by people throwing stones at the building. The police come and they move on. Even when these people have nothing they are still victimised for society not providing jobs or homes.

A lovely shower and a fried breckfast and some sandwiches given to me I will be of. This homeless centre is provided and financed by the parochial local church. When Simon came in he was truly liked and respected.

(6th Day Thursday)

Last night a middle aged man washed all my clothes and dried them. He has nothing, no material things yet he has a huge kindness.

The girl who is pregnant must feel very alone and scared. She does not talk much.

Again I realize that the Christian Church has provided for me. The is the living body of Christ. Giving love kindness and shelter.

Simon of St johns had no hesitation to help me.

The sun is shinning Ive had a good breakfast if I walk well today I could be in Norwich Friday. Im walking well and starting to speed up as I know the Cathedral is within reach. Im singing songs and whistling. The birds have been singing everyday on this pilgrimage. 4pm. And I brake into my last pound and buy a refreshing cup of tea in a roadside café. How wonderful a basic cup of tea is to taste. The lady and I talk and I tell her all about my pilgrimage. I go to the toilet and when I come out there is a big skone with butter on. Umm it was lovely.

Im about 23 miles from Norwich so I decide to push on for a couple of more hours. Then I know I will make Norwich on Friday. 5.30pm and its going to be a clear night so I decide to sleep in the open. Im looking in some woods standing by the road. A car stops and two men are in the front. The driver asks me if I would like a lift. I said no thankyou Im on a walking pilgrimage to Norwich. He said Im going to Norwich don't be silly a pilgrimage is not a walk of penitence. Anyway he says Im giving you something Im not asking. It was as if he knew my conscience and my aim of the pilgrimage. I got in the back and we started to drive. We started to talk about my faith. He was telling me about an appearance that keeps coming to Yogouslavia. Then he says that I should keep a normal job and not to go into ministry. I never mentioned ministry. He says that we are in God's image and that then God is and fails like us. That don't worry if you do bad. Just live. He talks very convincingly and I ask him if he studied theology and he says no and I don't want to talk about myself. Suddenly he says he has got to make a detour and drop the other man of. I feel a perception of evil and that something bad is going to happen. I look at the doors and realise it is a two door car. I am unable to get out if I need to. I look at him and he ouzes bad feeling and uneasiness. I even feel that they may try to kill me, the evil feeling is so strong. I know that I can handle two of them but this is different. I feel that I am in the dark and this is not physical but spiritual. I look around to see if they have any weapons. The driver says he has a flat tire, we are in the middle of a country road with no one in sight. Please lord I rest in you. Let go I rest in you. The driver stops the car and doesn't get out. Im terrified. I know theres not a flat. He tells the other man to get out and have a look. He hesitates as he knows there is no flat. Its like two wolves circling there prey building up courage to attack. Eventually the passenger gets out I jump out and stand next to him. He doesn't look at the wheels and just says he will tighten them up later. The driver says get back in. I do and Im terrified, Im stupid. We drive on and no one talks. The driver drops the passenger of. I get in the front seat. He stops at a little chief and buys me egg and chips. He looks at all the women in the little chief. Very brazingly at there breasts and bodies. He openly trys to chat the waiter up. We still don't talk. Again we get back in the car. Two hitch hikers are picked up by two young women as we pull out of little chief. He follows them into Norwich and around the town. Suddenly he says the car is over heating and stops. He says I am to get out here. I do and he waits a few minutes and drives of.

Im shattered, fed up that I took a lift, bewieldered, confused and sad.

I feel as if the devil himself was in that car. If God works through Christians and people then so must the devil.

Six days and I am in Norwich. Its not a glorious happy feeling, but a failing feeling. I walk to the Cathedral and see the sphire.

I sit on a bench and feel sorry for myself. I know that the evil has tried to make this pilgrimage seem a failure for Christ.

Yet it is Christs total triumph. I know that evil has tried to make my arrival to Norwich Cathedral seem a waist and to make Christ look like a God of pain, rather than joy and resurrection. I do feel bad and sad.

But I know that the triumph is Christs. I am here safe and sound, I left Feltham six days ago with only my faith. Tomorrow I know Christ will lift me up from this sorrow. For He hath Borne our griefs and carried our sorrow. I love you Christ.

I find a church that is a hostel for the homeless. Im fed and have a bed. Again I rest in Christs body.

(Friday 7th day)

0:800 We have breakfast and are watching T.V. There are about 20 men and 2 girls. The news of the conservative victory has shattered them. The mood is of depression and unhopeful. All the politicians make there speeches. I feel they should be sitting here with me and these lovely but helpless people. Maybe they should do a pilgrimage to see and feel what their decisions do to and affect the most vulnerable.

I shall go to the Cathedral and pray. 9:00AM

The stain glass windows by the entrance seems to be parallel to my pilgrimage. I feel very emotional as I see a cross with a snake around it. As if to say the devil will paint you the wrong picture and meaning of the cross. The stain glass windows I read so easily now. It is a very passionate Cathedral. 12.30 I have communion and the thorns on the deans gown brings tears to my eyes. I remember Easter is near. The Dean and I talk after the service, I then make my way to the Julian cell.

213

Hide Little Boy

There is a fresh aura in the cell. I feel it so strong. I look to see if anything is causing a draft. I pray.

My pilgrimage is coming to an end. Thank you lord for giving and blessing my faith in you. Let go Let go All will be well as Julian said. Let go and trust."

My poem:

"God of Love

God of Doubt,

I need to love you

Why do I doubt?

……...

In your wisdom

Our spirits are free,

Free to choose

What will it be?

…….

To love you truly

Is how you want love to be,

So, God almighty you set us free.

……

God of love

God of doubt,

In your wisdom we may doubt.

For if we knew,

God you are.

We would have no doubt.

……..

To choose to love you for true loves sake!

The mystery of god is always at stake.

……..

Doubt keeps us hungry,

Hungry for love.

Doubt feeds our souls

With the mystery, of God's love.

'Potential'

Soon after I completed my pilgrimage, my vicar began to talk to me about potentially having a calling to ordained ministry and the priesthood in the Church of England. He encouraged me to explore the possibility. My initial response to him was not positive; "How can that be? I am a divorced lone parent with four children in my care and I am living on Income Support. I have no qualifications and I did not receive much schooling. I can hardly read properly or spell and write. Yes, I have been teaching myself the basics of grammar and English with children's study books, but that is where I am at, probably at the standard of a not very good primary school-aged child with regards to spelling, English and maths."

My vicar told me to consider going back to school to get some qualifications. I did sense some sort of calling, but I thought the calling from God was to a monastic life, however, this could not be as I had four young children in my care. Little miracles occasionally happened in my life which kept me wondering and questioning whether I did, in fact, have a calling to the priesthood of the Church of England.

On one particular day, I remember having no money at all. I had no food for the children and they would soon be coming home from school. I was desperate and I had exhausted all my usual avenues of finding a few pounds for dinner. Sadly, this can often be the life of a lone parent on Income Support or a low-income family.

How was I going to give the children an evening meal and a breakfast?

Completely unexpected, an envelope popped through my letterbox with no name or writing on it. Inside the envelope was a five-pound note. With that five pounds, I was able to give the children an evening meal and some breakfast. Thank goodness for supermarket own brands!

I was baptised in the Holy Spirit in a field in Feltham in January 1991, and then my four children and I were all baptised by water into the Church of England on Easter Sunday that same year. I had a deep desire to help people, which continued to grow in me. My outlook on life had completely changed, from money and the pursuit of money, to compassionately helping people who were hurting. Before I took on the children on my own, I had embarked on various entrepreneurial pursuits with millionaires as my backers. Unfortunately, the projects failed to be successful for one reason or another.

The lovely lady who had come to visit myself and my children when I first enquired about church arranged for me to volunteer at a drop-in centre called Open Doors. Ironically, now when I think of the Open Doors Project, it is interesting, because the Project was a Mental Health drop-in centre. My role was to be a group worker with the people who dropped in. The role of the drop-in centre, and its aim, was to help and support people with mental health problems with their transition to Care in the Community following a change of government policy. This job and the hours suited me well as it fitted around my children. My youngest was at nursery for a few hours a day, and this relieved me to work in The Open Doors Project. Eventually, her nursery hours increased to school hours and I worked in the Open-Door Project from 9.30 am to 2.30 pm. I enjoyed the work and I understood many of the clients; I somehow knew their pain and I could empathise with the symptoms of their mental health conditions. At this time in my life, I did not know why I could do this, and certainly did not know that I myself was suffering from a mental health condition. Again, I was asked by the Open Doors drop-in centre facilitator to consider getting educated because she thought I had potential.

'Education'

As both my vicar and the Drop-in Centre facilitator had suggested to me that I should get educated, I began to make some tentative enquiries. I could not face starting at the bottom of the education system, and so I decided to ask my vicar what he thought. He told me that he wanted to put me forward for the selection process of the Church of England, to test the calling he thought I had. In order for him to put me forward, I had to have a couple of A-levels at least.

After this conversation, I went straight to Hounslow College and asked them if I could do a couple of A-levels in one year. After I shared my education experience, or complete lack of it, they, not overtly, laughed at me and said it was just not possible, and that I had to start with GCSEs first. I went away disappointed and prayed at home and at church about my situation. I felt I should not give up, and so I went back to Hounslow College and met a lovely Irish lady who was one of the lecturers. I shared with her my situation, and it turned out that she ran a one-year Access course. I told her I had been trying to teach myself to read and write for years now but that I was terrible at spelling and grammar. She looked me in the eyes and said, "Paul, I'm going to start you on the Access course, and I will coach you for three months. After three months I will be able to tell if you can continue or if I have to pull you off the course".

I started the Access course which, if completed, would give me two A-levels, one in Sociology and the other in English language and comprehension. I got over the three-month probationary period and stayed on the Access course. During this year, I began to have meetings with various Archdeacons and Bishops and 'lay' people to test my calling to the ordained ministry. I continued my A-level Access course and passed, all within a year! I just about had good enough grades to be accepted by King's College London to begin a BA(Hons) degree in Theology. I was still struggling with spelling and grammar, but I had gained the confidence that I was bright enough to understand various theories and concepts.

Education opened up a whole new world to me. Knowledge was thrilling. Every page I turned in a book excited me. I would get up at 4.00 am to read, study and write before I got the children up at 7.00 am to get them ready for school. My depression and anger seemed to be at bay during this time of study.

'Nervous Breakdown'

Then, out of the blue, it happened. I was getting the children ready to go out in the evening to support and watch my son who was in a school production. It was about 6.30 pm. I began to feel weak and faint. I slipped into a severe panic attack. My chest tightened and I thought I was having a heart attack. My breathing quickened, my hands began to curl up and I could not straighten them. I was now unable to function and I had three children with me (my son had gone early to school). I told my eldest daughter to go and get help, and a couple we barely knew came to help me. The husband helped me to his car, and his wife stayed with the children as he rushed me to hospital. I remember telling him that I had a life insurance policy for the children as I thought I was going to die.

When I got to hospital, a nurse hooked me up to all the monitoring equipment and told me to breathe into a brown paper bag. Gradually my breathing slowed, and my fingers, hands and arms began to uncurl from the curled up and twisted state they were in. I was kept in hospital for three days and underwent all sorts of tests. I was convinced I had had a heart attack and that it would affect me for the rest of my life. On the evening of my third day in hospital, the Cardiac Consultant and various other Doctors stood around my bed. I thought to myself, "Here comes the bad news."

The Consultant told me, "We have done every test there is to do, and I can categorically say that you have not had a heart attack. It felt like a heart attack to you, but it was not. You have had a nervous breakdown. Basically, your body and your brain are telling you they've had enough and cannot go on anymore the way you are living. Of course, we do understand, as a lone parent, you do not have many options. Please consider how you can help yourself. You can leave hospital this evening."

When I got home, my children were given back to me by the various people who had helped with their care. I was weak and my anxiety was overwhelming me. I had to go and shut myself in a bedroom and lie in the dark. I could not face talking to them or having any of the children moving about around me. Moving objects made me feel sick and I wanted to vomit. I felt terrible for the children. All they wanted to do was hug me, but I could not handle it. It was just too much. I gave instructions through my bedroom door to my eldest daughter as to what needed to be done, and just lay in bed feeling like I was dying and crippled with anxiety. We lived like this for a week. Eventually, I made myself come downstairs; it took all my might and willpower to overcome the stress and anxiety I was feeling and the weakness of my body, but I had to do it for the children's sake. I sat on a kitchen chair and told each child what they needed to do to get ready for school. My eldest daughter took my second youngest to school, and a neighbour kindly took my youngest to nursery. I went back to bed, drained, weak and full of anxiety. The weekends were difficult, but not too bad for the kids. They were effectively feral, but safe, going in and out of their friends' houses all day.

After three weeks, I gave myself some targets to achieve to help me get stronger. My first target was to be able to walk to the front gate of my house and back. This was approximately ten feet from the front door. After I achieved this target for a week, I increased the distances I wanted to achieve each week. The end of the road for three or four days, the shop around the corner for three or four days, taking the children to school for a week. Gradually, I built myself up again and I began to function. It took me four months to be able to get back into caring for the children properly and re-start my studies. There was nothing I could do to ease the stress in my life in the way the consultant wanted me to do. I knew I had had a nervous breakdown but I didn't realise the extent of my mental illness at this point in my life. I continued to live in financial poverty with no extended family support. I needed to pursue and test my calling, I needed to continue my education, and most of all I needed to do my best for the children.

'Yet another selection'

During my studies at King's College London, I was asked to attend a Church of England selection conference for the priesthood. I arranged for the children to be cared for, and off I went. At the beginning of the three-day selection conference, about twenty of us sat in a circle and introduced ourselves. We had to say who we were and what our occupation was. I was very embarrassed when it came to my turn. The people who had introduced themselves before me were doctors, solicitors, teachers, CEOs. I introduced myself as a divorced lone parent with four children in my care, living on Income Support, and doing some occasional hod-carrying for bricklayers to earn a little extra money. I thought if God is calling me, then I need to be honest. After I introduced myself, the stillness in the room seemed to me to be a mixture of disbelief and snobbery.

I had no idea if I would be selected; it seemed to me that I didn't fit the 'norm' for a Church of England clergyperson. However, during the selection conference, I was in my room and looking in the mirror, when suddenly my face lit up and shone brightly. It was weird, but I felt it was a confirmation and encouragement from God for me.

A few weeks later, I received confirmation that I had been selected for training for the priesthood in the Church of England. I was overjoyed and humbled by God, and I wanted to serve Him with all my might. It was in the spring of 1996 that I received confirmation of my selection for training, and I had to go and see the Bishop of London who, at the time, was Bishop Richard

Chartres, as he was my sponsoring Bishop. He very generously gave me a cheque for £400, £100 for each of my children, to treat them with. He also said he would like me to start residential theological college in the September of that year. I agreed. I had a four-bedroom former council house that I needed to sell so that we could move to theological college and pay off all my accumulated debts and be debt-free. The only problem was that none of the former council houses were selling on my estate. People had had their houses up for sale for years. Just one week after my meeting with the Bishop of London, I sold my council house and paid off my debt.

In the summer of 1996, I was honoured and proud to be awarded a BA (Hons) degree in Theology from King's College, London. Not bad for someone who had had little to no 'formal' education!

Canada

'Amber and Mark'

Regrettably, whilst I was still at King's College, I got a phone call from my big sister Amber, who, after the rest of the family had been deported, had stayed in Canada and made a life for herself. She rang to tell me she had cancer of the lungs; she had always been an extremely heavy smoker, and now did not have long to live. I arranged for my mum and myself to fly over to Canada together. After the long flight, we made our way straight to the hospital. We found Amber writhing on her bed in extreme pain. She had her eyes closed and seemed unconscious. Mum went home to Amber's house to rest and I stayed with Amber. There was no communication between us other than me talking to her and hoping she heard. I laid my hands on her and said the Lord's Prayer out loud. She stopped writhing and squirming and just lay, peaceful.

A group of doctors came in to observe her and they seemed confused that she seemed to be out of pain. Amber died that night; I believe she had been waiting for us to arrive before she gave up. David, her partner, said he did not want a funeral or anything for Amber. David had been nursing Amber at home before she had to go into hospital for palliative care. He was extremely angry and depressed. David and Amber were truly in love. My niece and nephews were staying at the house too. I sensed the house was going to explode with emotion and become out of control. They asked me to hold a little prayer ceremony in the garden for Amber because David would not allow a funeral. David did not want to take part.

Mum and I flew back to England. I decided that I needed to phone the Canadian social services and tell them that, in my opinion, the people living in Amber's house, her children and David, needed support or something bad would happen. I do not think I was taken seriously, and to my knowledge, Canadian Social Services did not do anything for the family.

A few weeks later, David sat on his bed and committed suicide by shooting himself in the head. The loss of Amber was all too much for him.

Many years later, I repeated the same scenario with my brother Mark. He, too, had lung cancer from years of heavy smoking, and many other health issues from the unhelpful life choices that he had made. I sat with him and supported him as he passed on.

What chaos my psychopath of a mother caused throughout our family and the extended family. The web of a psychopath reaches all; children, partners and grandchildren.

Statistically, I am now aware that children from a family who have suffered at the hands of a parent, in the way that I and my siblings did, die young.

Nottingham, Nottinghamshire, UK

'St John's College – Vicar Factory'

Myself and three of my children joined St John's Theological College in Nottingham for two years' theological training, or as it is colloquially known, 'Vicar Factory'. My eldest son had now joined the army so did not move with us. St John's College was good in some ways but lacking in others.

I was asked by the Church of England to stay on Income Support rather than receive Church of England funding for our maintenance, as this saved the Church of England money. I agreed because there was no difference in the amount of money that I would receive whether I was funded by the Church of England or the state via Income Support. However, this did make me feel unsupported and a bit like I wasn't completely accepted by the Church of England. Not much changed for me during my time at St John's. I still lived with constant depression and anger, feeling lost and very tired. I survived by living on my wits and did my best to care for the children.

In my first year at St John's, I studied for an MA in Theological Studies. This was very much a research degree and gave me a lot of time to rest and look after the children. As had been a constant pattern in my life, I never got the chance to wholly commit myself to my studies and to apply myself so that I could reach my full potential. At this point in my life, this was due to two factors; my mental wellbeing and my commitment to caring for my children. I did make some friends, but we didn't really stay in touch after ordination.

For the Easter of my final year, we were given six weeks off from college. These six weeks saved me because my back pain, which I had suffered following a bad parachute jump in the military, flared up and added to my already troubled depression and anger. The pain got so severe, I had to call an ambulance. I was taken to hospital but sent home again after x-rays were taken, with instructions to have complete rest. I took a door off its hinges and put it under the mattress on my bed for me to lie on. I was immobile for most of the six weeks, and from this position, lying on my back, I ran the house and completed my final dissertation.

Eventually, my back pain became manageable, so we visited my mum at her house for a couple of days because we needed a change of scenery but could not afford to go anywhere else. I was still endeavouring to give my children some sort of extended family experience.

Mum's house was a three-bedroom council house, but one of the bedrooms was permanently locked and Mum gave strict instructions that no-one was to go into this bedroom. I had no problem with her request; maybe I was being naive. A very bright light shone out of the bottom and sides of the locked door at night-time. This made me curious, but I was not going to ask her what was in the room; I still feared her.

While we were visiting, Mum went out of the house one day, and I noticed that she had not locked the bedroom door properly, the door to the 'shining room'. The children were occupied downstairs and in the garden, so I unhooked the padlock and pushed the bedroom door open. I was gobsmacked! Inside, cannabis plants filled every inch of the room. It was no amateur set up. On platforms, the plants had water irrigation pipes and above the plants, hanging from the ceiling, were strong heat-lamps. The brightness in the room caused me to squint. I suspected right away that my brother Mark had set the cannabis farm up in her bedroom, and that Mum, who was by now in her 70s, was happy to oblige.

This discovery plunged me into a moral dilemma. The house could potentially be raided by the police at any moment; the children and I could be caught up in a police raid. I was a lone parent who was at theological college studying to become an ordained priest in the Church of England! I felt angry that my mum would put my children and myself in this position without telling me. Just another example of the dross she brought into my life, all my life. I decided to leave in the morning and say nothing about it. It was not worth trying to explain the rights and wrongs of what she was doing, or the rights and wrongs of potentially involving myself and my children in a criminal investigation. Would the police believe I had no knowledge of the cannabis farm and I had nothing to do with it? I was stupid again to try and give the children an experience of extended family.

Not so long after this experience, I discovered that my mum was pimping my younger sister and using her council house to facilitate the liaisons. My younger sister had never been able to get away from the clutches of my mum, and she always succumbed to my mum's power over her. I was informed that the bedroom, and the bed I slept in during our visit, was the room and bed that my sister used to prostitute herself in, all facilitated by her own mother. I felt sick to my stomach. I was aware that she, my sister, had a drink problem; no doubt alcohol blotted out the pain of her existence, the pain that my psychopath mum inflicted on her, myself and all my siblings.

My sister gave me her permission to include the information about her prostitution in this autobiography, and the way in which my mum 'pimped' her when she was a young and very vulnerable woman. I had not had a lengthy conversation with my sister for some time, years even, and I had forgotten just what a lovely person she is. In our conversation she was open and kind, thoughtful and tearful as we reminisced about our experiences, both as children and adults, of our mother. Disbelief, tears and laughter were shared as we touched on and poked around a little of our pain. Deep pain. Pain inflicted on us by our psychopathic mother.

In giving me her permission, she said, "Truth is the only way."

She told me it broke her heart when I joined the army at sixteen. To her, I was the only rock and support she had. I became a little embarrassed when she said to me that I was a gentle, kind and 'angelic-faced' beautiful boy before I joined the army. She went on to say that although I had had to fight to survive, literally physically fight, I had always been compassionate. However, in her words, the army changed me, and not for the good.

When we spoke about how our mum had 'pimped' her, she told me that not only did Mum take her 'cut' of the earnings, but in addition, she also charged my sister for hire of the room! Most of the time, Mum would leave my sister and her 'client' alone in the house, vulnerable to attack, but always made sure she got her money.

My sister has had a life of pain cause by being raised by a psychopath. She has a deep ache and is searching for answers for her ruined life, with a history of many broken relationships. She is hoping the therapy that she is now undergoing will begin to heal her also. We both nervously laughed together when I shared that the statistics show that children raised by a mother like ours die young. We again nervously laughed when we realised our two other siblings died in their fifties. My sister is 54 and I am 61. We know now that we will keep in touch. I understand my sister, and also the many,

many others like her, who, when faced with tragedy in their lives and poverty, are pushed into a life of prostitution.

'Pre-Ordination'

I soon completed my theological studies and I had to find a curacy, a training post before becoming a fully-fledged vicar! I managed to secure a curacy at the Church of St Mary Magdalene located in the beautiful market town of South Molton in North Devon, and my children and I prepared to move.

Before my ordination, I was required to go on a pre-ordination retreat, and I was excited and full of hope about this new chapter in my life and my children's life. I very rarely heard from my mother; she only ever phoned me if she wanted money or to threaten me or tell me how evil me and my siblings were, or how evil the particular man she was with at that time was.

An hour before I set off for my retreat, the phone rang, and it was my mum. I knew as soon as I picked the phone up, she had phoned me with the intention of ruining my retreat and ordination. My mother could not tolerate it if any of her children succeeded in anything in life and would become extremely jealous. During this 'phone call, an hour before I was about to go on a spiritual retreat, she decided to tell me that she thought I ought to know that my brother Mark had been doing terrible things. The nature of what he had done was deeply troubling and sickening, and I felt completely crushed by this information. I went on retreat, but was unable to focus, my mind constantly going over the information I had been given. What should have been a happy and joyful occasion and the culmination of 5 years of study, was ruined, yet again, by my mother's psychopathic thinking.

I was, however, really pleased that many members of my sponsoring church, St. Dunstan's in Feltham came to support me at my ordination. I still felt like an imposter though. I felt I did not belong. I knew I was baptised in the Holy Spirit; I knew I was called by God, but I knew I was not OK. I had, throughout my life, learned to hide, to throw up smoke screens if you like. I was damaged goods, but this is what I knew Christ wanted of me, to know and see the damage in others, and to love, comfort and accept them.

PART FOUR

'A Holy Mess'

1998 – 2015
Aged: 39 – 56

"Going to church doesn't make you a Christian, any more than standing in a garage makes you a car."

Billy Sunday

South Molton, North Devon, UK

'Curacy'

I began my curacy in South Molton, and the children and I lived in an adequate house provided by the Church of England right next to the church hall. My time as a curate was not easy, and I had to face many difficulties and challenges, particularly with regard to finances and issues with the Parish.

I still did not know I had a mental health illness baying to be recognised, baying to scream and shout and be heard. My net monthly pay (stipend) was around £740.00 a month. Feeding the children, buying clothes, school trips, Christmas, birthdays and paying bills could not be covered by this small income. Most of the other curates I knew had wives who worked to make ends meet. Debt began to creep up again. I so wanted to give the children the life of happiness that I had never had, opportunities and experiences that I had never been able to know. I made a commitment to one of my daughters which I felt I could not go back on.

When we began theological college, my daughter, who was ten years old at the time, asked me for a horse. My dysfunction meant that I found it hard to say 'No' to my children, even though I knew I couldn't afford it, so I told her that if she wanted a horse, she would have to get a 'job' helping out at a stables on the weekends for two years. I promised her that if she did this, I would buy her a horse.

When we arrived in North Devon two years later, she reminded me that she had worked every Saturday and Sunday for two years at a stable in Nottingham, and could she please have her horse. So, I bought her a horse and she became a very accomplished rider, eventually heading up the eventing team at the university she attended. Of course, paying for the horse's upkeep was difficult, and beyond my means. Eventually, once she was old enough to earn money, my daughter was able to work at the stables in exchange for free livery for her horse. Thankfully, my other daughter only wanted a puppy, and we got a beautiful poodle who she called 'Febi', who was an integral part of our family for 16 ½ years.

During my curacy, my personal battle with depression, anger and sleepless nights continued. Sleep was virtually impossible, as the moment I closed my eyes, the 'images' came, images that were terrifying and tormenting. I tried fighting it with all my might. I would drink whisky after the children went to bed to try and blot everything out. On the odd occasion, I would have a glass of whisky or wine before I went out to a meeting. Debt, trauma buried deep in my mind and a difficult parish situation took its toll on me.

My financial struggles continued. I recall that one Christmas I had no money for presents, and all I could do was write IOU promises of money on sheets of paper and wrap them up in boxes. That is all that the children received that year. I wrote to a clergy charity to ask for help, and at the time, the trustees of this charity were Archdeacons and senior clergy in the Church of England. They put a lot of pressure on me to inform my Bishop of my debt and told me that they would not help me, instead just demonstrating judgementalism and indifference to my situation. I felt at the time that I could not inform my Bishop of my debt as it would potentially stop my progress within the Church of England and eventually finding a parish of my own. Even though I was working again, I could not escape the anxiety, stress and shame of poverty and debt.

'Stalked'

Life in North Devon was what I had hoped for the children. My eldest daughter had decided to stay in Nottingham to finish her studies, and St John's College helped me and her out by accommodating her for a while. I now only had my two younger daughters at home and in my care. The countryside, beaches, schools, and close-knit community of a market town like South Molton was good for the girls. They also got involved with the church choir, a local drama school and a youth group that I started, and both girls made life-long friends.

The three of us found it very amusing that when we arrived in South Molton, and I began my ministry in St. Mary Magdalene's Church, the congregation increased with the addition of several single women! My children had nagged me for years to meet someone else, but at this stage in my life, I was still comfortable to live a life of celibacy and serve my calling.

Curiously, while living as a single parent and being a newly ordained curate, I experienced something that I had never experienced before; I was stalked!

Wherever I went, whether to a meeting, a service or just sat at home, this lady would turn up. I began to receive letters from her, and little donations of money were put in envelopes and pushed through my letterbox, which were, I presumed, to help me with the children. Eventually, she asked for my help and asked if we could meet for a chat to discuss spiritual guidance for her. We met a few times, all in public places, and it became clear to me she wanted more than just spiritual guidance; she wanted a relationship with me. I did not want to give her any hope of a relationship, so I ended our meetings and asked her to not contact me. However, she kept turning up at events that I attended. I can only assume that she felt rejected, and I began to receive threatening letters from her. In one of her letters, she told me that she was going to blow my house up. It was really scary and gave me such an insight into the suffering of victims of a stalker. I did not go to the police, although I had the letters as evidence, instead I spoke with a friend of hers and asked her to help me, to persuade her to leave me alone. Although her friend agreed to speak with her, her response was quite dismissive, and she could not understand why I, an ex-Para and former SAS soldier, would be worried about a mere woman! Assumptions because of my background continued to make people think I was invincible. Little did they know of my mental health suffering.

Although the children were enjoying the benefits of living in North Devon, we still lived in poverty. Lack of money and the continued state of my mental health had its impact on us all as a family. I fought depression, night terrors and flashbacks each day and night. I was living in the nightmare of trying to be the real me. I knew my heart was a loving heart, a generous heart and a gentle heart, but rage and outrage, combined with the symptoms of PTSD, were unbeatable at the time and remained so until I eventually got my diagnosis and received specialist help in 2017.

I remember having suicidal ideation, seriously wanting to end my life. I had had enough of my sleepless nights and the horrors of my mind. I had had enough of feeling guilt and shame.

'Mask'

I can remember one occasion clearly when I had locked myself in the bathroom and determined to end my life. I was totally confused; my head was telling me 'enough is enough' but I could hear banging on the bathroom door, which brought me back to reality. My girls were banging on the door, begging me to open it, expressing how worried they were about me. I was lying on the floor, crying, exhausted with life, exhausted with my head, exhausted with the stress of poverty, exhausted with failing at doing my best for the children. After some time, I became stable and I came out of what I now know to be a dissociation. I then began the cycle of experiencing the guilt of failing my children and putting them through that. All I wanted to do was love my children and give them the life I never had. The roller coaster of my children one minute having a good and loving dad, and the next a dad who failed them, continued. I was always on my own in this fight. I forced myself to work and I forced myself to support the children.

Daily, I would sit at home with my whisky and fight my demons. The children played out whilst I sat in my room, curtains closed, in the dark. As soon as they came home, I would put on my smile, bring out my happy, funny dad persona mixed with the genuine love that I had for them. I hid me.

'True Love'

With the benefit of hindsight, it is clear that my mental health began to really deteriorate, albeit slowly, around the year 2000. It would not be until 2017, seventeen years later, that I would be diagnosed with CPTSD and latent onset PTSD with dissociative subtype.

During my curacy in South Molton, my home circumstances began to change. My children were getting older and did not need me so much. I found myself in a more 'free' position, so I began to pray and think about whether I should consider meeting someone again, perhaps even marry again. At this point, I was still not aware of the full extent of my illness, and in denial of my need for help. After all, a Para never shows weakness or asks for help.

Eventually, I concluded that it would be ok for me to meet someone again, and I joined a Christian dating site. Meeting someone is difficult when you are an ordained priest in a small community. There were the public expectations of a priest, alongside the complications of dating women in a community I served. This would not look good and would be frowned upon by the community and my seniors. Another complication for me was my children. I did not want their expectations raised and then potentially dashed. For these reasons, I joined a Christian dating site. I was 'successful', in that I had some lovely dates, but I never met anyone for which my heart felt a connection. Then, a link came through, which we believe was God-ordained, to Lois. Lois, in time, would come to be my soul mate, and the person who has, without a shadow of a doubt, saved me from my mental health and suicidal death.

Lois is a beautiful, stunning and loving Lioness of a woman! After months and months of emails and telephone calls, we decided to meet up. We realised very quickly that we were falling in love. At the time, I had not been looking after myself and was very overweight, and the drinking, lack of sleep and depression had taken their toll on me.

After a time of courtship, we made our way to a beautiful spot near South Molton, deep in the countryside. I chose this specific place to propose to Lois, as I felt it was symbolic of the separate paths we had taken in life and our journey forward together. We stood on a bridge over a river, and at this point, two separate rivers flowed down the valley from different directions and joined together to form one river under the bridge. This one river then flowed on into the distance on its journey through the valley. Lois and I had had very different life journeys up to that point. Lois had a stable, loving, happy childhood with two parents and financial security. To put it simply, I did not. However, our love for each other and our love for God, blended with our mutual desire to serve God, was profoundly meaningful. I felt safe and happy with Lois; I had never felt these emotions before in my life. At the time, we both felt our future was going to be amazing. We were going to get married, serve God and have adventures in ministry together. Our life was going to be blissful!

Of course, unbeknownst to us both, my mental health condition would be a terrible thorn in both our sides, as the symptoms began to manifest themselves in our relationship. Sometimes, these manifestations would be symptoms of CPTSD and sometimes symptoms of PTSD with dissociative subtype, and sometimes a mix of both. The hauntings in my head were not going to go or disappear just because I got married. The traumatic hauntings I had experienced in my life were not going to leave our newfound hope and happiness alone. Miserably, my illness was going to continue to deteriorate and drastically affect our marriage and ministry. With the slow and gradual deterioration of my mind, there arose the increasing symptoms of PTSD in our relationship.

Lois chose to love me and understand me. She knew the real me, and although at the time we did not know that I was mentally ill, Lois knew there was some sort of a problem. She offered me nothing but grace, the grace she understood God gave.

Our wedding day and marriage service was a beautiful and holy occasion. At the time, I was part of a team of clergy who were conservative in their views on marriage and divorce. It was only in the previous year, 2002, that the Church of England had changed its policy and began to allow divorcees to remarry in their churches. I had, for a while, at staff meetings, shared with the other vicars that life is not always so simple for many people, and for one reason or another, marriages don't always work out. I was pleased that my colleagues decided to come and support Lois and me at our wedding despite their reservations.

As the curate of South Molton Parish Church, I was loved and supported by the town's folk. They were so happy that I had met someone, and they wished the best for me. The town and our church community supported our marriage in many different acts of kindness. They organised our reception, decorating the church hall and providing the catering, and came to the wedding service. People lined Lois' walk from my curate's house along the pebble paths to the church. When Lois entered the church, I was overcome by her beauty. She was stunningly beautiful, and her beautiful soul radiated outwards to all around her. I could not believe how blessed I was. Tears of joy and thankfulness trickled down my face. At one point in the service, we both knelt together for our blessing, and a lady came forward and wrapped a silk scarf around us and blessed us. It was a powerfully spiritual moment.

'A two-edged sword'

When PTSD symptoms were triggered in me, the symptoms varied in how they showed themselves. I felt such intense shame and guilt, had difficulty controlling my emotions, including rage and anger and had periods when I lost concentration or even awareness of where I was and who I was with (dissociation). After my marriage, I did not want Lois to know that I had a drink problem, so I could not rely on alcohol to dull the mental pain and also the physical pain that I felt across my body at times. My PTSD symptoms increased. My nightmares, flashbacks, hypervigilance and paranoia at times were extremely frightening for Lois. Lois had, and has such a wonderful and beautiful heart. She loved me. Many times, since our marriage, I wished that she did not love me. This would have freed her from the many years of pain my illness would bring her.

Eventually, with time, my dissociations would involve re-enactments of traumas that I had previously suffered, and during these dissociative episodes, I now know that I was totally unaware of what was going on in the present, and completely unable to control what was happening. I was not in control of my brain; the brain will not let the trauma disappear. Triggers for a dissociation for me were perceived fear and perceived threat, as well as sights, sounds and smells that would stimulate memories of a past traumatic experience, transporting that trauma into my present living moment, rather than it just being a recalled memory. So, in reality, I was re-living that trauma.

Although my PTSD caused times of great trouble and distress for Lois and myself, our marriage was not, and never has been, 24/7, 365 stress! Sadly, the Church of England, I suppose to try and justify their actions somehow, made it out that Lois had lived in constant fear of me for the whole of our marriage, but this simply was not true. In the years running up to my breakdown and diagnosis, we had many, many times of great joy, fun and laughter together, enjoying each other's company and journeying through life together.

Not long after our marriage, following a particularly traumatic dissociative episode, Lois, quite rightly, sought help for me and her. At the time, my paranoia did not comprehend that what Lois was doing was helpful; to me, it was disloyal. My military training to survive at all costs, combined with the paranoia and hypervigilance that came with my mental health condition, was never going to accept that Lois was trying to help me. It was not until many years later when I hit a crisis point and could not go on and started therapy, that I came to see the reality of her actions.

At this stage, that 'crisis moment' was still a long way ahead of me and would be the moment when Lois would finally decide that unless I got help, she could not go on with me. This would be the time when I would begin to accept that I needed help and I had something seriously wrong with me. This would be the time when God brought many 'angels' into our lives to help and support us; a caseworker from a veteran's charity who would be a rock for our family and traumatologists who wanted to help me. This would be the time when a psychiatrist and psychologist wanted to help me. This would be the time when professionals had no other sinister agenda other than to get me healed and help me. This would be the time when I would start my journey to recovery, but this time was not yet here.

Hurst & Winnersh, Berkshire, UK

'Hurst & Winnersh'

After our honeymoon, we settled into the process of looking for my first 'living', my first appointment as a priest and not a curate, with a parish of my own to lead and grow. After interview, I was offered the post of Vicar of Hurst and Winnersh in the Diocese of Oxford. We moved with excitement and anticipation of happiness in our future, and our family at home now consisted of my youngest daughter from my first marriage and Lois' daughter from her first marriage. My other daughter stayed in South Molton to finish her A-levels.

My mental health continued to deteriorate even before I was licensed to the parish. Depression was prominent, along with paranoia and hypervigilance. At times, to my utter shame now, I was aggressive towards Lois. Lois was concerned for the wellbeing of all of us and asked the Diocese of Oxford for help. Of course, my paranoia and hypervigilance wrongly perceived this as disloyalty; in my mind, Lois was being disloyal to a cohort (me), and that just wasn't done in the military. I flipped in and out of various states of dissociation. I was a nightmare for Lois to live with.

My licensing service proceeded. Neither Lois, myself nor our children were safeguarded by Oxford Diocese.

Life in this Parish did not help our situation. The majority of the church members in this Parish were entrenched in 'tradition' and did not want to be progressive or change in any way. They were perfectly happy with the way things were, and although they acknowledged that they could do with some 'new blood', they did not want to do anything to encourage new members of the Church.

My appointment was made on the understanding that I was to work towards bringing change in the Parish to make it more progressive, relevant to the younger population and inclusive; to develop a church model of shared ministry. In other words, a model of church that empowered the lay people (the church members), with responsibility, and shared ministry and leadership, so that everything wasn't left to the person in the dog collar! Like many Church of England congregations which are comfortable with their lot and resistant to change and growth, there is a phenomenon that these congregations become resigned to decline and close rather than change. I remember an elderly lady saying to me, "I know we need to change, but not until after I'm dead!"

Lois and I were progressive, and we were asked to grow the parish congregation in numbers and spiritual maturity. This meant we needed support from the congregation, support to enable a vision of growth. We were very quickly informed that previous vicars in this Parish had tried to bring about change and growth and had either become ill trying or given up in the face of strong opposition. The opposition was not just 'agreeing to disagree'; for us, and for previous vicars, it became malicious and dangerous. We were told that one of the previous vicars, who left ministry altogether because of this Parish, woke one morning to find that a goat they had in the garden had had its throat cut in the night and had bled to death. We had our computer hacked into, our house alarm tampered with and dead birds placed ritualistically under our bedroom window, a male and a female bird, placed directly under where the head of our bed would be, and disturbingly, in accordance with the side of the bed on which each of us slept. Our youngest was bullied at the local village school, and we discovered that some parents were encouraging their children to bully her. We received many threats.

This did not help my mental health. I was told to my face by a prominent parishioner, just before I was about to start a service, "If you continue to want to make changes, the whole front row of the congregation will leave".

This was eighty percent of the total congregation of about thirty people.

I remember my spiritual director once saying to me, "Paul, some of the nastiest people around are in the Church of England".

I was naive and did not expect to find it to be true, but sadly, my story, our story, is all too common in Church of England Parishes and is ignored, in our experience, by those in the hierarchy of the Church of England, with the opinions of parishioners being believed over that of vicars.

I soon experienced a hard lesson in so-called 'holy' congregations. It was Annual General Meeting time, and unbeknownst to me, a group of parishioners had organised themselves to deliberately disrupt the AGM. The AGM was a meeting open to the public. At the AGM, several people of this group, intermittently and from different areas of the Church building, stood up and shouted and hurled abusive comments at me. I tried to talk with them, but it soon became evident that it was planned, and communication was not their purpose. This group of people, organised by one prominent parishioner, refused to be civil and discuss their issues. They would not sit down, and they continued to interrupt the presentation of a vision for growth that I was giving. I knew their intention by disrupting the AGM was to try and rile me so that they would have a reason to make a complaint to the Bishop. Some members of this group were experienced campaigners for other causes, and they knew how to disrupt a public event. I ended the meeting as soon as I could.

Lois and I now had in our lives, my mental health (as yet undiagnosed), an aggressive and actively hostile parish, and no senior staff support.

Although I did not lose my temper at the AGM, the orchestrated disruption of the AGM resulted in this group getting what they wanted. A few days later, I received a phone call from my Archdeacon, who told me that, "In two minutes I am meeting with some of your parishioners who are disgruntled. I apologise I did not let you know earlier".

I was beginning to see how senior staff operated in the Church of England. This was effectively a meeting being held behind my back, and I was given no prior warning that it was going to happen (other than 2 minutes before the meeting started). To me, this was totally dishonest and not transparent. It caused huge anxiety for Lois and myself. I never had the opportunity to be part of the discussion they had behind closed doors.

During the year in Hurst Parish, my weight ballooned up to nineteen stone and three pounds, and I became extremely ill, physically as well as mentally. After a severe bought of 'flu, I was diagnosed with type two diabetes. I had put on over six stone in weight. My relationship with food has always been a problem for me. As a child I witnessed my mother deliberately poison the food that she gave to her husbands/partners, and then as an adult, I too became a victim. My mum poisoned me, and I was seriously ill, needing medical attention. Even today, I still am very cautious about what I eat and how it has been prepared.

'The Plot Thickens'

During this time, a new Bishop of Reading was appointed, Bishop Stephen Cottrell, who is the current Archbishop of York, and he was my suffragan Bishop. His appointment came in the aftermath of the 'Gay Bishop of Reading' scandal when Jeffrey John, a gay senior Church of England clergyman, was appointed as Bishop of Reading but then had his appointment rescinded amid homophobic protests.

My mental health difficulties became scary for Lois and me, and Lois approached Bishop Cottrell for help. Bishop Cottrell did not instigate any safeguarding procedures to safeguard Lois, myself or our children and made it quite clear to her that 'he did not want another scandal as the diocese had just got over the gay Bishop of Reading scandal'.

Prior to his recent appointment (2020) as Archbishop of York, Stephen Cottrell publicly apologised for not taking the correct action in a domestic abuse case concerning a member of clergy whilst he was Bishop of Reading. In this statement, the then Archbishop-elect states:

> "In my new position as Archbishop of York, it is absolutely essential that I am open and transparent about the need for the whole of our Church to be scrupulously honest with each other about any failings in safeguarding."

He goes on to state that the Church of England needs to stop being:

> "too quick to protect its own reputation and slow to admit its failings."

The case referred to was not what happened to us in 2004, and although we have been in contact with Archbishop Stephen during the summer of 2020, we have not received an apology for his failings at the time. We have complained, and my medical team has complained, about serious failures of safeguarding of me by the Church of England to the National Safeguarding Team, but no action has been taken to date, other than to 'protect its own reputation'

In light of Lois' request for help, we both went to see Bishop Cottrell. I admitted what had happened, but really did not recognise that I needed help and I certainly did not recognise I had a mental health illness. Bishop Cottrell was also aware of the difficulties the parish and I were having, but he had never asked to see me or help me. One of the results of our discussions with Bishop Cottrell was that I agreed to move to another parish and work with the vicar of that parish. My role was Assistant Priest in the parish of St. Sebastian's, Crowthorne. The brief from Bishop Cottrell was for me to work with the vicar of this parish to learn and recover from the opposition Lois and I and my children had experienced in Hurst and Winnersh.

'St Sebs'

The Vicar at St Sebastian's was, and is, a most integral and holy man, who I have the utmost respect for, and the most important and life-lasting teaching and role modelling that he gave me was this: 'Never give up on anyone, just as God never gives up on anyone.'

This man never gave up on anyone. He did not give up on me. I worked alongside him, but my mental health continued to take a downward spiral. This continued to affect Lois. All the symptoms of CPTSD and PTSD with dissociative subtype got worse. My paranoia and aggression particularly increased.

Sadly, Lois had to go back to Bishop Cottrell once again following a more serious dissociative episode, and at this point, I was told to stay at home and not work. Again, no safeguarding measures were put in place; I was not suspended or put on sick leave. Bishop Cottrell arranged for me to see someone who I was told would help me. This person carried the title 'Dr', and I was never told that they were not a medical doctor.

I waited at home for my first appointment whilst my mental health continued to deteriorate. Lois was working full-time whilst, at the same time, having to contend with my state of mind. It was terrible for her. She continued to hang on and cope because she thought I would be getting the help I needed. This was the desperate situation she was in. Lois was very much caught in the middle of the Bishop of Reading and me. Bishop Cottrell was telling her that they didn't want a public scandal, and to effectively keep everything under wraps, and I, in my paranoia and hypervigilance, was putting pressure on her not to trust the Bishop. It was intolerable what we both did to Lois.

I merely sat at home with no support and waited. I had no mental health support and no safeguarding support for Lois or me. A month went by, and I just wandered up and down in the living room all day and night procrastinating with my mental health. Lois endured good days and bad days with me. Another month went by and we heard nothing. Lois and I were locked into this nightmare each day. Another month went by and nothing. I was now severely depressed and suicidal, although I did not reveal this to anyone, including Lois. All we were told was that the 'Dr' was busy. I eventually sat at home in my nightmare for over a year. I hardly left the house. In hindsight, and now knowing how the Church of England works, I believe this prolonged time was a tactic to wear Lois and myself down, so that we would walk away from the Church of England and, with that, their responsibilities towards us would be gone. During this year we both suffered from my mental health.

'Tragedy'

To add to our misery at this time, something terrible happened which potentially could have finished off both me and our marriage. My eldest daughter was killed in a road accident on the 22nd of October 2006. Hell, upon hell was upon us during the tragedy. I was trying to manage my mental health, still undiagnosed. Lois was trying to hold our marriage together when every bone in her body was telling her to walk away from me. Together we tried to support all the children in their loss. My daughter's death was devastating for all of us, but yet again, Lois stepped up and supported me trying to support the other family members.

The support that we received at this time from our church family at St Sebastian's and Lois' colleagues from school was overwhelming; we couldn't have felt more loved and cared for; it was very humbling. In the Church of England, a Bishop is supposed to be a Priest's 'Father in God', the person who cares for and provides pastoral support for the clergyperson. My daughter was killed, and all I received from Bishop Cottrell was one answerphone message telling me that he was 'sorry to hear about my daughter's death'. That was it. No return phone call later, no visit, nothing. In my opinion, this lack of concern for me from my 'Father in God' told me I was just a problem he wanted to get rid of.

'Hypocrisy'

Finally, over a year after I was first referred, I got an appointment to see the Church of England appointed 'Dr', who I shall refer to as Dr X. At our first meeting with Dr X, I was asked to sign some papers. These papers gave permission for several Bishops and Archdeacons to have access to Dr X's final report on me.

I questioned Dr X and said, "I thought you were going to help me and give me therapy? I didn't know our meetings were for you to give a report to all these people!"

Dr X told me to sign the papers. I refused and was told to wait in the room while Dr X went to do something. I was left there, alone, for thirty minutes, just stewing. Dr X came back into the room and told me to sign the papers but I again refused. I was living in a state of paranoia and hypervigilance, so this encounter did nothing to enable a relationship of trust to be fostered between us. I wondered what Dr X was up to; I wondered what the Bishop was up to. Bishop Cottrell had said he wanted to help us, but this encounter with Dr X did not feel right, paranoia or no paranoia.

We ended the session there and Dr X informed me that it would be necessary to talk with Bishop Cottrell. I was asked by Bishop Cottrell why I did not want to sign the consent form, and I told him I was under the impression that I was seeing Dr X so I could be helped with my mental health, and if there was going to be a report, and I had not previously been told that there would be an official report, then that report was for him only. Bishop Cottrell was clearly frustrated with me, but he told Dr X to go ahead with meeting me and it was ok if I did not sign the consent form.

I was on my guard now with Dr X. I did not trust Dr X, and Dr X let it be known to me they found the fact that I would not sign the consent form annoying. When I met with Dr X, I decided that it would not be good for me to answer any questions or fill in forms and questionnaires that I was given to complete. I could not trust Dr X, and I wondered now what Bishop Cottrell was up to. I also couldn't trust being myself, something which I came to learn was borne from the paranoia of my mental health condition.

I thought, surely Jesus would be found to be ok if He sat in front of Dr X and answered the questions? I knew the bible stories of Jesus and how he answered questions and the answers He gave. This is how I answered Dr X's questions, and this is how I answered the questions on the forms I was given. I made the strongest attempt I could not to answer any verbal or written questions as me, Paul. I chose to answer the way I thought Jesus would answer! I also tilted the paper I wrote on so that my writing was slanted extremely forward-facing. I normally wrote with my writing upright and it always looked childlike to me, so I decided to change my writing to make it look more adult! I was hiding myself from, in my mind, the enemies, Dr X and Bishop Cottrell.

Bizarrely, my mental health state thought that Dr X and Bishop Cottrell were up to something, and in reality, there was something dishonest happening to me and Lois. All Lois and I wanted was transparent and honest support and help to get me well, but sadly we came to realize the Church of England, rather than being supportive and empathetic, can be a destructive force to be reckoned with, and in my opinion, not fit for purpose.

Later on, Dr X told me that my handwriting had been sent off for analysis, and my handwriting was a cause for concern!

Eventually, Dr X put together a report for Bishop Cottrell. The three of us met together to discuss the report. At this meeting, myself and Bishop Cottrell were given a bland A-4 sized piece of paper, with what I was led to believe was Dr X's report. This was not in fact true, and I only became aware of their dishonesty in 2017 when I had my breakdown.

In 2017, I found out Dr X had put together a much more detailed formal report, which I had previously not been made aware of and was not given a copy of. It took two years and the involvement of the Information Commissioner's Office, for me to receive a copy of the report, which I did in 2019.

I believe that the reason that the report was hidden from me was that there was never any intention by Bishop Cottrell to help me or my ministry. Dr X was a means to an end of getting rid of me and the 'problems' that I caused.

In 2017, my NHS Consultant Psychiatrist eventually managed to obtain a copy of this report, and things began to become much more clear about what exactly happened in Reading. Dr X was not a medical doctor. Dr X did not involve my GP, although Dr X stated that I was suffering from a mental health condition. Dr X did not refer me to a psychiatrist. It was all kept very much in-house! Although Dr X had concluded that I had, in Dr X's opinion, a mental health problem, the diagnosis that was come to was incorrect.

In one of the reports presented to the Church of England Tribunal in January 2020, it was clearly stated:

> 'Mis-diagnosis in January 2006 by Dr X, commissioned by the Bishop of Reading but not shared with Rev Parks, his GP or referred on to a Consultant Psychiatrist. This process, which appears to have been inappropriately managed by the Bishop of Reading, seems to have induced further shame and stigma for Rev Parks and has likely impacted delay in appropriate treatment for a combat-related C-PTSD mental health condition for a further 11/12 years. This delay has clearly contributed to the significant escalation of Rev Parks' PTSD symptoms, and furthermore experienced a number of stressful events that were mental health-related that have re-traumatised him, and traumatised Mrs Parks. In retrospect, this level of PTSD symptom escalation and the re-traumatising psychotic

episodes could have been avoided if proper due procedure had been followed by the Bishop of Reading.'

In other words, had Bishop Cottrell and his appointed 'Dr' followed proper procedure in 2004 -2006, then the years of suffering that followed for both Lois and I could have been avoided.

'Time's running out'

Bishop Cottrell allowed me to return to work, but advised that I needed to find another post as Oxford Diocese could not continue to support us and gave me a time limit in which to find a post. The house that we were living in at the time was a lovely house, rented by Oxford Diocese, and eventually, as time went on, Bishop Cottrell said they could not afford to pay the rent on that house, and moved us to a smaller and rather grotty house. We had no stove or oven in this house, so we cooked on a small camping stove that we put on the worktop. We were not able to unpack properly because the house was very small.

I had been applying for jobs and was being short-listed a lot, but after interview, was never offered the job. On some interviews, it was clear that I was wanted by the panel, but I was never appointed. Our time limit was getting close, and as a teacher, Lois had a small window of opportunity in which to hand in her notice, otherwise, she would have been obliged to continue on into the next term. I had two interviews lined up. We attended an interview in Coalville in Leicestershire, and felt that everything had gone really well, so we were very disappointed to receive the call to say that I had been unsuccessful. We then received a call from one of the parishioners who had been involved in the selection process, who wanted me to know that they, the parishioners on the panel, had really wanted me for the post, but that they couldn't appoint me because of my Bishop's reference, and he advised me to speak with my Bishop if I wanted to get another post. Parishes need a recommendation by a Bishop before they can appoint. We didn't know what to do, but I had one more interview lined up. If I didn't get this post, my pay would stop, and we would be made homeless. With hindsight, it is evident to me that Bishop Cottrell was deliberately trying to get rid of me by the reference he gave, and not recommending me for posts, yet I was not aware of this, and the time he gave us was running out. This was, I believe, a dishonest and cruel act by Bishop Cottrell, and certainly showed no honesty or transparency. He knew we had children at home too.

We went for the next interview, and after the interview process had concluded and we had spent time meeting the parishioners, Lois and I were asked to wait in the study in the Vicarage. The Archdeacon, who had been conducting the interview, came into the room and sat down opposite us, and asked, "Paul do you get on with your Bishop?"

I said, "As far as I know I do."

He then went on to tell me that I had got the job.

'Good News'

Lois and I were delighted with the news and we thought Bishop Cottrell would be too. We decided to surprise Bishop Cottrell with our good news at a function we knew Bishop Cottrell was going to be attending, the 'blessing' of a refurbished building in St Sebastian's parish. At this function, there were about fifty people standing around the building which was being blessed. We stood next to Bishop Cottrell. I suppose we hadn't really taken on the full extent of what Bishop Cottrell had done, and we were naive in thinking that he would be so pleased for us. We told him that we had some good news, that I had been offered a parish and that we were moving in a matter of weeks.

When he heard this, Bishop Cottrell looked shocked and immediately fell to his knees directly in front of us and the other people, with his head bowed. It seemed like he did not fall to his knees as a cognitive thought; it looked like he was flung to his knees. Lois and I believe it was his complete contrition and guilt that confronted him that day and made him fall to his knees.

It may have been at the 'eleventh hour', but we knew that as we were faithful to God, He was faithful to us and was on our case no matter what.

Wolverhampton, West Midlands, UK

'Wolverhampton'

Our move to Wolverhampton and my licensing as Team Vicar of St Albans Church was, for Lois and me, to be a new start. Little did we know, at the time of our move, the difficulties that the parish had had in its history over the previous fifteen or so years. Sadly, this is a common experience for many clergy when moving parishes, or applying for posts; full disclosure is not given in order to assist with the decision-making process or prepare for the work ahead.

St. Albans Church family had experienced the coming and going of many team vicars, some of whom had only stayed for a short time. We were told by the Archdeacon that he thought we would thrive in our new role, and he was right, we did thrive. Nonetheless, we had to face up to and help the church family to face up to and deal with some serious issues. Some of these issues had been buried and not dealt with in the past, and we were told by members of the church family that the difficulties had been too difficult to deal with and the team vicars had not been supported by senior staff, so they just left. This is an ongoing culture problem within the Church of England. Senior staff only think of their own position and, much of the time, let vicars and their families sink under the challenges of parish life.

St. Albans Church family was part of a team ministry of three churches. Due to a lack of money in the deanery and dwindling congregations, one of the team churches needed to close. This would be either St Albans or St Cuthberts. My brief for leading St. Albans was that we had a couple of years to grow the church family of St Albans or risk its closure. At the time, the church family consisted of about thirty mainly elderly people, and within this group, there were one or two children. The church was extremely poor financially, and at the time of my licensing, I was only one of about four people in the church family who had a regular income. The estate was, in parts, a tough working-class estate, and many people in the community had few or no educational qualifications. Previously, mining had been the main source of employment.

The estate was not ethnically diverse, with around 97% of the population describing themselves as Caucasian. I remember walking our miniature poodle dog around the estate with my clergy collar on, and being stared at. Most of the estate's young men walked around the estate with Rottweilers or Staffies. I did laugh about the looks I got.

Our vicarage was in the heart of the estate, and our front 'garden' was the church car park. It was often used by the local school to show the children what a detached house looked like, as there were no other detached houses on the estate.

On one occasion, Lois spotted a car parked in the church car park right in front of the kitchen window, with 2 men seated inside. She went outside to ask what they were doing and was quickly flashed ID badges and told that they were plain-clothes police on a stakeout! They had been tipped off that there was a planned robbery of the post office in the precinct of shops across the road. That day, nothing happened! About a week or two after, however, Lois and I were driving out of the car park, when in front of us we saw a person carrying a large bag running towards a car, with the postmaster running behind him shouting and screaming. It was evident that a robbery was taking place. We watched the robber get into his 'getaway' car, and for an instant, I thought about blocking their car with our car. I suppose old habits die hard! Lois saw the look in my eye and shouted at me not to do anything. Against my nature, or training in a situation like this, I listened to Lois and stayed at the entrance of our vicarage. Two Police Community Support Officers were, by chance, standing on the opposite side of the road. They were panicked and seriously confused as to what to do. I jumped out of my car and told them to radio it in with a description of the car. We then carried on with our journey.

I can honestly say that life was never dull in Wolverhampton!

'Difficulties'

There were three serious issues that I had to deal with during my time in Wolverhampton. The first, and most serious, was a paedophile in my congregation. This was horrendous, and I had to deal with and guide the church family through their pain. Lois and I had not been in the parish that long when this problem arose. Spiritually, it was interesting in that every time I had prayed for this person, at their request and before their arrest, I always sensed I should say to this person, "The truth will set you free".

The person had a prominent role in the community and church, and if I was to handle this situation badly, the publicity could seriously affect any chance of growth in St Alban's Church for years to come. The diocese was slow to support me, and my Rector (senior Vicar) at the time did not have a clue what to do. No senior staff invited me to meet with them, and no senior staff came to visit Lois and me to support us. Everything the diocese did with regards to this situation was held at a distance from me. I supported an angry and hurt church family. I liaised with the diocese to organise pastoral support for the person once their two-year jail sentence was over, however, this support needed to come from someone outside of our church. Overall, in the end, the fallout from this case was minimal. I suppose this issue coming to light early on in my ministry at St Albans helped my ongoing ministry there.

Soon after this incident came to light, another problem reared its head within the church family. This particular problem had seen off a few team vicars in the past. It nearly saw us off too due to the incomprehensible lack of support from senior staff. The problem was a bullying culture, or more specifically, a bully within the congregation. We were told that previous vicars had been scared of this bully, one vicar having locked herself in the vestry as she was so scared. The church family lived in fear of this person. Lois and I soon became the target of this bully. This person would regularly try to intimidate us by walking up to me whilst I was leading a service and only stopping when we were nose to nose, to standing outside my study window and vicarage shouting and threatening to get a shotgun and shoot me. Spiritually, I knew the church family would not grow with this oppressive bullying culture ingrained and accepted within it.

One day, I was sitting in my study praying and thinking about what conflict resolution principles I could apply to this situation, when the local community policeman knocked on my door to say hello. We sat and chatted, and he asked how I was settling in. I shared with him my problem. He immediately said, "Look, this is bullying and harassment you are experiencing. I will go and see this person and tell them to stay away from your church and home or I will arrest them."

"Wow!" I thought, "that is great."

This, however, was not the end of it. The bully made a complaint to the Archdeacon and Lois and I had to go to see him. This was not the same Archdeacon who had appointed me, but his replacement. We thought it was a simple case of explaining the situation to the

Archdeacon so he would be informed. No, this is the Church of England! Lois and I sat in the Archdeacon's office for three hours while he tried to pressure me into writing a letter of apology to the parishioner who was bullying me and the congregation, stating it was all my fault and inviting him back to church. After explaining to the Archdeacon time and time again it was the policeman who banned the bully from our church and not me, the Archdeacon threatened me, in front of Lois, that if I didn't write the letter, there would be serious consequences for me. I refused to write the letter of apology and we left his office.

The Archdeacon called us back again and the content of the meeting was much the same. I refused again to comply. He had no compassion for us, only concern for the Church of England's reputation. I decided to ask the Bishop of Wolverhampton for a meeting. Lois and I had a meeting with the Bishop and explained what the Archdeacon was doing to us. We never heard from this Archdeacon again about this matter, and it was agreed with the Bishop that the bully could come back to church as long as he signed a contract of expected behaviour. This was done and the person gradually came back to church. The person did not have the same power over the congregation or me as they previously held.

A little while later, a very honest and reliable parishioner came to visit us to tell me that money was being stolen from the offertory plate. I was already aware that money had gone missing from the safe. A parishioner was helping themselves to cash! The matter was dealt with pastorally, the problem was resolved, and practical steps put into place to allow the money counting procedure to be more open and public.

Although my mental health problems had not been identified correctly or treated in any expert way, I did not seem to suffer so much in Wolverhampton, and the deterioration of my mental health seemed to slow down. I did have some periods of depression and other symptoms of PTSD and CPTSD while there, but for some reason, they were not as severe.

In spite of the difficulties that we had to deal with, we loved our time in Wolverhampton and were very happy there and sad to leave. The congregation supported us and loved us and our children, and also supported the vision to enable growth of the church family.

An incredibly beautiful gift the congregation arranged for us was to kit out a nursery for us for the birth of our son. These people did not have a lot of money, but through their love for us, they chipped in to supply our nursery room with all that was needed. We felt so loved and cherished by this church family.

'Chris'

An interesting character Lois and I came to know well was a young homeless man who was only twenty-five years old but looked about fifty. He slept rough all year round in and around Wolverhampton. He did the rounds of visiting and asking different churches for help with money, and we were one of his regular stops. He had had a very abusive childhood, and he was an alcoholic and drug user. He was in and out of jail for minor offences on a regular basis. When he visited us, we would give him a hot meal, let him have a bath or shower and regularly give him a pair of my shoes to wear, as he was always losing his shoes or had them stolen when passed out drunk or drugged. Over time, I must have given him many pairs of shoes. He regularly collapsed in the streets and he was taken to hospital and was warned countless times by the hospital staff that if he didn't change his lifestyle he would die soon.

Lois and I became fond of Chris, and he liked us and trusted us. Occasionally, he would come to church on a Sunday morning.

This was wonderful; however, it did cause a few issues, as he didn't always smell very sweet! A group of our lovely parishioners in Wolverhampton were very gracious towards Chris, and would sit with him at the back, although the smell must have been suffocating. He would always sit quietly and listen intently to the sermon and join in with the singing.

I would often give him work to do in the vicarage garden, and he would work hard for the whole day. His 'payment' would be a hot bath, hot dinner, washed, dried and ironed clothes and £1. It was futile to give him any more money as it would just be spent on booze and/or drugs. He worked so hard to impress us and he really appreciated that we valued him.

As we got to know him more, we came to learn that his history was that he had been a victim of child sexual abuse and violence. Sometimes he would sleep in an old trailer we kept outside our garage. In winter, I would find him curled up asleep, with a blanket of snow on him and with his bare feet sticking out of the bottom of the trailer.

Sometimes, but not often, Chris would turn up sober and sit and chat with us. One day, he turned up and was sober, and Lois was getting our towing caravan ready for us to go away on holiday for a week. Chris asked her what she was doing, and, letting her guard down, she told him that we were packing up to go away for a week. This turned out to be a big mistake as no sooner had we set up camp in Devon than we got a phone call from our Churchwarden to say that the Vicarage had been broken into and various items, including our bikes, had been stolen. From the blood on the broken window, the police were able to prove that it was Chris who had broken in. We were devastated; not so much by the loss of our belongings, but by what we saw as a betrayal by someone we had tried to help. In reality, his addiction and need for drink and drugs overrode his care for us. He was sent to prison and told to write us a letter of apology, which he did, the contents of which were heartfelt. He was, we believe, truly sorry for what he had done. When he was released from prison, we were told that he had been given an order to stay away from us and our home.

We often thought about Chris, and when we moved away from Wolverhampton, our hearts hurt for him. I knew he could not fight the battle in his head and that his liver and kidneys were failing. I am sure he would die in the cold one winter, totally alone and without shoes.

'Revival'

Revival and the healing ministry interested Lois and I. Revival, because church congregations across the UK were declining, and the healing ministry because I knew from my own experience and my own pain that people's lives needed hope and healing. Our interest in the revival and healing ministry inspired Lois and I to visit a revival which was happening at the time in Florida in the USA. We wanted to learn from and experience an actual revival.

When we came home, I felt that God was wanting me to offer a healing service where people would have the opportunity to come forward and members of our congregation and myself would lay hands on their shoulders or heads and we would pray for God's grace to heal them and give them hope for whatever the need in their life was. We opened this service up to all the churches in the Wolverhampton area.

I was praying in the vestry half an hour before the start of this service, and my Churchwarden popped in to tell me that a few people had arrived. I thanked him. Then he came back in again and said some more people had arrived. This sequence of events carried on, with my Churchwarden becoming more excited and worried each time he came in. He eventually came in to tell me that the church was full, with around 250 people in attendance. They'd never seen anything like it in St Alban's Church before!

The service was phenomenal, full of hope and people requesting prayer. Some people lay down in the presence and peace of God. Other people sang with joy. The service was profoundly different from anything I had led before in my ministry. A few days later, feedback came to me about the service. People claimed they had been healed of various ailments. People found a new hope in life and in God. Lois and I, with the help of St Alban's congregation, facilitated three or four more services like this. Numbers attending remained high, and then began to dwindle over time. This phenomenon brought a new interest in the Wolverhampton area of the Christian healing ministry.

Out of the blue, we were invited to go and lead a healing service in a church which was extremely different to ours. It was in a very wealthy part of Staffordshire, and a large imposing traditional church building. A group of us from St Albans Church went to lead this service. Our team consisted of people who were at the completely opposite end of the educational and wealth spectrum to the people from this upper-middle-class Church of England congregation. When we arrived at the church, they felt somewhat intimated by the building and the people. However, members of our team had personally experienced the healing grace of God in their lives, and they desperately wanted to share their experience with others. Each one of us shared a short testimony with the congregation of how God had touched our lives, and we then asked the congregation to stand and if they wanted us to pray for them, we would. Lois played the keyboard and sang heavenly songs over us all. Members of the congregation began to fall down in the gentle and powerful loving grace of God's presence. Soon, most of the congregation were lying on the floor and we went around to each person and prayed God's grace upon them. This went on for a few hours! It was an amazing experience of God's gentle grace and healing.

'Leaving Wolverhampton'

Our time and ministry were brought to an end in Wolverhampton by a difficult choice. The person who had been sent to prison at the start of our ministry there was released, and the proximity of their house to ours made it difficult for us to stay. We felt it was not possible for us to stay, knowing what we did about the case, and having a little boy of our own. We shared our concerns with our Bishop and told him it was unfortunate, but it was an intolerable situation for us. We had no way of resolving this problem, so our only option was to move. The Bishop understood and we began to look and listen to God as to where he was calling us to move to next.

Lois and I made some wonderful lifelong friends in St Alban's Church, and we were sad to leave them. St Alban's continued to go from strength to strength, and the church family there are still ministering faithfully to the people of Ashmore Park.

Hoddesdon, Hertfordshire, UK

'Hoddesdon'

We arrived in the parish of Hoddesdon and I was licensed as vicar of St. Catherine and St Paul's Church, known as Hoddesdon Parish Church. This parish was located within a commuter town in reach of London. The congregation were mostly professionals who commuted to London for work. Other members of the congregation were retired. Again, as is common in many Church of England churches, unfortunately, the congregation was declining in members and the decline caused concern. My brief was once again to grow and increase the Church membership. This was the reason for my appointment.

Opposition to growth and change in order to enable growth reared its head quite fast after our arrival at Hoddesdon Parish Church. We soon realised that this was another entrenched congregation, who would hold on to their rituals and traditions at all costs, even the cost of continued decline. Indeed, we were informed that once my appointment was announced, the inevitable 'googling' of me happened, and one parishioner openly declared, "I don't like him. I don't want him. I will get rid of him."

I naively endeavoured to take on the challenge to help this church family. I developed an understanding and taught about the need to change to enable the church family to be accessible to non-church people. Society was miles away from the traditional church service. Schools now taught with large interactive screens, and children sat around tables and learned to listen to each other. The idea that people wanted to join a model of church which was structured hundreds of years ago was naïve.

With debate and presentations by me, and in line with the diocesan policy of needing a vision for growth, the Parochial Church Council agreed to introduce a new service which would follow on from the traditional service and would not interfere with the way the traditional service was run, except for a small change to the start time. The traditional service could stay as it was. This was an achievement, so I thought.

The new informal service began to attract new people. Many of these new people were not Christians. They varied from recovering drug addicts to teachers and retired headteachers. Many families began to join us. Some of these families were gay and lesbian families, ethnic minority families and single-parent families. They felt accepted. This new congregation grew and grew, with many more children attending church on a Sunday. This began a big problem. I gave new people jobs and involved them as much as possible in the life of the church family.

The new members who attended the new service caused concern for the long-standing members of the church. New members were actively discouraged and made to feel unwelcome by some of the 'traditional church' members.

Then, a member of the congregation approached me to off-load about something that they had, to their now regret, been involved with previously. I was informed that a group of people in the traditional congregation had previously organised themselves to hound out one of the previous vicars. I was told that this same group had decided to do this to Lois and myself. A horrendous time for Lois and myself followed during our time in Hoddesdon parish, as the history of that church repeated itself. I was still unwell, and I believe the stress of what was going on caused dissociations to flare up again during our time in Hoddesdon.

Complaints started to be made about me to the Bishop, a slow drip-feed of complaints found their way to the Bishop's desk. People also visited the Archdeacon and complained. They knew he was sympathetic to them. Evangelicals were not his flavour of the month. This organised and hostile group tried to catch me out by checking everything I wrote in magazine articles or preached in my sermons, to see if I had plagiarised anything. They meticulously used software to try and catch me out. They could then make a complaint to the bishop. Formal complaints were made to the Bishop many times. This group would not meet with me to work things out. They refused to talk with me. On occasion, they disrupted church services. Church council meetings were made extremely difficult for me, and things only got worse when the 'leader' of this group organised for people in opposition to me to be voted on as members of the church council. This person even accused Lois and I of having our youngest child purely to garner sympathy from the congregation. Lois and I, at times, felt the opposition made us feel like we were dying, literally dying.

PART FIVE

'Suicide does not mean there is no killer.'

2015 – 2020
Age: 56 – 61

'The course of justice often prevents it.'

Edward Counsel

Hastings, East Sussex, UK

'Hastings'

Our move to Hastings came quite unexpectedly in many ways. We had realised that it was time to move on from Hoddesdon, so I had met with my Bishop in January 2015, and started to look for another post. I had a sabbatical planned for May/June of 2015 so we weren't in a hurry to move, and it can take, on average, 12 – 18 months to find a new Parish. We didn't start looking at the 'job' adverts until spring and the post in Hastings was the first job I looked at.

I showed the parish profile to Lois, we prayed about it and decided to apply, believing and trusting that God would make the decision for us. To my surprise, I was invited for interview. The parish had been looking for a new Rector for some time and this was the fourth round of interviews, having not appointed in the previous three. At the end of the 2 days of interviews and meetings, I was offered the post. Both the Parish and I felt that this is where God was calling us as a family.

Now, looking back, I still believe that God was in my appointment, and that was the place where He wanted us to be. My question now is, did He want us to go there just so that I could be healed, or did He call me there for a ministry as well, which the Church of England has now taken away from me? I suppose I shall never know the answer, but I do know that God is faithful and the new opportunities that He is opening up for me give me a 'hope and a future' (Jeremiah 29 verse 11), which, at one stage, I felt the Church of England had destroyed.

We arrived in Hastings in September 2015, and it was a good feeling for us both to be joining a church family with the same spiritual tradition as ourselves. We're not too keen on 'labels', but if we had to apply a label to the style of worship that we feel most comfortable with, it would be the charismatic, evangelical tradition.

The Rectory, our new home, was a very opulent house, quite unlike any other Rectory/Vicarage we had seen! However, the garden was not at all 'child-friendly'; indeed, it was quite dangerous as it sloped down a hill in a tiered fashion and was severely overgrown. After many requests to the Diocese of Chichester for help to make the garden safe, a contractor deemed the garden dangerous for children, and the Diocese finally and reluctantly did some work to make it functional and safe. For some reason, which we never really got an answer for, the Diocese had removed the fire and the fireplace in the living room of the Rectory, and left us with a large 'blank' wall, and no form of heating, other than two small radiators, in what was a very large room. We asked the Diocese if they would replace the fireplace and fire so that we could have secondary heating (a requirement in the 'Green' book relating to Vicarages/Rectories), but also to give us a feature in the living room for aesthetic reasons. We were somewhat surprised by their response when we were advised to buy a 'fan heater or portable oil-fired radiator which can all be purchased for around £30.00.' This attitude of the Diocese was an early insight for Lois and I into the uncompassionate culture of the Chichester Diocese. We both would suffer tremendously from this culture later in our ministry in Hastings.

Nevertheless, Lois and I were filled with a sense of hope as we started serving the church family of St Helen with St Barnabas in the Parish of Ore. The church family had hope in us too.

My brief, what was wanted of me, was yet again, to grow the church family into spiritual maturity and increase numbers of people attending and becoming part of the church family. An issue Lois and I encountered very early on within our new church family, was a 'fear' of a few of its members, who were dominant and overpowering. Sadly, this is often the case in many Church of England churches and causes clergy a great number of problems. Of course, one of the ways to deal with this was to show them that I was not fearful or going to be dominated by these people. This inevitably led to complaints against me to the Archdeacon; people who are used to getting their own way and being in control really don't like it when they are challenged! Typically, the Archdeacon merely told me to learn lessons, rather than congratulating me for showing leadership to help the church move forward.

Gradually, my leadership team, church family and Lois and I created a good Mission Action Plan together. We organised a Parish Away Day to explore the Mission Action Plan and the plan was accepted by the church family. There was a wonderful time of God's presence being felt and experienced during worship times and whenever we came together for services and fellowship.

One very special moment was during a funeral that I led for a member of the congregation who had bravely battled illness and who was an amazing woman. I had the privilege of being with her in the moments shortly before she passed, and her faith was evident right to the very end. The service was incredible, like nothing many of us had experienced before at a funeral, and a beautiful fragrance lingered in the church. After the funeral service ended, a lady approached Lois to ask what the lovely fragrance was. The lady had realised that it was not coming from the flowers because she had gone around the church and smelled every flower to see where the smell came from. Lois simply responded, "It is the fragrance of God's presence." The lady left the church with a smile on her face.

'Suicide does not mean there is no killer.'

'My deterioration'

Although we were very happy with our move to Hastings and our new church family, disastrously, my mental health continued to deteriorate. We lost our pet dog soon after moving; she was 16 ½ years old and had been my constant companion, and it devastated me. Depression, along with what I eventually came to learn were the symptoms of CPTSD and PTSD with dissociative subtype, increased. Most days, nearly every day, I found it almost impossible to get out of my bed. I wallowed in a dark, dark, depression, curled up on my bed, procrastinating, fighting and losing the battle for my mind. I never knew at the time, but have since been told by the mental health experts, that I would never have won the battle for my mind until I had completely broken down.

My paranoia and hypervigilance were off the scale. All these symptoms caused me to live in a cycle of aggression, followed by guilt. My flashbacks increased to many times daily, and intrusive thoughts annihilated me throughout the day. I could not sleep. I did not sleep. At the most, I would sleep for an hour a night and some nights I never slept at all. On the rare occasions when I managed to fall asleep, Lois would inevitably have to wake me, as I would be screaming out loud. Screaming in a pitch so high, that Lois described as seemingly physically impossible for me to reach. I started having suicidal thoughts. My hypervigilance put Lois on edge. I was constantly looking for 'the enemy' around me; to me, to my paranoid perception, nothing and nowhere was safe.

My type 2 diabetes was completely out of control, and I found comfort in sugary food and take-aways. My sugar levels were off the scale and the readings were in the thirties. I should have been hospitalised with these readings, but I never admitted 'defeat'.

There was no way out of the vicious cycle of my mental health slowly killing me and, at the same time, ruining Lois' life. Moment by moment, the battle in my mind was now constantly, 'if I commit suicide, then Lois will be free of me'. Death, too, would end the guilt; guilt that I survived whilst many of my friends lost their lives in Northern Ireland, guilt over my outbursts of anger and aggression to the woman I deeply loved. Gone too would be the shame, depression and stigma. I could rid myself of my night terrors, flashbacks, dissociations and every other trauma I had experienced in my childhood and adult life. I could free others of me. This would be a good thing to do.

Lois continued to carry me in my work. She loyally prayed for me, gave me pep talks and even after she had been on the receiving end of the symptoms of my mental health, she would hold my hand and calm me in my terror. I made 'appearances' at the church family duties I had to attend, but would quickly return to my bed, angry, depressed and extremely ill. I was able to think of a sermon in a few minutes because, strangely, I knew the character of Jesus. I knew the message of grace in the Bible. I did know Jesus in my personal relationship with Him. Lois answered my emails and did the parish administration. I just could not move unless I really had to.

Then the beginning of the end happened. Time went on and I was deteriorating more and more, living in this nightmare. The beginning of my healing started in a back to front way. Lois and I were both in my study, and the tension in the room was palpable. Lois was at the end of her tether with my illness, with its cruel symptoms. She was tired of carrying me. She had had years of my illness, me swinging in and out of dissociation, wallowing on my bed, fighting my demons and just getting worse. Lois could see I had no understanding or self-awareness of the severity of my mental state, and any attempts that she had made to get help had resulted in her being told that unless she had serious concerns for my safety then I had to seek help myself. She knew that there was no way I would reach out for help; I only knew how not to give up. The mere fact that she had tried to get me help would, in my mind at the time, have been seen as an act of disloyalty. This was the sadness of me. I just kept going on, putting one foot in front of the other, just like the army selections I passed. It was my DNA. I had no perception of the reality of my state and its consequences for Lois.

Fear and perceived threat triggered a disassociation in me. We don't really know what the 'trigger' was, but I went into self-preservation mode. I left my body. I hovered at the top of my study door. I have absolutely no memory of what happened next.

The next thing I remember is talking to Lois in the kitchen about what we were going to try and do for the rest of the day. It was some while later that Lois had the courage to tell me what had happened; what I had done in my dissociative state. At the time, we knew nothing about the damage that trauma can do to the brain or resulting dissociations. I was absolutely floored by what she told me; sick to my stomach yet also questioning her as I had absolutely no recollection of what she was telling me. I found it hard to believe what she was telling me, but at the same time, I knew that she was not someone who would make something like that up!

Lois told me that I had become extremely aggressive towards her, that I did not hit her or harm her physically, but that I had threatened her and kept her in my study. She went on to explain that I had picked a letter opener up and threatened to gouge her eyes out, and that I would not let her move from the chair in my study for more than 2 hours, all the time scanning the window to see if anyone was around. What she was telling me was an exact replication, a re-enactment if you like, of what had happened to me around 40 years earlier, as a young Para being tortured by two other Paras. On hearing Lois tell me this, horror, shame and guilt consumed me.

"Was I going mad? Could I have physically hurt her?"

That night I didn't sleep, just walked up and down in our lounge despairing at what Lois must have felt like during my dissociation. The next day, I was due to run a half marathon for charity. I had not trained, was completely unfit and my diabetes was completely out of control. Added to that, I hadn't slept! I merely drew on my Parachute Regiment mindset and 21 SAS mindset and determined to complete it. Every step of the way, I punished myself by pushing through the pain. I was exhausted in my mind from my years of deterioration, and the horror of what I had put Lois through the day before. The pain I felt on the run was, to me, a deserved punishment. To the outside world, to my parishioners, I smiled and waved, but inside I was dying.

After the half marathon, I lay on my bed for weeks, back into depression and PTSD. I never moved. My Sunday appearances were becoming harder and harder for me to navigate through, and my paranoia got worse and worse. Three months after the last and most severe dissociation, Lois began to have serious concerns for my safety. I was, by now, not hiding my suicidal ideation, and having experienced what she had experienced the day before the half marathon, she had concerns for her safety should it happen again. She went to a church friend, a trained Counsellor, for help, who felt that she needed to involve others from the church. The result was that Lois was advised to contact the police.

'Suicide does not mean there is no killer.'

It was absolutely right that Lois went to get help for herself and for me. She had suffered many long years because of my dreadful illness. I had reached a crisis point and needed help. Reaching a severe crisis point is, unfortunately, for many, many veterans with mental health conditions and their families, the only way that they come to realise there is something wrong with them and they need help.

Initially, Lois went to the police first rather than seeking help from the senior staff of Chichester Diocese, Bishops and Archdeacons. Lois was so badly let down in the past by the then Bishop Cottrell, now the Archbishop of York, when she asked him for help for us in 2004.

After contacting the police, Lois did, as a matter of courtesy, contact my suffragan Bishop at the time, Bishop Richard Jackson. Even with the past experience of the Church of England, she expected help and compassion for the situation, but instead, we were persecuted and isolated so that the Diocese of Chichester/ Church of England could achieve the outcome they wanted- my removal from office and protection of their reputation.

Following on from Lois' telephone call, Bishop Richard asked for my blue file (personnel file) to be looked at, and he reported back to Lois that the paperwork relating to what went on in Oxford Diocese, was, in his words, 'so well hidden' in my blue file, that 'you wouldn't have known about it unless you were specifically looking for it'. Oxford Diocese had 'covered up' what had happened, even in an 'internal' file, rather than being open and transparent.

I want to make it clear at this stage, that at the time of the writing of this book (September 2020), both Lois and I have tried to get the Church of England National Safeguarding Team to undertake an independent review into what went on in my case. Lois has been in contact with Archbishop Stephen to ask for his help but to no avail. We were told that an investigation was taking place, which filled us with great hope, however, when we requested a copy of the 'brief' given to the 'investigator' (a person paid for by the Church of England), his instructions were only to investigate the 'risk' that I had posed, and whether mistakes had been made in effectively allowing me to continue in ministry. There was nothing in the brief which referred to my medical diagnosis or the opinions of my medical team. Nothing that demonstrated that they took the serious safeguarding issues concerning my mental health seriously, issues concerning why I, as a vulnerable adult, was not safeguarded. It was, yet again, an exercise in protecting the reputation of the Church of England.

What follows is a testament to the brutality and, in my opinion, the corruptness of the Church of England and its ability to close ranks when it wants to and seek to destroy rather than help. I recall at a meeting Lois and I had with Archbishop Cottrell when he was Bishop of Reading, that he said, "If the Church of England wants to close ranks, it is very good at it, and it will".

'Breakdown'

My mental health state at this time was extremely dangerous for me. I had been suicidal for many years and increasingly so during the last several months. After an initial conversation with the police, Lois decided to stay at a friend's house with the children. This was the first time Lois had stayed away from home, and later, I was informed that she was told not to let me know where she was or what was going on. Paranoia and suicidal ideation is not a good combination for an escalating crisis.

I wanted to end my life that night and I prepared to drive to Beachy Head to jump off as so many people have so tragically done

'Suicide does not mean there is no killer.'

before. I was about to leave the house when the police knocked on my front door. They wanted to check if I was ok. Lois had asked the police to see if I was ok because she thought I might be suicidal. I immediately jumped into 'show no weakness' mode and gave the police an assurance that I was fine, so they left me on my own.

After the visit from the police, my thoughts changed from suicide to needing to see my children and hug them, and to say sorry to Lois, but I had no idea where they were. I thought that they may have gone to stay with Lois' father on the Isle of Man so, in my confused mental state, I got my passport and caught a plane from Gatwick airport to the Isle of Man. I had nothing with me, other than the clothes I was wearing and my wallet, car keys and passport. Desperation, depression and all CPTSD and PTSD symptoms haunted me and crushed me as I struggled to put one foot in front of the other. I arrived on the Isle of Man and made my way to my father- in-law's apartment. Although I didn't knock on the door, I could not see the children or Lois in the apartment or around anywhere, so I decided to find a field to sleep in for the night. I had sent Lois a text message telling her that I was in the Isle of Man, and she phoned me as she was concerned about me and my state of mind. The conversation was short, but she encouraged me to stay in a hotel and confirmed that she and the children were not on the Isle of Man. I found the hotel she directed me to, spent the night and caught a flight back to Gatwick the next day.

When we landed at Gatwick Airport, three policemen came onto the plane, arrested me and took me to a police station. I was put in a cell and told that they were waiting for a detective from Hastings to come and interview me. I was interviewed by the detective and I answered all the questions directed to me as best as I could. I did not feel well, and I was deeply, deeply depressed. I basically told the detective that I didn't know what had happened, but if Lois said it happened then it did. The detective told me that he thought I needed help. I remember acknowledging this and agreeing that I needed help. I was charged with 'coercive and controlling behaviour' and told that Archdeacon Edward Dowler would be collecting me as I was not allowed to go home or see Lois.

What I later learned was that when Lois was interviewed by the detective, she had made it very clear that she had serious concerns for my mental health and wellbeing, and that she wanted me to be helped and not punished. She was contacted later that evening by the detective to be told that I had been arrested and released on bail, but that he agreed with her, that I was a good man who desperately needed help. The detective, who had previously worked for the Metropolitan Police in London, was the first person who made the connection between my military service and my mental health.

'Burrswood'

Archdeacon Dowler picked me up from the police station and drove me to a retreat centre, 'Burrswood', where he booked me in and left. I had one very small room to stay in. I began to procrastinate while lying on my bed on my own, and a desire to end my life once again overwhelmed me. Paranoia and mental health symptoms fell on me, covered me, consumed me as I lay on my bed in the dark. I was determined to find a way to end my life. I had been told by the police that I could not contact Lois, and this was part of my bail conditions. I lay on my bed through the night, and the next day I got a message to go downstairs and meet Archdeacon Dowler in a small room.

I went to meet him, and he gave me some official papers telling me that I was suspended from duty and I would be facing a disciplinary. As soon as he had 'served' the papers, he left. No care was shown for me, no compassion or Christian love, just the formality of the start of a disciplinary process.

I went back to my room and lay on my bed again. Lois let me know by text that she had spoken to Archdeacon Dowler and that he had said he was going to contact the organisation 'Combat Stress' because he acknowledged I needed mental health support. Archdeacon Dowler only came back to see me again to serve yet more disciplinary papers, as the original papers had incorrect information on them, and to ask me where I could go and stay because the Diocese of Chichester would only pay for me to stay in the retreat centre room until the end of the week. I told him that I had nowhere to go, and that I would not embarrass any of my family with my presence. I mentioned to him that I thought Lois may stand by me and be supportive of me, and his facial response was one of alarm. He left straight away, again with no words of comfort or even offering to pray with me. I was rather taken back by the look on Archdeacon Dowler's face, I thought he would be pleased that Lois was going to support me. With what I know now, his reaction, his face, was a mirror of how the senior staff of Chichester Diocese would behave towards me and my family. I went back to my bed and kept the curtains drawn so I could lie in the darkness.

What I came to discover, years later, as a result of documents received from a Data Subject Access Request that I made to Chichester Diocese, shocked both Lois and I to the core. What is evident from the paperwork in our possession is that, initially, Archdeacon Edward Dowler, in conjunction with Bishop Martin Warner, took advice on what he, Archdeacon Edward should do to get me help immediately following my breakdown. Advice was given by Rebekah Golds-Jones, a psychotherapist, who at the time was the Pastoral Care Officer for Chichester Diocese. Ms Golds-Jones clearly, and quite rightly, advised getting me a psychiatric assessment and help.

It is then evident from an email written by Archdeacon Edward, a non-clinician, that he makes a 'clinical' decision, and decides that I do not pose a 'high level of risk' to myself, as I seemed, in his words, 'fairly calm'. He does, however, suggest that an organisation called 'Combat Stress' be contacted as they specialise in PTSD-related conditions, and he, Archdeacon Edward thought that my 'background in the parachute regiment is very likely to be significant'.

Rebekah Golds-Jones then makes it clear in an email to the Archdeacon, Bishop Martin, Bishop Richard, Colin Perkins (Diocesan Safeguarding Officer), and other senior staff at the Diocese of Chichester, including their legal advisor at the time, that I will no doubt need long-term support, which 'sits within her remit', and points the recipients of the email to the 'pathway' that she had created as, 'any therapeutic support would be via herself' and 'the external therapists' who would work alongside her.

Again, and in response to this email, Ms Golds-Jones encourages the Senior Staff to 'follow the pathway' that she 'has spent time setting up in order to provide pastoral and counselling support to clergy and their families, if for no other reason than to ensure that therapeutic support is provided in a joined-up way and with the appropriate reviews in place where [she] I have the opportunity to meet with those in therapy and spend time reassessing their progress. Given the situation, it also automatically facilitates a review of risk'.

I was never given Ms Golds-Jones' contact details and was effectively left to fend for myself.

'Suicide does not mean there is no killer.'

What is interesting to note, and, with hindsight, 'set the tone' for Chichester Diocese's attitude towards me, is wording in an email written later the same day by Mr Colin Perkins, the Diocesan Safeguarding Officer, who states:

'I was beginning to get a little worried that a number of the people involved had already diagnosed PP as suffering from PTSD and that the abuse was a symptom of that. I just wanted to slow things down before we ended up focusing on 'treating' PP rather than responding to a crime'.

This was the attitude that the Diocese of Chichester took; they acted upon the 'opinion' of a former probation officer, rather than the mental health expert, and that attitude continued for almost another three years. In their eyes, I was a monster, a criminal who needed to be gotten rid of, a 'bad, mad man'. It is well documented that Combat PTSD is not a character flaw, it is a recognised medical condition, and just as with any other mental health condition, sufferers need help and support, not punishment and judgementalism.

'The Deep Pond'

The next day, I walked down to the field located at the back of the retreat centre near to a large, deep, and isolated pond. I sat on a bench beside the pond. The signs around the pond clearly stated that it was dangerous and deep. It was, to me, deep enough to go to sleep in and drown in peace. Sitting beside the pond and knowing I was going to step into the pond and sink to the bottom gave me a huge amount of peace. I had no concern about drowning or death, I just longed for peace. My mind, head, mental health, whatever was wrong with me, would not hurt anyone else or myself again. I was just so, so tired of life. I knew I only wanted to love my family and love people, and I was at peace with that. Everything was settled in my mind. Then, two police officers walked towards me from behind some bushes. I think the local mental health team or someone from the retreat centre had phoned them to come and check on me. They sat with me to try and persuade me to go back to my room whilst they got help for me.

One of the police officers contacted Lois at home in Hastings and told her that they were with me, that I was by a pond, and that I was intent on killing myself. They advised her that they didn't want to section me as that can be a difficult process and have implications for my future, so they asked her to arrange help for me. Thankfully, Lois was able to contact the Mental Health Triage team at the Conquest Hospital in Hastings, who rang me, spoke with me and then advised Lois to make arrangements to get me to hospital.

I was now in a state of complete breakdown and constantly sobbing. I could not stop myself. My father-in-law and my stepdaughter came to collect me from the retreat centre and to take me to Hastings Hospital for a psychiatric assessment. I was assessed by the psychiatric team and told that it would be better for me if I volunteered to go into the psychiatric ward, and if I didn't go voluntarily, they would have no option other than to section me. This began a six-week stay for me in the Woodlands Centre for Acute Care (secure psychiatric unit) at the Conquest Hospital in Hastings.

'Sunflowers'

Interestingly, about 12 years before, Lois and I had visited a church in London where a friend of mine was a curate, and a group of people there asked if they could pray for Lois and me. We agreed, and this group of complete strangers prayed for us. During the prayer time, one person said that they believed God was telling me to take off my military uniform. This person did not know me, and definitely did not know I had been in the military! Another person simply said, "Sunflowers will be very important in your life".

We, Lois and I, never really understood the 'word' about sunflowers, but we felt that it was from God and we kept this image of a sunflower close to our heart and mind, without knowing the relevance. We have a beautiful painting of a sunflower above our mantelpiece, which was given to us by the church family at St Sebastian's in Crowthorne.

When Lois was desperately trying to find out what she needed to do to get me help when I was at the retreat centre, she was put in touch with a psychiatrist and sent an email. When the response came into her inbox, the first thing that she saw was the word 'Sunflower' in the 'from' column. It transpired that a relative of this psychiatrist had been instrumental in the biological processing of oil from sunflowers and therefore the Psychiatrist used 'Sunflower' as a contact name on personal emails. God is good!

From that email contact, Lois was able to get me to a place where I could start my slow journey to recovery. At that stage, we did not know just how important another 'Sunflower' was to become in my journey to recovery.

'Woodlands'

During my stay in Woodlands, I was given what I came to understand from the other patients was called the 'Kosh'. The 'Kosh' is administered by either a needle full of drugs to calm you down and make you sleep, or pills which achieve the same result.

This 'Kosh' was administered to me twice a day, morning and night. Its contents comprised of a large dose of anti-depressants and anti-psychotic drugs to make me sleep. I had not slept for years. I slept from 10.00 pm until 8.00 am every day whilst I was in Woodlands. The sleep was wonderful, but I could hardly think or function because the 'Kosh' made me drowsy and lethargic all day.

I made some good friends with the other patients on the Woodlands ward. There was the person that I describe as 'the cutter'; this person had neat knife cuts horizontally across every part of their body. All the cuts, which were now scars, were about four inches wide and two inches above each other. These cuts started from the bottom of their legs and led upwards in what can be described as a neat and tidy staircase. The staircase of scars went up to this person's neck. This person was very bright and soon worked out what my background was.

Then there was the person I call 'the grinder'. This person ground their teeth all day long and the sound it made was loud and disturbing. There was the 'cuckoo person', who could become rather aggressive and saw imaginary cuckoos flying around them and made a 'cuckoo' sound as they walked around the ward. I met many other patients, but one person I remember particularly is a person who deteriorated more and more while I was there. One afternoon, some heavily built men came and took this person away in a black van. I guessed this person was going to a more secure hospital. I hoped beyond hope that my mental health did not deteriorate to the point at which I would be escorted away in a black van. I spent most of my days in Woodlands sleeping or walking. It was great to get some sleep.

At the time I was a patient in Woodlands, the place was in chaos. The nursing staff was mainly made up of agency nurses, who were different people every day. This caused confusion for the regular staff and for the patients. Every time a different staff shift began, a different regime and a different way of doing things commenced. Each shift had different rules. We, the patients, were checked on average about every twenty minutes to see if we were a suicide risk or harming ourselves in some other way. Our rooms were checked for items which could potentially be used to harm ourselves or other people, and at night-time, nurses would look through the vent on the room door or come into the room to check on you. Chaos prevailed.

On two occasions, the psychiatrist that I was assigned to mistook me for another patient on the ward. Firstly, the psychiatrist thought I was a person who had started a fight in the unit and asked me why I decided to start the fight with the other patient. I quickly corrected them and told them that I had not been involved in a fight with anybody! Secondly, I discovered that the psychiatrist wrote in my notes that I was a regular cannabis user. I have never used cannabis in my life!

The behaviour of this psychiatrist became more and more bizarre, and on one occasion whilst meeting with Lois, the psychiatrist became aggressive and shouted at her and caused her to cry. Lois reported to the nursing staff that she was concerned about the psychiatrist's mental stability! On another occasion, the psychiatrist made Lois and I stand in a corridor opposite their office for two hours, whilst the psychiatrist ran up and down the corridor sweating profusely. I was then told I needed to speak with another psychiatrist, who talked to me for around 30-40 minutes, and then walked out of the building, got into their open-topped sports car and drove away. This psychiatrist later produced a letter which contained inaccuracies and was based on only spending a very short time with me.

I have been informed that since my stay as a patient in Woodlands, it has been transformed and has become much more efficient and less chaotic. As for the psychiatrist, whilst I was an in-patient, the psychiatrist went off sick and the last I heard was that they had suffered a breakdown and had not returned to work.

Whilst I was in Woodlands, Lois met someone who was to become, in our eyes, an 'angel', although being a formal Royal Marine, he probably didn't like this description! Lois had to attend a meeting at the local food bank on behalf of our church. With everything else that was going on in our lives, she did not want to go but felt that she should. The decision to attend turned out to be a blessing! When the meeting started, the person leading the meeting asked everyone to introduce themselves by saying their name and which organisation they represented. At the opposite end of the row to Lois was sat a gentleman, and when it came for his turn to speak, he said, "I'm Bernard Stonestreet and I support Military Veterans and their families in the Hastings area, particularly those suffering from PTSD."

Lois couldn't believe what she was hearing and, as soon as the coffee break arrived, she made a bee-line to speak with him. That was the start of our journey into understanding PTSD and having the support of someone who 'got it', who totally understood the condition and its symptoms, and wanted to support and help us. We thank God for Bernard and his wife, Pat, as without them and their input into our lives at that moment, things could have turned out very differently for us.

'Disciplinary'

While I was still a patient in Woodlands, Bishop Martin, the Bishop of Chichester, had more disciplinary papers served on me. He did this twice. On one occasion, the senior nurse told the clergyperson who was wanting to serve the papers on me that he was not allowed to do so as I was extremely ill and he, the nurse, needed to safeguard me. Chichester Diocese had no regard for safeguarding me at all.

The detective who had charged me came with Lois, to tell me that the Crown Prosecution Service had decided not to prosecute me and that my bail conditions were lifted. Lois was now free to visit. Lois had withdrawn her statement against me after I had been in Woodlands for about 10 days, with the full support of the police, and the CPS believed it was a mental health problem and there was no public interest in prosecuting me. Lois and I could be together for the first time since my breakdown. At this time, an official informed us that the Diocese of Chichester was gunning for me in a big way. Lois and I soon came to realise that this was true.

What follows are details of what happened to us between May 2017 and March 2020, a period of almost 3 years. The contents of these writings are from our own personal experiences, but mainly sourced as evidence from copies of documentation that we received as a result of Data Subject Access Requests that we made under the GDPR regulations.

'Cruelty and Incompetency'

Whilst I was in the secure psychiatric unit in Hastings, Lois received a visit from the local Children's Services. Whilst we absolutely recognise the need, due to the complexity of my dissociation, for Children's Services to undertake an assessment/initial investigation, what we and our children suffered at the hands of Hastings Children's Services (East Sussex County Council) was appalling. This eventually resulted in a finding by the Local Government and Social Care Ombudsman that they, East Sussex County Council, had failed to follow proper procedure and their actions caused our family undue stress and worry. East Sussex County Council were ordered to write us a letter of apology, which they did, and pay us the sum of £500 in compensation, which they also did. Although £500 is hardly anything compared to the suffering we endured, we were told that this amount is more than the Ombudsman usually awards.

The incompetency of Social Services was evident from the start. Lois received the first visit from a social worker some 10 days after I had been admitted to the Psychiatric Unit. The social worker demanded that Lois take the children to a 'safe house', and when Lois questioned why she should do that, she was told, "because your husband is roaming the fields of Groombridge and he is dangerous."

Lois responded by saying, "My husband is securely locked up in the local psychiatric unit and has been for the last 10 days!"

Lois then challenged the social worker as to why she didn't know where I was, and if I was, as they believed, a dangerous person who was 'roaming the fields of Groombridge', why had it taken 10 days for them to make contact with her? The social worker again insisted that Lois move herself and the children to a safe house, and when Lois asked to see under what legal authority she, the social worker, was making the request, Lois was told, "There is no legal authority; we just expect you to comply!'" Lois and the children remained at home, and I remained in the secure psychiatric unit.

What we came to realise quite quickly, is that Hastings Social Services did not like being challenged or questioned and certainly could not cope with someone who was articulate and intelligent.

However, we happily complied with the request for our children to be visited and 'assessed', and allowed the social worker access to our children. I should make it clear at this stage that my children did not witness what happened in my study that day, and other than occasional angry outbursts, had not witnessed or been adversely affected by my mental health difficulties. We had, and have, a very good relationship, and they know that they are loved and cherished.

We did not expect any other outcome of the Social Worker's findings about our children other than what she found. Her assessment stated that she had not identified any current concerns regarding the children's development. She said time spent with our children indicated they had a positive relationship with both parents, and they were not aware of my dissociation. She stated that interactions with my step-daughter supported this view. The social worker also stated that our children were not displaying any emotional or behavioural difficulties, that they both presented as relaxed and happy, that they were chatty and able to express their views and both presented as well cared for, relaxed and enthusiastic.

After six weeks in Woodlands, I was discharged back home and under the care of an NHS Consultant Psychiatrist. I stood many times by myself on Hastings seafront with a sense of peace and a desire just to swim out to sea, fall asleep and drown. I stepped into the sea up to my knees on a few occasions, but for me, the thought of my wife and children and the suffering and pain my actions would cause turned me around and stopped me from going any further.

Again, in June 2017, at a meeting we had with Children's Services, at which representatives of the Diocese of Chichester were present, the same social worker recorded in writing that 'there are no concerns relating to A* and B* with regards to Neglect, Emotional Abuse, Physical Abuse, or any other abuse,' and further stated that our children 'are presenting really well at school.'

The meeting at which this report was presented was an Initial Child Protection Conference to determine whether there were grounds to put our children on the Child Protection Register. Representatives of the Chichester Diocese Safeguarding Team, including Mr Colin Perkins, were present at this meeting. We, Lois and I, were not allowed to speak unless spoken to, and our lawyer was not allowed to speak at all, only being allowed to attend the meeting in order to make notes. We felt utterly powerless.

At this meeting, Mr Perkins, who had never met with or spoken with Lois, asserted that in his opinion, Lois was a weak and fickle woman, completely under my spell, and could not be trusted. Anyone who knows Lois knows that this is so far from the truth! It was evident from this meeting that the Diocese were determined to keep up their mantra that I was a 'bad, mad man', and we soon discovered that they would stop at nothing to get what they wanted.

The outcome of the meeting was that, until further medical advice could be sought and more meetings with the children could be had, our children would be placed on the Child Protection Register and a meeting would be reconvened in three months' time. After the meeting was over, our experienced family lawyer, who attended this meeting, told us, not to worry too much, as in her opinion, the children would be taken off the register at the next meeting. Although this was devastating for Lois and myself, we understood, and naïvely expected our case to be dealt with in a professional way. Sadly, this was not to be the case.

It is my opinion, that the Diocese of Chichester heavily influenced, if not controlled, the meeting, and as we were to learn, our children being put on the Child Protection Register would help the Diocese to prevent me from returning to work and to label me as a 'risk'.

We next discovered that the Diocese put pressure on the police to re-submit evidence to the Crown Prosecution Service for a second time to try and get me charged with an offence. Thankfully, the CPS rejected their request.

Myself, Lois and my children needed help and support from the Diocese in our time of crisis, but instead, Bishop Martin Warner and the senior staff not only rejected us completely but began gaslighting us in any way they could. They 'used' institutions such as the police and Children's Services to attempt, I believe, to destroy our marriage and family, so that we would no longer be their problem. We needed help and the Diocese of Chichester behaved like Judas and betrayed my family.

From this point on, what we experienced from the Diocese, under the authority of the 'Core Group', was silent rage. Why did they rage at us? Because Lois and I dared to stand up for ourselves. We were meant to be submissive and go away quietly. This is what the Diocese expected, and this is what the Diocese was used to. Lois and I came to realise the culture of the Church of England and the Diocese of Chichester; if they decided to, this culture could crush clergy and their families with the power that Bishops have and which the Church of England regulations give them, to enable them to do this. The Church of England is an expert at self-preservation, something which has been heavily criticised and described as an 'organisational culture which puts reputation before protection.'

Millions of pounds of parishioner's money given to the Church of England is spent on paying an army of lawyers, barristers and media experts to protect Archbishops, Bishops and the Church of England's reputation. This army's sole aim is to crush all who stand in the Bishop's way, and who could damage the Church of England's reputation. This wicked aim has been very well documented in television documentaries and writings, which has publicly exposed this corruptness.

It was devastating for Lois and me to realise that the Diocese of Chichester had become actively hostile to me and my family. It was distressing for us to learn that the Diocese was putting pressure on Children's Services to impact my family in the strongest possible way in order to assist them.

During the three-month period assigned by Children's Services, we complied with any requests that were made of us. By the time of the next meeting, in September 2017, I had been assessed in August 2017, by a Consultant Psychologist who was an expert in military mental health, who had confirmed that I was indeed suffering from PTSD related to my military service and that my actions were attributable to the symptoms of PTSD, and more importantly, that I did not pose a risk to anyone other than myself. The psychologist deemed me to still be at risk of suicide.

I was also now under the care of an NHS Consultant Psychiatrist who concurred with the Psychologist's assessment of me.

My psychiatrist attended the next Child Protection Meeting with me. At this meeting, although it was the 'mind' of those people present that our children should not be kept on the register, the Chair decided that he wanted to 'err on the side of caution' and requested that an in-depth psychiatric assessment be undertaken and reported back to a meeting in six months' time. At this stage, although I had had an assessment with the psychologist, no lengthy detailed assessment had been undertaken by a Consultant Psychiatrist, so I was happy to comply.

The chair of the meeting made it clear that should the psychiatrist conclude his assessment within six months, he would be happy to reconvene the meeting early, and should the assessment determine that I was indeed suffering from PTSD and that I posed no risk to anyone, the children would be removed from the register.

'Suicide does not mean there is no killer.'

'Diagnosis'

As I've already detailed, in August 2017, I was assessed as suffering from military PTSD by a Consultant Psychologist who is an expert in this field. This assessment was also affirmed by my NHS Consultant Psychiatrist. This information was given not only to Hastings Children's Services but also to the Diocese of Chichester. The Diocese of Chichester were fully aware in the Autumn of 2017, that I, in the opinion of medical experts, posed no risk to anyone other than myself. Had the Diocese followed the advice of Ms Gold-Jones, their in-house mental health advisor, at the start of my breakdown, then her involvement would have 'automatically facilitated a review of risk' from the start.

The report by the Consultant Psychologist was ignored by the Diocese, and we later discovered in the paperwork we received, that in November 2017, the media advisor to the Diocese wrote to Gabrielle Higgins, who is the Diocesan Secretary, and posed the question as to when the PTSD diagnosis was confirmed (i.e.; the date of diagnosis), going on to state that that would 'be critical in media terms'. The response he receives from Ms Higgins states that, "It [PTSD diagnosis] hasn't been. A psychologist, who doesn't have the qualifications to make the diagnosis, 'diagnosed' it in September......"

The Consultant Psychologist that Ms Higgins (a former barrister) so rudely dismissed, had had 20 years' experience working in mental health, undertaking assessments and treatment of military veterans presenting with mental health issues, and had worked extensively as a psychologist for the Ministry of Defence and, in particular, with members of the Special Air Service (SAS).

It seemed clear again that Chichester Diocese had a number of staff who arrogantly believed that they knew more than medically trained and qualified persons!

In reality, the information given to the Diocese did not fit with the outcome that the Diocese wanted. What they wanted was me and my family gone, and their reputation protected.

All this time, we were not just living under the shadow of Children's Services, but we also had a Church of England disciplinary procedure hanging over my head. It is stated that,

"The Clergy Discipline Measure 2003 ('CDM') provides processes for dealing efficiently and fairly with formal complaints of serious misconduct against members of the clergy." [Copyright: Public sector information licensed under the Open Government Licence]

The Code of Practice for dealing with Clergy Discipline Complaints states:

"Overriding Objective of the Clergy Disciplinary Procedures

14. The overriding objective when dealing with formal allegations of clergy misconduct under the provisions of the Measure is to deal with all complaints justly.

15. Dealing with a complaint justly includes, so far as reasonably practicable: (i) ensuring that it is dealt with in a way that is fair to all relevant interested parties, including the complainant, the respondent, the respondent's family, the church, and members of the wider community, (ii) dealing with the complaint in ways which are proportionate to the nature and seriousness of the issues raised, (iii) ensuring that the complainant and the respondent are on an equal

footing procedurally, (iv) ensuring that the complainant and respondent are kept informed of the procedural progress of the complaint, (v) avoiding undue delay, (vi) avoiding undue expense." [Copyright: Public sector information licensed under the Open Government Licence]

My experience was that the process was dealt with neither efficiently (over two and a half years to complete), nor fairly. The issue of fairness will become evident further on in this book.

More shockingly, we were to discover from the Data Protection paperwork we received that on the 21st of November 2017, 6 months after my breakdown, and at a time when Bishop Martin and the senior staff of Chichester Diocese were aware of the diagnosis that I had been given and had been advised that, at that time, I did not pose a risk to anyone other than myself, meaning that I was still potentially at risk of suicide, a discussion was had amongst the senior staff of Chichester Diocese, concerning whether or not they should start a more 'aggressive legal and PR strategy' against me, and whether they should 'go public' about my 'misdemeanours'.

From the paperwork that we have been given, it is reported that Archdeacon Dowler was 'really keen to find a way forward to make public the true extent' of my 'misdemeanours'. With regard to 'going public', the email goes on to make reference to ascertaining exactly what 'he' (Archdeacon Dowler) and Bishop Richard Jackson were thinking.

Putting aside the sheer immorality of what was suggested, i.e.: exposing me publicly at a time when I was very fragile mentally, the safeguarding implications of what was being discussed are astonishing. It would appear that Archdeacon Edward Dowler and Bishop Richard Jackson were prepared ("keen") to shame me publicly about my PTSD symptoms, to stigmatise me publicly about my PTSD symptoms and disgrace me publicly about my PTSD symptoms. Had they done so, my reputation would have been irreparably damaged, my vocation finished, and, given my mental state at the time, my medical team are of the opinion that I would have taken my own life. The consequences for my wife and children would have been devastating, as well as the consequences for my church family. I would have been the collateral damage in order to protect the Church of England's reputation.

At the time, I had also become involved with a local veteran's support group which met every other Saturday morning and was facilitated by Major Bernard Stonestreet. The meetings consisted of teaching about mental health, PTSD and wellbeing. It was, and still is, a hub providing friendship and support for veterans and their families, and Major Stonestreet's incredible work with the East Sussex Veteran's Hub has, quite rightly, been recognised by the UK Prime Minister, Boris Johnson.

I duly complied with the requirement to undergo an in-depth assessment and met regularly with my psychiatrist for 6 months. I met with my psychiatrist both on my own and also with Lois. Lois also had individual meetings with my psychiatrist.

My psychiatrist completed the report, which confirmed the diagnosis of Combat-Related PTSD, and gave recommendations for ongoing treatment/therapy and also confirmed that I was not a risk to anyone. In light of this, Lois and I had no concerns that, at the next Child Protection Meeting, our children would be taken off the Child Protection Register.

Unfortunately, the Diocese got wind that the Child Protection Conference Chairperson was going to remove our children from the Child Protection Register and cease their involvement with our family, should the Psychiatrist's report be accepted. Potentially, this was going to happen by Christmas 2017.

At this stage, I was being suspended from my post approximately every 3 months on the grounds that, under the Clergy Discipline Measure, the Bishop was satisfied "on the basis of information provided by a local authority or the police, that a priest or deacon holding any preferment in the Diocese presents a significant risk of harm." [Copyright: Public sector information licensed under the Open Government Licence]

The Bishop was relying on Children's Services advising him that I 'presented a significant risk of harm' so that he could prevent me from returning to work. This became much more significant as time went on.

From the paperwork that we have received, both from the Diocese of Chichester and also Hastings Children's Services following Data Subject Access Requests, it is apparent that the information that our children potentially could have been taken off the Child Protection Register by Christmas 2017, caused the Diocese concern. This would remove their reason for suspending me and could mean that, potentially, I could go back to work. This is not what the Diocese wanted!

We were made aware by a concerned Trustee of St Helen's Church, our church, that Archdeacon Dowler, who was the complainant against me in the Clergy Discipline Measure, had approached the parishioners who had supported Lois some eight months previously when I suffered my breakdown, and requested that they write statements to be passed on to Children's Services. Two of the people agreed to this, and the statements were passed on to Children's Services by the Diocese. In reality, the statements didn't give any new information, but we felt very betrayed; betrayed on behalf of our children who would suffer because of this. The old cliché, 'you find out who your friends are in a time of crisis', was certainly true for us. However, the mere fact that the Archdeacon got two people to write them, and they were given to Children's Services, meant that Children's Services could use them as an excuse to stay involved with my family. This, in turn, gave the Diocese a reason to keep me suspended from office and unable to work. Using our children was, and is, an abuse of the highest depravity. The Diocese were using our children as 'pawns' to get their desired outcome.

This became the 'modus operandi' of the Diocese of Chichester. Every time I was suspended, I appealed each suspension, as was my right, and each time there is evidence of Mr Perkins frantically trying to get help from Children's Services to justify the suspension. On one occasion, Mr Perkins blatantly stated;

> "For the avoidance of doubt, if the President of Tribunals overturns the suspension, Mr Parks is back at work".

and;

> "we're under quite a bit of pressure as the only legal grounds for continued suspension depend so much on local authority advice…"

All the suspensions were upheld; the Deputy President of Tribunals for the Church of England had no choice. The legislation clearly states that if a Local Authority deems a clergyperson to be a 'risk', then suspension must follow. The Deputy President of Tribunals, Sir Mark Hedley, did, however, note that, in my case, 'Suspension has in truth become a staggered dismissal' and also acknowledged that, 'The appellant clearly suffers from PTSD relating to his earlier extensive military service. He says that the matter, now to be the subject of a Tribunal hearing under the Measure, occurred in a dissociative incident, which has now been satisfactorily addressed by treatment and therapy. It is right to acknowledge that he has participated thoroughly in that process.'

However, his hands were tied.

I was in a Catch 22 situation. I was re-suspended every three months, and sometimes a week or two at a time, from May 2017 to January 2020.

'Schemes'

Prior to the next Child Protection Review Meeting, scheduled for February 2018, the meeting at which we were expecting the Child Protection Plans to end, my psychiatrist finalised his report. This report clearly stated that I had Military PTSD and did not pose a risk to anyone. It detailed how I (and Lois) had co-operated fully with all help offered and with the assessment, that I had begun specialist therapy and that the psychiatrist was working closely with my therapist, and I was responding very well to the treatment.

Prior to this meeting, we had had a 'core group', and we were given the impression by the social workers that their recommendation was that our case would move from 'Child Protection' to 'Child in Need', although the Social Work Manager was not sure what they could do to help our family under a Child in Need plan as she knew that our home was not 'in a constant state of chaos and arguing like some of the families they deal with', and that our children were 'cared for above and beyond what Children's Services expected'.

We did not receive a pre-meeting report prior to the meeting scheduled for the 21st of February 2018, and although this was in breach of law surrounding Child Protection conferences, we had become accustomed to the total incompetence of the social work team, so it was not unusual for us to not receive reports, and any reports that we did receive were generally completely inaccurate.

What happened was that on the Monday before the meeting (the meeting was being held on the following Wednesday), we received a text message asking us to meet with the social workers the next day, the day before the review conference. Unfortunately, Lois was at a conference in London that day so we were not able to meet with them until 9.15 am on the morning of the conference itself. I was asked to stay in reception and Lois was taken into a separate room by two of the social workers.

It was explained to Lois that the senior Children's Services Management had decided to recommend that our case go to pre-proceedings; effectively we were being threatened with court and the possibility of our children being taken into care. This was completely unexpected; we had been expecting the Child Protection plans to end, not to go up a notch! The social worker 'blamed' the senior managers and said that she had no involvement in the decision and really didn't know what was going on. She also told Lois, who by this stage was in floods of tears, that 'we had a strong case and we should fight it'. At that point, less than 3 hours before the review meeting, we were given the pre-meeting report. We felt utterly powerless yet again.

We learned early on in our involvement with Children's Services that we needed to have an independent witness with us at all the meetings, as minutes of meetings were produced sometimes six months after the meeting had taken place and were incredibly inaccurate, containing fabricated information. Indeed, in the paperwork we received, we came across an email from the Head of Children's Services to our social workers, telling them to ensure that they only included the truth in their reports in our case! You have to question why a department head would instruct his staff to 'only include the truth'; was he aware that sometimes his staff didn't always write what was truthful?

Major Bernard Stonestreet attended the majority of our meetings with Children's Services, and eventually, a retired senior CAFCASS Officer, who had 20 years' experience in Child Protection, also attended to support and witness how we were being treated.

At the review meeting later that day, we discovered that the 'goalposts' had been moved in more ways than one! A new chairperson had been appointed, and he took a much more aggressive approach toward me.

'Gaslighting'

Early on in our involvement with Children's Services, they had requested verification of my military service; they wanted proof that I had actually been in the military. To expedite this for them, Major Stonestreet, in his role as a SSAFA Caseworker, had written and obtained a copy of my Verification of Service Record from the Army Personnel Centre in Glasgow. The letter was on headed paper and addressed to Major Stonestreet. As is normal practice, it was not signed but it did have the name of the Administrative Assistant who had compiled the record. Major Stonestreet is now the Executive Secretary and Founder of East Sussex Veterans' Hub.

At the start of the meeting, one of the social workers assigned to our case, who had shown a great deal of incompetence and also personal dislike towards us, put it to the meeting that he wasn't convinced that I had ever been in the Army, that I was a 'Walter Mitty' type character, and that I had not experienced the traumas that I had claimed to have experienced. The new Chairperson agreed with him, that he too, was not satisfied that I had served in the military or experienced what I had experienced. Sadly, Major Stonestreet was not able to be present at that meeting, although, in subsequent meetings, he made his feelings clearly known about the accusations that had been levied at me!

Lois pointed out that they had been given an official document by the Army Personnel Centre, which demonstrated that I was indeed in the Army and detailed where I had served. The social worker, rather incredulously, responded by saying that as the document wasn't signed, it could be a forgery. He went on to accuse Lois of having used her computer skills to create the document! We were completely dumbfounded by this behaviour! What soon became obvious was that this change of approach, i.e.: questioning my military background, was so that Children's Services could undermine the psychiatrist's diagnosis and report. At this meeting, reference was made to the two statements provided by the parishioners (at the request of the Diocese), and although, as I've said before, the 'statements' did not provide any new 'evidence', it gave Children's Services an excuse. In procuring these statements, this is exactly what the Diocese of Chichester wanted.

The meeting continued for some considerable time, and at one point the Chair decided that we needed to have a break. During the break, one of the social workers spoke on the telephone to Colin Perkins of Chichester Diocese. It was obvious Mr Perkins had made himself available for this meeting and it was becoming more and more obvious of his, and the Diocesan Core Group's involvement with, and influence over, Children's Services. This was something that we were only able to 'prove' once we received the paperwork from the Data Subject Access Requests.

When it came to the part of the meeting where recommendations were made with regard to whether or not Children's Services should remain involved with our children, although we were told that this meeting had the power to override Senior Management's decision to escalate our case to pre-proceedings, it was obvious it was already a 'fait accompli'. In her summing up, one of the social workers, the one who had previously said that she didn't know what was going on, and who had acknowledged that our home was not chaotic and our children were very well cared for, stated, "I am torn between humanity and protocol, but I have to go with protocol."

My psychiatrist, who was present at the meeting, stated that I had Military PTSD, that he did not consider me to be a risk to anyone and that in his opinion, Children's Services should be supporting us as a family and not putting us under more stress and pressure. My psychiatrist went on to express concern about the pressure being put on both of us, and the effect that this may have in slowing down my recovery and stopping me from returning to work, which he, and the other mental health experts, believed was an essential part of my recovery. Had I not been put under such pressure by the Diocese of Chichester, Church of England and Children's Services, my recovery would almost certainly not have taken so long.

All the reports that had been produced stated that I was not a risk to anyone other than, at one stage, to myself, and that I was engaging in all that was required of me by Children's Services. Added to this information, Children's Services had not found any concerns for the wellbeing of our children. They had met with the children countless times, visited them at their school, talked to their teachers, and visited them in our home. They only received information that our children were thriving in all aspects of their lives, physically, emotionally and intellectually.

Lois and I went home from this meeting totally confused, deflated and at our wit's end. How could professional people be so cruel? How could my Bishops, the people who are supposed to have pastoral care for me and my family, be so cruel? Their actions had nothing to do with care for our children. Our children were merely pawns. They were out to get rid of me, destroy me even, and they would stop at nothing to achieve this.

'Big Stick!'

We now found ourselves in the situation where we were being threatened with court and had to appoint lawyers to fight our corner. Firstly though, we and our lawyers had to attend a 'Meeting Before Action.'

The first Meeting Before Action took place on the 15th of March 2018. Having met with our lawyers before this meeting, both lawyers believed we had a very strong case, that Children's Services did not have a viable case against us, and that we should push for Children's Services to start court proceedings. We were happy with this decision. The meeting started and my lawyer simply told the meeting that we shouldn't waste everybody's time, that we wanted to go to court, and invited the Children's Services' lawyer to start court proceedings. The look of shock and surprise on their lawyer's face was quite interesting; I don't suppose that they get many people who call their bluff! Their lawyer quickly replied that they would rather avoid court if possible, and perhaps we could come to a mutual agreement about the way forward. After much discussion, it was agreed that I would undertake yet another risk assessment and that I was to arrange the risk assessor, as it needed to be somebody with experience of Military PTSD, and the Children's Services' lawyer acknowledged that he did not think that the person they usually used would have the necessary experience and expertise to do the assessment. Interestingly, the person that the Children's Services' lawyer was speaking about had been previously contacted around the time of the meeting in September 2017, and he had agreed that it was best for my NHS psychiatrist to undertake the assessment of me.

It was agreed that a further assessment of me would be arranged by a military psychiatrist through my therapist, and the meeting ended.

'Assessment #3'

As agreed, I met with a Military Psychiatrist, and yet again, the conclusion was that I had Military PTSD and my actions were as a result of a dissociative episode and that I was not culpable or a risk to anyone. During this time, social workers continued to meet with our children, Lois and I attended all meetings that were requested, and the Clergy Discipline Procedure still hung heavily over our heads. We also had to incur a lot of legal fee costs surrounding our 'fight' with Children's Services, and for various reasons, not just the Clergy Discipline Process, the Diocese of Chichester. This put another huge pressure on us, but we felt that we had no other option than to get into debt to fight our corner.

At the second Meeting before Action on the 11th of May 2018, we, with our lawyers, felt confident that, with the information contained in the latest risk assessment, Children's Services would be satisfied that I did not pose a risk to anyone. As soon as the meeting started, Children's Services' lawyer advised us and our lawyers they would not accept the assessment undertaken by the expert Military Psychiatrist because they had not agreed on a letter of instruction. The matter of the requirement of a letter of instruction had never been raised prior to this meeting by Children's Services. Children's Services were stalling again, and this stalling definitely helped Chichester Diocese.

Between the March Meeting before Action and the Meeting Before Action in May, Children's Services never wrote to us or to our lawyers to say that they would not accept the expert report without a letter of instruction, and they never sent us or our lawyer a letter of instruction.

My lawyer slammed her paperwork on the table in utter disbelief and immediately terminated the meeting, merely stating that they should take us to court, and we would await the issue of proceedings. Our lawyer asked the social worker present at the meeting what order they were seeking, and he was unable to give her a response! We heard nothing, no court papers were served, and our lawyers were totally confused and in agreement that Children's Services seemed to be deliberately stalling for some reason.

While we were waiting to hear from Children's Services, my therapist suggested it might be better for my ongoing recovery just to agree to another risk assessment rather than go through the court process. I think we all naïvely thought that if we did as they asked, then surely Children's Services would leave us and our children alone, and I would be free to focus on my therapy and recovery.

Following her advice, I agreed to yet another risk assessment, on the basis, as advised by my family lawyer, that any appointed assessor be agreed by my lawyer, and that the assessor had experience of Military PTSD. We informed Children's Services of my decision.

'Suicide does not mean there is no killer.'

After a wait of seven weeks, Children's Services provided details of the assessor they wished to undertake my assessment. My lawyer did not agree to the person chosen, because the person was not a psychiatrist and had no experience of Military PTSD. Along with details of the proposed assessor, Children's Services had also sent the documentation that they proposed to send to the Assessor. My lawyer quickly 'flagged up' to Children's Services that they were effectively 'cherry-picking' the documentation in order to support their case, rather than providing all the documentation and allowing an assessor to make their own assessment!

Prior to this, Lois had agreed to undergo a mental health assessment herself, by an assessor appointed by Children's Services. The result of this assessment showed that Lois had no mental health conditions, that she was a fit and able mother who could protect her children and that she had an excellent understanding of Military PTSD and its symptoms. Two of the documents that Children's Services were going to omit to give to the proposed assessor were the six-month assessment of me by an NHS Consultant Psychiatrist, and the mental health assessment of Lois! Unbelievable does not cover it! Actually, with the 'games' that Children's Services had been playing, it was believable. This was not a moral or fair fight; this was, at worst, utter incompetence and, at best, institutional corruption!

In the meantime, we had had to attend another Child Protection Review meeting (July 2018), with the Chairperson who saw me as a 'Walter Mitty', and again it was a 'fait accompli'. The Chair believed that there was 'an impasse' and instructed that 'a way forward needed to be found.' He then gave Children's Services one week to either start court proceedings or propose an alternative assessor. The timeline was agreed to by the social worker present at the meeting. The requirement from me was to continue therapy, which I did.

A week came and went, followed by many weeks and months, and it wasn't until November 2018 that we heard again from the legal team at Children's Services, some seventeen weeks after the 'one-week' deadline set by the Chair.

We felt that we were right back at square one! Children's Services were proposing that the assessment be undertaken by the same person who had been contacted in September 2017 and had agreed to the NHS Psychiatrist undertaking the assessment. This was the same person who we were told by the Children's Services' lawyer early that year, did not have the expertise to undertake an assessment of someone with Military PTSD! Again, they were proposing to leave out the two important documents – the six-month assessment of me and the mental health assessment of Lois, and to make matters worse, the person that they named as their legal lead in our case had sadly passed away during the summer! You couldn't make this up if you tried!

It seemed like we were trapped between two large vices, the Diocese of Chichester and Children's Services, and they weren't going to stop until we were completely crushed. Both institutions had the power, money and time to do this.

We were not going to be crushed; we totally relied on God's justice and our faith in the truth. This was mental health; no matter how much these institutions didn't like it, this was mental health. I was still in therapy. I had admitted what I had done, albeit without really cognitively knowing what had happened; I had reached a crisis point and just wanted help and support. Instead, what I got was isolated, persecuted and humiliated.

'Suicide does not mean there is no killer.'

'Occupational Health'

Whilst all this was going on, in March 2018, I was also requested by Chichester Diocese to attend an assessment by a Church of England Occupational Health doctor, and I gladly complied. Their doctor received a medical assessment from my NHS Psychiatrist, and the Occupational Health doctor also completed his own assessment of me. His assessment informed the Diocese that I had a mental health condition, PTSD, and that I should begin returning to work part-time leading into full-time work. This assessment was ignored by the Diocese of Chichester, as the report did not fit in with Bishop Martin and the Core Group's desire to crush me and my family and rid them of a problem. They were still able to use the 'excuse' that Children's Services, a local authority, deemed me to be a risk!

During the time that Children's Services were actively involved with our family, Lois and I attended ten core group meetings with social workers; we never missed one meeting. We also attended Child Protection Review Conferences and Meetings Before Action, never missing one. I complied with having a six-month assessment by an NHS Consultant Psychiatrist, a psychological assessment by a psychologist who was an expert in Military Mental Health, an occupational health assessment by a Church of England appointed assessor, a risk assessment by a military psychiatrist, and weekly therapy of one and a half hour sessions each. I don't think I could have done any more.

Lois also attended some of my therapy sessions with me, as it was important for her to support me in my recovery, and to contribute to my therapy. I attended fortnightly support meetings on a Saturday morning with the local veteran's hub, and Lois became involved with a support group for wives and partners of military veterans who have suffered physical and/or mental disability due to military service.

We permitted Children's Services (we had parental responsibility throughout), to see the children 33 times on their own, not in our presence, at home and at school. The children did questionnaires and worksheets, and one social worker, without our permission, subjected one of our children to a psychological assessment. The result of this assessment was that my son loved me tremendously and had no issues with me. Not being happy with this outcome, the social worker tried to twist the results saying that it was not right for a child to express his love for his father that much! All of this occurred even after the social worker at the very beginning, in 2017, wrote that our children were 'not presenting emotionally or behaviourally in a way that suggests they have already experienced significant harm."

Children's Services did not comply with their statutory requirements. At one point, Children's Services did not attempt to see our children for six weeks, when the statutory requirements were that they should see them at least every ten days. Interestingly, this six-week period fell within the time when East Sussex County Council Children's Services were being inspected by OFSTED! Yet, they were still threatening us with court proceedings to attempt to take our children away! If they had a real concern for our children, then why not take action?

The truth was that they had no real concerns for our children; this was not about risk to our children; this was about assisting Chichester Diocese to get rid of me. We even travelled abroad on a holiday gifted to us by concerned friends. We informed Children's Services of our intention to go away and where we were going, and they were not at all concerned. Even when we went on holiday in the UK, they did not follow the statutory requirements and advise the local authority near to where we were staying of our presence there. Such was their concern! We had a core group meeting with the social workers in September 2018, and at that meeting, we were advised that they were 'either going to start court proceedings or draw a line under things.'

We, and our children, had had difficulties with one of the social workers that was assigned to our case (I think we had at least 5 social workers involved in our case), and our children had expressed concern at some of the questions they were being asked by this particular social worker.

On one occasion, following a family holiday to a Christian Conference which had been sponsored by 'Compassion', a leading children's charity which empowers children left vulnerable by poverty, our son had told this social worker about how concerned he was for children in India who were poor and had to live in orphanages. Our son told him that he would like to give them money to make them feel better. In his next report, the social worker stated that he was concerned about this comment as 'often, parents with Children's Services' involvement can coach their children not to discuss home life', the inference being that somehow, we were 'coaching' our son to lie to the social workers about life at home, otherwise he might end up in an orphanage. This was despicable behaviour on behalf of the social worker, grasping at straws to try and find something negative to report.

This particular social worker, much to our relief and that of our children, seemed to disappear from our case, and this particular social worker did not see the children for a period of six months. Suddenly, this social worker re-appeared in their lives in December 2018. This caused distress and confusion for our children.

In December 2018, after eighteen months of being involved with our children and our family, Children's Services had not been able to provide any factual evidence that our children were at risk, or demonstrated any evidence of emotional abuse. From the paperwork we received, we discovered that they had tried their best to find some evidence though, and the social worker, in an internal email to Children's Services, Lawyer admits that he was 'going outside of his remit'. There was, however, plenty of evidence to demonstrate that our children were happy and thriving.

School reports were given to social workers, which clearly showed that our children were well-rounded and achieving above what was expected of their age group. Our son's report stated:

'...has had a positive year of learning and approaches all tasks with positivity and enthusiasm...... is determined and will persevere with a task until ...has succeeded. ..... gentle nature and positive attitude to learning have made him a delight to teach this year..... listens attentively to feedback and with support, acts on this to challenge himself and improve. ..... has made a good circle of friends and gets on well with everyone in the class. ..... is friendly, enthusiastic, helpful and a hugely reliable pupil who deserves success. I have no doubt that ..... will succeed in whatever path.... chooses for the future and I wish .... the best. ....., well done for a fabulous year! I have thoroughly enjoyed teaching you, thank you for making me laugh! I wish you every success. Good luck!"

Our daughter's report was in the same vein:

"..... has been a pleasure to teach this year and a great asset to the class....... is a good role model to others and always conducts herself well, following classroom expectations. ......

'Suicide does not mean there is no killer.'

is a good friend to others and plays well in the playground.
......behaves responsibly and is always willing to help us
with classroom jobs that we might have. ....has worked hard
in all areas of learning and has taken on board the feedback
she is given about how to improve her work. ...... always tries
her best and works well independently. We are confident she
will continue to thrive."

Children's Services were asserting that our children were at
risk of emotional abuse. The Pan Sussex Child Protection and
Safeguarding Procedures Manual, which is readily available to read
on the internet, lists the child presentation concerns with regard to
a child who has suffered or is suffering emotional abuse as follows:

    a. Delay in achieving development, cognitive and/or educational
       milestones
    b. Failure to thrive/faltering growth
    c. Behavioural problems, e.g., aggression, attention-seeking
    d. Frozen watchfulness, particularly preschool children
    e. Low self-esteem, lack of confidence, fearful, distress, anxious
    f. Poor relationships with peers, including withdrawn or isolated
      behaviour

    After eighteen months and 33 visits, Children's Services did not
identify one of the above in our children.
    It was so obvious that this was purely a witch hunt.

'Abuse of Power'

It was, I firmly believe, the aim of the Chichester Diocese and
Children's Services to keep perpetuating the myth that I posed

a risk to stop me going back to work. Whilst I recognise that legislation is put in place to protect people, the power that is given to authorities can easily be abused. We suffered, and I expect many other families suffer, by the way in which Children's Services can use and abuse their power, ignore any evidence they wish to and keep a family on Child Protection 'hanging in the balance' without any real right to recourse. There is no accountability for Children's Services' actions until it gets to court, but getting to court isn't, as we experienced, easy.

Lois and I made many complaints to East Sussex County Council, as well as the Church of England, which were a waste of time and energy. The complaint systems operated by The Church of England and East Sussex County Council are merely geared up to protecting the institutions and their staff.

Our MP became involved, making contact with the Archbishop of Canterbury, Justin Welby, directly, but he merely hid behind ecclesiastical law, stating that he could not get involved as it was the Bishop of Chichester's responsibility. Lois also wrote directly to the Archbishop of Canterbury, as well as other family members and parishioners, asking for help on my behalf, hoping that, as someone who had spoken out about his own battles with mental health, he would help, but they all got the same response.

Archbishop Justin Welby, a man who has spoken publicly about his own battles with mental health, and those of his daughter, and who is the patron of a mental health charity, walked by on the other side of the road. In the 1980s, there was a popular acronym, WWJD, this stood for 'What Would Jesus Do?' Jesus did not hide behind the law; he broke the law, much to the Pharisee's disgust, in favour of ministering to and helping those who were ill and broken.

'Suicide does not mean there is no killer.'

In a statement that Archbishop Justin Welby gave on World Mental Health Day, 10th October 2019, he stated;

"I'm so pleased to be able to give a message on World Mental Health Day. Every day here at Lambeth Palace we read some of the Psalms as part of our worship and when we get to Psalm 88 you find a Psalm of someone who I think was really depressed; it's tough but they're still looking outwards. Last year, I realised that I was depressed and, thanks to the fact that one of my children, who has been very public about it – understands these things and had taught me that there's no stigma to this, it's just life, I went and got help. It's not always easy but it made a huge difference. I want to say to anyone who feels they're walking in darkness, don't walk alone, you never need walk alone. It is so difficult; the Psalmist talks about that sense of isolation. **But increasingly, thank God, people draw alongside you and know that mental illness is no different to physical illness except it's invisible and it has a stigma. We need to get rid of that stigma, we need people to get help. We need people to know that their friends will go on loving them, that it's not a disgrace to suffer from mental ill-health.** I pray that God will give you strength if that's where you are to know that there's hope, that people still care for you and they will still stand with you. And if they know someone in their family and friends, just reach out and connect with them. Thank you."

I have deliberately highlighted two of the sentences in his message, as I completely agree with what he was saying, but unfortunately, this is not what I experienced in my treatment by Bishop Martin and the senior staff of Chichester Diocese. In fact, I experienced quite the opposite.

At a mental health conference held at Lambeth Palace, Archbishop Justin is quoted as saying that he had found it *"quite easy"* to talk about his mental health challenges, but was concerned that many people would worry *"because you don't know how your boss will respond"*. Although my 'boss' was God, my 'earthly' Father in God, Bishop Martin, had responded to my mental health difficulty with judgementalism, stigma and disgrace, and caused me to feel bullied and intimidated, humiliated, disgraced, an outcast and someone whose personal dignity had been violated. The conference, 'Faith and Mental Health: a Christian Response', was intended to raise the profile of mental illness and ensure the Church of England responded well to challenges. The Archbishop of Canterbury was quoted as saying that, *"along with the rest of society, the church had a history of not knowing how to deal with mental health issues"*.

In my experience, the Church still does not know how to deal with mental health issues, and deeply failed myself and my family. How can the Church of England promote a 'Christian Response' to mental health, when it has treated one of its own so appallingly?

PTSD in veterans is very much a topic under discussion in parliament with finances being put into mental health provision specifically for veterans. The subject of veterans with PTSD is also receiving a lot of media attention and coverage, and we have been approached to take part in a documentary about our experience of Military PTSD, its effects and the way in which we have been treated by the various agencies, including Children's Services, the Diocese of Chichester and the Church of England.

'Suicide does not mean there is no killer.'

The Archbishops, the current Archbishop of Canterbury, Justin Welby and the previous Archbishop of York, John Sentamu, on behalf of the Church of England, covenanted to:

"commit to honour the Armed Forces Covenant and support the Armed Forces Community. We recognise the value Serving Personnel, both Regular and Reservists, Veterans and military families contribute to our organisation and our country. Those who serve in the Armed Forces, whether Regular or Reserve, those who have served in the past, and their families, should face no disadvantage compared to other citizens in the provision of public and commercial services. Special consideration is appropriate in some cases, especially for those who have given most such as the injured and the bereaved. This obligation involves the whole of society: it includes voluntary and charitable bodies, private organisations, and the actions of individuals in supporting the Armed Forces. Recognising those who have performed military duty unites the country and demonstrates the value of their contribution. This has no greater expression than in upholding this Covenant."

It would appear, however, that for some reason, this Covenant didn't apply to me.

'Please, please, please, take us to court!'

We requested that Children's Services take us to court on four separate occasions, yet they failed to do so. The so-called 'Independent' Chair appointed by Children's Services made the same recommendation on two occasions, yet Children's Services did nothing. We and our legal team believed that the reason why they did not, is that they knew that they had no evidence, whereas we were able to provide overwhelming medical evidence. We sought legal advice to see if there was anything that could have been done to move our case forward and bring our case before a Judge. Yes, you can apply for a judicial review, but the costs surrounding that are immense and were certainly out of our reach.

Throughout all of this time, Bishop Martin Warner was suspending me from office and stating that he was 'satisfied' that I posed a 'substantial risk' based on the information provided by the Local Authority. I would question, and did question, whether Bishop Martin or his advisors had obtained any concrete evidence to support his assertion. Bishop Martin, it would seem, was purely basing his decision on what Children's Services (Local Authority) were saying, without determining whether what they were saying was true or not. We did, however, have proof that Children's Services had lied, deliberately stalled and failed to undertake their statutory obligations. It would also appear that Bishop Martin was blindly following the advice of his safeguarding advisor, Mr Perkins, without seriously considering the consequences of his actions.

We were advised to contact the Local Government and Social Care Ombudsman (LGO) with regard to our complaints against Children's Services, but first, we had to exhaust the Local Authority's own internal complaints process. We started the LGO process at the beginning of 2019.

We filed complaints about Bishop Martin Warner under the Clergy Discipline Measure, and, in particular, his failure to safeguard me, a vulnerable adult with a mental health condition, but were told that we were 'out of time'. Our complaint that Bishop Martin

'Suicide does not mean there is no killer.'

Warner had failed to pastorally support us was considered, however, it transpired that legally, he had done enough to comply with the legislation, but the question must be, had he morally done enough?

'January 2019'

We were facing yet another Child Protection Review Conference in January 2019. 19 months had now passed since Children's Services had got involved with our family, yet no action had been taken by them, although they kept that 'threat' over us. We were becoming very angry that an organisation had the power to do this to us and our children, and frankly, we were feeling abused by Children's Services, the Diocese of Chichester and the Church of England. Nobody, it seemed, wanted to help us, and we felt very alone.

The facts at the time of the meeting were that I had a diagnosed mental health condition, Military Combat-Related Complex PTSD, which is treatable. My medical records show that that is the only condition that I had. My medical records show that I had completed phase 1 of Complex PTSD treatment and that there was a significant reduction in my symptoms of depression and dissociation, and risk was now sub-clinical. My mental health disability determined that I was a vulnerable adult, and therefore, under adult safeguarding protection. According to numerous highly qualified medical professionals, who assessed me thoroughly and followed proper procedure, I did not pose a risk to anyone, including myself. I was deemed fit to return to work by the Church of England-appointed Occupational Health Advisor.

Also, my therapist reported in 2019, that, "…change is clinically meaningful (Monson et al, 2008). Risk (harm to self or others) is now mitigated and of no concern now…. There is good prognosis for full recovery."

Eventually, over three years, I would have around one hundred sessions of therapy. Some of this therapy was needed to help me deal with the bullying by the Diocese and Children's Services. This specialist therapy is not available on the NHS, and initially, following pressure from my psychiatrist, the Diocese of Chichester agreed to fund my therapy. However, only a few weeks into my therapy, we were very abruptly told that they could no longer fund my therapy, and that, 'as it was the Army that caused my PTSD and not my work as a Priest, I should ask the Army for money'. Thankfully, the Parachute Regiment stepped in and funded the rest of my therapy. Had they not, I would have been left with no way of funding therapy and in a very serious state mentally.

I was determined not to be bullied into complying with any requirements that may cause harm, abuse or injury to either myself or my children or my family in general. I was then, and am now, prepared to expose the despicable way in which myself and my family had been treated by the Diocese of Chichester, the Church of England and East Sussex County Council, in the hope that no-one else will have to suffer what we have suffered and that there will be a greater understanding of the damage caused to the veteran community who have fought for their country, and the effect that that has on their families.

We in the UK are currently decades behind the US in our understanding of Military PTSD and treatment of veterans, but the information and expertise are available, and ignorance should not be used as an excuse to mistreat people.

I chose to circulate my situation to a wide group of people, including members of the House of Lords, and House of Parliament for the purposes of exposing the plight of veterans who have served their country in the armed forces, and the plight of their families in trying to get Military PTSD more widely understood by the various agencies. Also, I did this to highlight the need for expert therapeutic help to be made more readily available. Not one person helped me. I realised the Establishment is a very closed shop.

The Review Conference was scheduled for January 8th 2019, and for our part, the requirements of the Child Protection Plan formulated at the meeting on the 19th of July 2018 had been met, the three requirements being:

1. Letter of instruction to be agreed – TIMESCALE one week (From the 19th of July 018) [No letter was proposed until 15th November]
2. If the impasse continues the Locality team are to consult with senior management and there should be consideration of placing the matter before the Courts. TIMESCALE one week (from 19th July 2018) [No action was taken to take our case to court]
3. Paul is to continue accessing therapy. TIMESCALE - from now (from the 19th of July 2018) [I had continued with weekly therapy sessions]

Out of the blue, we received a letter from the Customer Services Manager of the Local Authority, in response to our complaint, but not actually answering the points raised in our complaint, and yet again moving the goalposts immediately prior to a Child Protection Review Conference!

The January 2019 meeting then played out just as the meetings before it had. The Chair stated that he was not able to remove the children from the Child Protection Register whilst there was still an impasse.

What were we to do to protect our children? By this point, our two previous solicitors had closed their files, saying that there was nothing they could do, except for a judicial review, which was financially out of our reach. We sought the opinion of another very experienced solicitor from outside of East Sussex, who told us that, in their opinion, Children's Services and the Diocese were not going to stop bullying and gaslighting us until they got what they wanted.

The situation was personal to me; neither the Diocese of Chichester nor East Sussex County Council had any interest in the wellbeing of our children now. Our solicitor was of the opinion that we and our children were now being abused by Children's Services and advised us to write to Children's Services and tell them that we were withdrawing permission for them to see our children and that we would no longer attend or engage with any future core group meetings and there would be no contact at our house, school or anywhere else. Her advice was that if Children's Services thought our children were at risk and I was a risk, that they could take us to court, and we would have a chance of justice there. We wrote the letter with fear in our hearts and waited for a summons to court. The children never had another visit by social workers again from that point onwards. The letter had worked, and our children reaped the benefits from this rather scary decision.

We heard nothing again from Children's Services until the next Child Protection Review meeting in July 2019.

In the meantime, Lois and I spent days in my study responding to the continued attempt by Bishop Martin and his team to crush us personally and financially. We had no money. Our debt had become out of control with all that we had had to pay out. Our credit cards were all maxed out because we had to use them to buy food and attempt to pay bills. The pressure heaped on us by the Diocese was unrelenting. One tactic which the Diocese of Chichester employed, which we have been told is prevalent in the cut-throat business world, was to hand-deliver important and sometimes threatening letters to me at 5 pm on a Friday afternoon. This meant that I had no access to legal support or advice until the following Monday, giving me the weekend to worry about the contents. This did nothing to help my mental health. Hypocritically, the mission statement of the Diocese of Chichester is 'Know, Love, Follow Jesus'.

The Church of England continued to stall on setting a date for my tribunal. From speaking with other clergy members who have had difficulties with the Church of England, and also representatives of victims of abuse by Church of England clergy, it seems to be a common tactic amongst Dioceses to put so much personal and financial pressure on people that they will walk away and the problem then disappears for the Diocese.

Although the CPS did not prosecute, and I faced no criminal charges, the Diocese was determined to humiliate me and demonise me and perpetuate the view that I was a dangerous, bad, mad man.

In an email written in November 2017, the Diocese of Chichester's media adviser advises the Diocese that, "...*what we should be looking for is a dramatic change in our approach as employer once the diagnosis is medically proven/confirmed.*" My diagnosis was medically proven/confirmed multiple times, yet the '*approach as employer*' never changed or improved over the 2 ½ years. Rather alarmingly, the media advisor went on to state, "*The terms "war veteran" and "disabled" are consequential to this diagnosis and should not be used even by senior staff as emotive terms as the media would use them retrospectively.*" The response to this by Gabrielle Higgins, Diocesan Secretary, is even more alarming and downright offensive,

"Isn't war veteran independent of the diagnosis? War might be putting it too highly, though."

I find the latter part of Ms Higgin's comment utterly deplorable and highly demeaning. The majority of my military service and experience took place in Northern Ireland in the late 1970s and early 1980s. What happened in Northern Ireland may have been referred to as 'The Troubles', but it was, to all intents and purposes, a war where countless people were killed, maimed, tortured and subjected to horrific traumas. I personally lost 21 of my friends in my tours of Northern Ireland, including the Warrenpoint Massacre.

'July 2019'

Between January 2019 and the next Child Protection Review Conference scheduled for the 9th of July 2019, we had no contact with Children's Services. No court papers were served and no attempt to meet with our children was made.

On the 9th of July 2019, over 2 years after Children's Services became involved with our family, Lois and I, along with Major Bernard Stonestreet of East Sussex Veterans' Hub and a retired Senior CAFCASS Officer, attended another Child Protection Review Conference. As usual, no paperwork had been given to us in advance of this meeting, which was in breach of the statutory requirements surrounding Child Protection Meetings.

The Chair of the meeting was the same man who had chaired all meetings since January 2018. From the outset, his attitude was confrontational and both he and the social worker were flippantly dismissive of any issues that we raised or concerns with regard to statutory requirements having not been met.

At around 11.15 am, the Chair proceeded yet again to question my military service and, in particular, my involvement with the

Parachute Regiment at the Warrenpointmassacre in Northern Ireland in 1979. He leant forward towards Lois and myself and aggressively accused me of not having been at Warrenpoint, and that no evidence had been produced to clarify this. Lois informed him that evidence had been given, on a lawyer to lawyer basis at the first Meeting Before Action meeting in March 2018, and that two social workers present, one of whom was at that meeting, had acknowledged that they were happy for the evidence to be passed to the lawyer without them needing to see it. The Chair merely ignored this comment and proceeded to state that he had used the internet to obtain evidence of the names of those persons who were killed and injured at Warrenpoint. He began to read from a document (obtained from a website called 'paradata'), but was quickly warned by both the former CAFCASS Officer and Major Stonestreet that his actions were inappropriate and could result in harm to myself. The Chair was fully aware of my medical diagnosis of Military PTSD, and that I was, as defined in legislation, a vulnerable adult.

The Chair chose to ignore the warnings and continued to aggressively point to the piece of paper in front of me, saying that he did not believe I was at Warrenpoint as my name wasn't listed. The social worker present did nothing to safeguard me; even after further warnings to the Chair to stop what he was doing, the Chair continued to goad me. Lois intervened and informed him that my 'role' at Warrenpoint was as a response after the incident and that I had gone out after the 2 bomb explosions. More detail was given to the meeting; however, I do not want to document it here out of respect for the widows and children of those who lost their lives. He merely dismissed what I was saying.

The Chair continued his aggressive assertions and continued to put the list of names right in front of me. These were the names of my friends and colleagues who were slaughtered by the IRA on the 27th of August 1979. I began to feel threatened and I began to panic. His behaviour evoked feelings of guilt and shame in me because I survived and my friends didn't, and his actions reminded me of this fact and reminded me that my friends had been blown to bits.

At that point, my breathing and heartbeat became very fast, my head was swimming, and then, as he read out the name of a person I knew well, a friend I had journeyed through Junior Paras to battalion together with, I began to have a full-blown panic attack, which for me, was extremely frightening. At that point, I had to leave the room. I was violently sick and my body collapsed into a question mark stance and I sobbed and sobbed uncontrollably. I roared out loud with pain and grief and survivor's guilt. Major Stonestreet came to my aid to safeguard me and ground me in this episode by using traumatology techniques. At no point did either the Chair of the meeting (a former Social Worker) or the social worker present attempt to do anything to help me or safeguard me.

Given the seriousness of the incident, Lois telephoned my therapist to seek advice as part of the safeguarding/crisis protocol that was in place, and to ascertain whether emergency services were needed as medical support. My therapist advised Lois to ensure that the meeting was brought to an end and that she (Lois) was to call the police immediately to report and stop the 'vexatious abuse' being levied against me by the Chair. My wife contacted the police and made a verbal complaint which was followed up by a visit to our home. The two witnesses, Major Stonestreet and the Retired CAFCASS officer were both happy to provide witness statements, and the Retired CAFCASS Officer stated that in over

'Suicide does not mean there is no killer.'

20 years of work within the field of Child Protection, they had never experienced anything so appalling and unprofessional.

We also made a complaint to Children's Services, but, as usual, this achieved nothing.

Some weeks after we made the complaint, we discovered from Children's Services that the police were not pursuing our complaint against the Chair. The police had not informed us directly of this fact. We then contacted the police on numerous occasions, as we were not happy with the way our complaint had been handled and were concerned that this was just one institution covering the back of another. We eventually had a lengthy conversation with an Inspector at Hastings Police Station who oversaw dealing with complaints, and he told us he would look into what had gone on and get back to us. We heard nothing more.

After I had left the room and Lois had telephoned the police, all that then happened was that the Chair made the statement that the Child Protection Plans were ended, uttered the word 'shit', and quickly left the room by an alternative door, with the social worker in tow, so that he didn't need to walk past me.

What makes this even more disturbing is that we found out from the paperwork we received as the result of a Data Subject Access Request that the Chair knew before the meeting even started that the Child Protection Plans were going to end. The decision to end the plans had been made at a management meeting in March 2019, yet he chose to take the action he took and cause the distress he caused. The fact that Children's Services kept our children on Child Protection Plans for over 3 months after the decision to end the plans had been made was criticized by the Local Government and Social Care Ombudsman. Again, the question must be asked, why did they do this?

Throughout this time, Lois, myself and the children all lived happily together, yet I remained labelled as a 'risk' by the Local Authority and, therefore, was suspended from my role as a Vicar. How convenient for the Diocese of Chichester?

'Ombudsman & Data Subject Access Request'

Soon after the July 2019 Child Protection Review Conference, and the ending of the Child Protection Plans, we received the decision of the Local Government & Social Care Ombudsman in regard to our complaint against East Sussex County Council (Hastings Children's Services), and also part of the paperwork relating to a Data Subject Access Request that we made to East Sussex County Council under the GDPR Regulations.

As I've mentioned before, East Sussex County Council were found to be at fault in the way in which they conducted our case, and were instructed to write us a letter of apology, pay us £500 and circulate the findings to ensure that improvement in practice was undertaken. Normally, findings of the Local Government and Social Care Ombudsman are made public on their website, however, East Sussex County Council did not want these findings to be made public, and we agreed, as, at that time, we felt publication would be detrimental to our children. Little did we know that just over six months later, the Church of England would happily publish detailed information, against safeguarding advice, which would be extremely distressing for us all as a family.

One concern that the Local Government and Social Care Ombudsman raised was with regard to the level of consideration that was given to the assessments that had been conducted. This had been our difficulty all along; Children's Services had kept ignoring assessments and moving the goalposts, we believe, to assist the Diocese of Chichester in keeping me suspended.

We were also pleased that the Local Government and Social Care Ombudsman flagged up the inappropriate behaviour, or lack of professionalism, of one of the social workers. This was the social worker with whom we and our children had had difficulty, and the one who had admitted to going 'outside of his remit'. As mentioned before, Lois had, at the request of Children's Services, undergone a mental health assessment in April 2018, which stated that Lois understood the potential risks posed by someone with Combat PTSD and how she could mitigate against them if I was to relapse, and had discussed the coping strategies available to her. It was highlighted by the Local Government and Social Care Ombudsman that in December 2018, 8 months after the assessment, and another 8 months down the line of my therapeutic recovery, the social worker had stated in a case note file that Lois had, "very little capacity to protect herself and her children". The Ombudsman quite rightly highlighted that the statement of the social worker conflicted with the opinion of professionals 8 months previously. This was the problem that we kept on coming up against; in their desperation, Hastings Children's services would deliberately record false or misleading information.

Our experience of Hastings Children's Services was that they objected to Lois and I when we intelligently articulated our case and questioned their motives and actions. Indeed, the social worker assigned to our case complained about the fact that we were intelligent people! This resulted in behaviour that can only be described as malicious, and did not centre at all around potential concerns about the welfare of our children, but around working with the Diocese of Chichester to actively prevent my return to ministry.

The Child Protection Plans were not ended until July 2019, however, on the 5th of October 2018, over 8 months before, advice was given to the Social Work team from their legal advisors, which stated;

> 'Father is also said to be doing work - has this led to improvement? The evidence that the last event was 1 1/2 years ago suggests yes. So, is the risk present at time of issue? Threshold would be weak........a very expensive way of getting a further assessment and which may in fact achieve very little at a hearing."

It goes on to say,

> "Court also needs to be satisfied that an assessment is necessary in light of all the existing reports.'

Yet, our children were held on Child Protection Plans and I was deemed to be a 'risk' for another 9 months! For those 9 months, we had no idea if, at any moment, we would be issued with court proceedings, yet the legal advice to the Social Work team was that 'threshold would be weak' (case might not be strong enough to even get a court hearing), and it would be 'a very expensive (cost to the taxpayer) way of getting a further assessment' which the Court may say is not necessary in light of all the other reports!

We also discovered in a file note of a conversation between two senior members of East Sussex County Council, the statement, "…

in reality, we have no evidence of harm to put before the Court, given the children are fine at school."

Although rather scary, Lois and I would have welcomed the matter being placed before the courts, yet it would seem that the threat of court was just a 'big stick' that Children's Services could wave at us to try and intimidate us.

'Brinkmanship'

What we were to discover in July 2019, as part of the Data Subject Access Request paperwork shocked us to the core. What to us was the most serious and appalling discovery was that, on the 11th of May 2018, the Head of Children's Services sent an email to the Local Authority Designated Officer (the person who liaised directly with Colin Perkins at Chichester Diocese) which stated:

> "We would not meet threshold for separation at this time. We're playing brinkmanship ....and seeing how that goes down..."

The sentence that horrified us in that was 'We're playing brinkmanship...'.

The Merriam-Webster definition of Brinkmanship is 'the art or practice of pushing a dangerous situation or confrontation to the limit of safety especially to force a desired outcome' ["Brinkmanship." Merriam-Webster.com Dictionary, Merriam-Webster, https://www.merriam-webster.com/dictionary/brinkmanship. Accessed 20 September 2020]

The Head of Children's Services was deciding to push us to the limit to force their desired outcome! Where was the care for our children in this decision? Where was the safeguarding of me as a vulnerable adult with a diagnosed mental health condition?

As a result of discovering this horrific information, we made a formal complaint against the Head of Children's Services and we received a personal apology from the Director of Children's Services, who agreed to investigate, stating,

> "The use of the term brinkmanship is completely unacceptable and I share your dismay that it is being used in relation to you and your family."

We heard nothing more.

I have referred to our 'assumption' that Children's Services were working closely with the Diocese of Chichester to assist the Diocese in keeping me suspended. With the receipt of the Subject Access Request Paperwork, our assumption was confirmed. There are many emails from Colin Perkins of Chichester Diocese to the LADO, demonstrating the mutual relationship between the two. Without the help of the Local Authority, the Diocese had no reason to keep me suspended. The Local Authority had no grounds to keep our children on Child Protection and to pursue a court case, yet they had the power to do so, and so did! This was very helpful for Chichester Diocese.

We also discovered that the Diocese (Colin Perkins) were informed on the 1st of March 2019 that the Child Protection Plans would be ending, yet Bishop Martin Warner continued to issue 2 more suspension notices on the grounds that he was 'satisfied' that I presented a 'significant risk of harm'. Indeed, even after the Child Protection Plans ended in July 2019, and Children's Services' involvement with our family completely ended, Bishop Martin continued to suspend me on the grounds that he was 'satisfied' that I presented a 'significant risk of harm'. These suspensions continued right up until the tribunal in January 2020. Interestingly, the chair of the tribunal, a judge, during the tribunal, questioned Archdeacon Dowler as to why the suspensions continued after Children's Services involvement ended.

All that time, from May 2017 onwards, Bishop Martin did not attempt to take any steps under the powers afforded to him under Ecclesiastical Law to have the 'risk' independently assessed for himself. The reality of why he did not order a risk assessment would become clear as we read through the paperwork!

'Risk Assessment'

A question, which kept raising its head, was 'why has Bishop Martin not taken the steps afforded to him under ecclesiastical legislation to 'test' the information provided to him, and obtain an independent risk assessment?'

At no point did Bishop Martin attempt to use the powers available to him to commission an independent assessment of risk; instead, he solely relied upon the "information provided by the local authority".

The Safeguarding (Clergy Risk Assessment) Regulations 2016 give a Bishop the right to direct that a Risk Assessment, by a House of Bishop's appointed Risk Assessor, be undertaken on a Clergyperson in their Diocese. In doing so, the Bishop works with his Safeguarding Advisor with regards to the preparation of the terms of reference of the assessment. This is where it all went wrong for me!

From the start, back in May 2017, Colin Perkins, the Diocesan Safeguarding Advisor, had perpetuated the mantra that I was a bad, mad, man! Colin Perkins, a former probation officer, had form in this respect, and he seemed to be willing to make assertions about matters that would appear to be outside of his area of expertise as Diocesan Safeguarding Adviser or purely based on presumption.

One of the well-documented cases involving Chichester Diocese is the case of Bishop Bell. In September 2015, Chichester Diocese paid compensation to a woman who had alleged that she had been sexually abused by Bishop Bell, and a public apology was issued by Bishop Martin Warner. The next year, the Church of England announced that it would hold an independent review of how the church handled the allegations (not the truth of the allegations themselves), and Lord Alex Carlile, a QC and a member of the House of Lords, was appointed to undertake the review.

In his findings, Lord Carlile found that,

> "there was a rush to judgment: The church, feeling it should be both supportive of the complainant and transparent in its dealings, failed to engage in a process which would also give proper consideration to the rights of the bishop."
>
> [Bishop George Bell, The Independent Review,
> By Lord Carlile of Berriew, CBE, Q.C.]

The report also found that the available evidence did not suggest there would have been 'a realistic prospect of conviction' in court, the standard that prosecutors in England and Wales use in deciding whether to pursue a case. The Church of England released a statement with the report in which it apologized to Bell's relatives for the way it investigated child abuse claims made against him, acknowledged the mistakes highlighted by the report, and promised to implement all except one of its recommendations.

'Suicide does not mean there is no killer.'

In the Carlile Review, there is a direct quote from a letter written by Mr Colin Perkins to the Sussex Police, where Mr Perkins suggests that,

"it is unlikely that Bishop Bell only abused this one person",

and goes on to say,

"It is known, for instance, that Bishop Bell had evacuees staying at the Palace during the war, and he inevitably would have had access to many children over the 3 decades of his ministry in Chichester."

These comments were made by Mr Perkins before any substantial investigation had taken place and the facts from Bishop Bell's standpoint had been taken into account. Indeed, in Bishop Bell's case, Lord Carlile goes on to say that,

"Had Bishop Bell still been alive, unless there was evidence that he appeared to represent a danger to the public, he would not have satisfied the arrest conditions...".

There is also reference, in the Carlile Review (paragraph 231), to a newspaper article, referenced by Colin Perkins, in which Bishop Bell was spoken of very highly by a former evacuee. Mr Perkins' response to this praiseworthy reference is (paragraph 232):

"Clearly Mrs Suneps recalls GB in very positive terms. As we know this does not undermine the conclusion we have reached. What this evidence does show, however, is very clearly that GB had considerable access to children during a long period during the war, and whilst he was not living at the Palace for much of this period, he was a sufficiently regular visitor."

Lord Carlile criticises Mr Perkins in the following paragraph (paragraph 233) by saying:

"I regret that I do not understand the above comment, that the conclusion of the Core Group was not undermined. The fact that Bishop Bell had access to many young girls during WWII, that he had contact with them, and that no complaints had emerged from that period, could have been the source of evidence in court proceedings. Certainly, it should have been regarded as a factor in the Core Group's decision-making process. It was not so regarded."

Why reference the Carlile Review? It would appear that lessons have not been learned in Chichester Diocese and judgemental and destructive behaviours still continue.

In the 'Promoting a Safer Church' document issued by the House of Bishops, it states:

"The Church in exercising its responsibilities to suspicions, concerns, knowledge or allegations of abuse will endeavour to respect the rights under criminal, civil and ecclesiastical law of an accused Church Officer including the clergy. A legal presumption of innocence will be maintained during the statutory and Church inquiry processes."

'Suicide does not mean there is no killer.'

My experience of Bishop Martin and his senior staff (including the Diocesan Safeguarding Officer) was not one of "a legal presumption of innocence" but one of guilty, full-stop! Early on, following my breakdown, in November 2017, Bishop Martin states in an email,

> "….A future announcement could be that P will not be returning to work."

At this stage, the Clergy Discipline Measure process was only in the early stages, so how could Bishop Martin make such a conjecture?

Colin Perkins also tried to get me added to the DBS Barred List, which would have meant immediate dismissal from office, thereby by-passing the clergy discipline process. His scheme did not work, as there were no grounds to do so.

As I ploughed through the paperwork sent to me from the Diocese, the real and shocking reason why Bishop Martin did not commission a risk assessment became very obvious.

On the 12th of December 2017, Colin Perkins (Diocesan Safeguarding Officer) wrote to the Church of England Deputy National Safeguarding Adviser with regard to organising an independent risk assessment on me, saying that he would really like a specified doctor to undertake the risk assessment of me; however, that particular doctor was not on the list of clinicians approved by the House of Bishops. He then goes on to ask if this particular doctor could be added to the list, 'even if only for this one case'. Mr Perkins explains,

> "I'm going to find it a lot easier to move this case forward if I can instruct *[he refers to the doctor by his first name] rather than anyone else but I can't without him being on the list!"

The response he receives indicates that he, Colin Perkins, had already tried to facilitate this, as it is mentioned that he had already 'talked this over' with another member of the National Safeguarding Team. Colin Perkins is told, in no uncertain terms, that somebody who is not currently on the approved list in accordance with Church legislation cannot be used.

This response does not deter Mr Perkins and he continues with his determined stance to have an assessor of <u>his</u> choice added to the list, stating;

> "Operationally, not being able to use * in this assessment will make our job much more difficult......Please could you consider being flexible on this one; operational considerations must surely take priority over process matters?"

Again, the response is in accordance with policy and practice, and Mr Perkins is reminded that the approved process ensures 'a fair approach to all potential independent assessors to ensure consistency and quality as we move forward together.'

Mr Perkins is still not happy with the response he receives and responds rather angrily, however his request is not granted.

Colin Perkins was determined to appoint 'his man'!

Mr Perkins finally reports back to Bishop Martin, and this is where it becomes obvious why no risk assessment was commissioned. Colin Perkins writes about his frustration as,

> "process is clearly getting in the way, here, of the best outcome. I cannot give you the advice I want to give you, which is that we should instruct * [named doctor] to do the risk assessment..."

'Suicide does not mean there is no killer.'

The phrase 'the best outcome' was what immediately jumped off the page at me, and answered the question as to why Mr Perkins was so determined to add Dr * to the list. It would appear that the reason why Bishop Martin failed to use his powers to commission a risk assessment was because the risk assessment would have to be undertaken by someone other than the Safeguarding Officer's 'preferred' assessor, and if undertaken by someone else, would potentially not result in the 'best outcome' for the Diocese! The immorality of this is just shocking! Any other clergy person of whom a risk assessment is required would be assessed by someone who is on the list approved by the House of Bishops. So why did it have to be different for me?

'Data Protection'

Article 10 of the Human Rights Act - Freedom of expression, states:

> 'Everyone has the right to freedom of expression. This right shall include freedom to hold opinions and to receive and impart information and ideas without interference by public authority and regardless of frontiers.'

One of the best things that I did was to evoke my rights under the General Data Protection Regulation, and request copies of my personal data from both East Sussex County Council and the Diocese of Chichester. As I have already mentioned numerous times, what I discovered in this paperwork was both disturbing and infuriating. I have chosen to quote excerpts of this information, as I believe disclosure is justified in the public interest. Both institutions, East Sussex County Council (Children's Services) and The Church of England (Diocese of Chichester) hold positions of power and authority in the United Kingdom, and when that power and authority is abused, the repercussions are abhorrent and dangerous.

There is a well-known saying, "Power corrupts; absolute power corrupts absolutely", which has been attributed to Lord Acton, the 19th Century historian. In my dealings with both East Sussex County Council, the Diocese of Chichester and the Church of England, this saying could not have been more true! Indeed, in July 2019, the former Archbishop of York, Dr John Sentamu, said, "Bishops must be aware that if they have absolute power, it will corrupt them," and that "unquestionable authority" is no longer acceptable in the Church."

I first started trying to obtain a copy of my personal data from Chichester Diocese in June 2018 and found the Diocese to be obstructive, secretive and, ultimately, in breach of the Data Protection Act.

The first file of paperwork that I received from the Diocese of Chichester's lawyers basically contained papers that were 90% redacted and therefore of little use to anybody, and many important documents were missing. Unfortunately, at the time, I was still in the early stages of recovery and was not able to take matters further with the Diocese.

I then made a further Subject Access Request on the 8th of April 2019 (at the same time also making a Data Subject Access Request to East Sussex County Council, which enabled me to 'compare notes' as to what information was missing), and I received a response from the Diocesan Secretary, Gabrielle Higgins, informing me that she was restricted from disclosing certain information in the interests of my health.

I wrote again to Ms Higgins on the 23rd of April 2019 as I had a suspicion that they were using the 'health restriction' erroneously, and in order to deliberately withhold my personal information. I was also aware that none of my medical team had advised the Diocese of Chichester that to release data to myself would cause harm to my mental health.

There then began a 'chain' of correspondence between Ms Higgins and myself, and as I was aware that no-one from my current medical team had advised that to release data would cause harm to myself, I was concerned that the Diocese of Chichester were deliberately misleading and being obstructive and secretive. It is well documented that this is a tactic the Diocese had previously used with regard to abuse victims, even going as far as destroying paperwork!

The communication centred around an 'opinion' by a 'relevant health professional' that Ms Higgins claimed to have, and upon whose opinion she was relying, and that the 'serious harm test' was met. On one occasion, Ms Higgins arrogantly responded, "With respect, the opinion of your current medical team is irrelevant". How can the opinion of my medical team be irrelevant?

I continued to assert that they could not possibly have an opinion from a 'relevant health professional' as defined by the Data Protection Act, but Ms Higgins refused to allow me access to the 'opinion' or details of who had written the 'opinion'.

I finally received an email from Ms Higgins on the 14th of June 2019 which stated,

"Your assertion that the relevant medical professional is not a relevant health professional for the purposes of the Data Protection Act is incorrect. As I have previously explained, the health professional was directly involved in your treatment. Under the Data Protection Act 2018 Sch 3 Part 2 paragraph 6, the Diocese cannot disclose the report to you."

Ms Higgins then goes on to say,

> "The Diocese's decision not to release the medical report to you is final and is in accordance with legal advice from external counsel and direct guidance obtained from the ICO (Information Commissioner's Office). I do not believe continuing correspondence with you on this issue will be helpful, so as far as the Diocese is concerned. this matter is closed."

At 11.15 am on Friday the 14th of June 2019, I informed Ms Higgins that I would be progressing my complaint to the ICO and asking the ICO to investigate, after all, that shouldn't be a problem for her as she had already told me she had 'direct guidance from the ICO'.

At 17:54 on Monday the 17th of June 2019, I received an email from Ms Higgins, in which she suddenly decides that they had, all along, been quoting the wrong paragraph of the DPA and that the serious harm test was, in fact, not met! Ms Higgins laid the blame at the foot of their legal advisers. She then went on to admit that they had not obtained a "recent opinion from an appropriate health professional that the serious harm test is met". By this stage, I was fuming!

The following day, I received an email from the Diocese's lawyer who personally apologised to me 'for the error' and 'any frustration it would have caused me'. I proceeded with a complaint to the ICO.

The Data Protection legislation is not difficult to interpret or understand, and I fail to understand how a former barrister and her legal adviser could not interpret and apply it properly. I felt that I had been deliberately misled in order to attempt to prevent me from accessing my personal data.

I have since received a copy of the 'medical opinion' referred to (having been judged by a relevant health professional as defined, that to issue the same to me would not 'be likely to cause serious harm to my physical or mental health'), and the author of the report did not fall within the category of 'health professional' as defined, was not part of my medical team and indeed at the time the report was written, did not follow proper diagnostic protocol, did not undertake a thorough assessment and did not arrive at a correct diagnosis.

The ICO came to a judgement on the 10th of July 2019, concluding that the Diocese had not complied with its data protection obligations and had been unfair to me. In the opinion of the ICO, the Diocese had not made sufficient effort to resolve my complaint, and the Diocese was asked to revisit the way it handled my complaint and consider what further action it could take to resolve it.

'Sheldon Report'

Our involvement with Children's Services may have come to an end, but I still had the Church of England Tribunal hanging over me. I had not worked for nearly three years, and for that time, I had been isolated from my parishioners and spent my days just walking and thinking.

The Diocese had been told by various medical professionals, including their own Occupational Health Assessor, that a return to work was essential for my ongoing recovery, but that is not what they wanted. During this time, nobody from the Senior Staff of the Diocese had come to speak to me, and even the 'prosecuting' barrister ('Designated Officer'), had not come to speak to me to hear my side of the story. Lois and I were now in serious financial debt in the region of eighty thousand pounds. Each month, we paid off our credit cards and loans and were left with not enough money to buy food with or pay our bills. We had some amazing, godly friends in our congregation who gave us handouts and offerings of money now and then. If it wasn't for their kindness, I don't know how we would have survived. Lawyers were needing to be paid, and we needed more lawyers to help us with the tribunal.

All the time, Bishop Martin had access to a team of lawyers and barristers for which he did not have to pay a penny. We were up against an enormous giant with huge financial power over us. Suddenly, after nearly three years of trying to crush Lois and me, we got a date for a tribunal to be held in January 2020. We were given six weeks to prepare. After almost three years, we were given just six weeks. We had no money; we were worn out and we could not afford a defence lawyer. We were eventually granted ecclesiastical legal aid. The Church of England decide if they will give you money to help you fight The Church of England! A limited amount of money was granted, which did not pay for a lot of lawyer time.

I requested that the tribunal panel have someone on it who was medically trained in dealing with mental health issues. My request was ignored, and I was told it was not necessary for a medically qualified person to be on the panel. It became clear that the tribunal panel members would be handpicked by the Church of England. The tribunal seemed like it was going to be a kangaroo court. And it was.

I was asked if I objected to any panel members, and when I did, my objections were over-ruled. I had no power in the process and was most definitely the underdog. The whole process of getting to the tribunal, which took over two and a half years, was a farce from beginning to end. In the whole of the time, all the medical evidence was ignored, and all mine and my medical team's complaints were ignored. The Church of England regulations ensured this would be the case.

Some friends paid for Lois and I to stay in a hotel in London so that we wouldn't have to travel back and forth between Hastings and London each day of the four-day tribunal. Lois and I arrived at the tribunal feeling done, finished personally and finished financially.

The tribunal was set up as if they were hearing a criminal court case, yet we had to rely on ecclesiastical lawyers to defend us and support our barrister. They are not defence lawyers and are not equipped to defend someone.

We had a barrister who was a mental health/human rights barrister, but who did not have experience of an Ecclesiastical Court. She was assisted by an ecclesiastical lawyer.

It was interesting that a Sheldon briefing for the Parliament Office for Academic Research was published on the 14th of January 2020, a few days after my tribunal. There is much in the Sheldon report, which is publicly available, that Lois and I can testify to in the way in which we have suffered at the hands of the Diocese of Chichester and the Church of England throughout the Clergy Discipline Measure process. Our sufferings mirror the findings of the Sheldon briefing and it highlights faults in the Church of England which we too have experienced.

The report begins,

'We at Sheldon started observing an unexpected emergence of harrowing personal stories through direct pastoral/counselling ministry and online forum. Confidentiality, shame, isolation and both loyalty to and dependence on the institution appeared to be keeping the stories as isolated 'anecdotes' which could be disregarded individually. Some of the things that particularly concerned us, including in cases which were clearly vexatious and resulted in 'no case to answer' or 'case dismissed', are:

1. *People getting into significant debt through legal costs* – In my case, we got into a considerable amount of debt over the two and a half year years.
2. *Cases taking a very long time to resolve. Timescales in the Measure being disregarded.* – In my case, timescales were totally disregarded.
3. *Significant mental health impacts up to and including suicide* – In my case, I was already suffering with a mental health condition, and the CDM process exacerbated that and prolonged my therapy. At the beginning, I suffered with suicidal ideation.
4. *Long-term effects on employment prospects in the church (the 'blemished blue file')* – In my case, not only is my 'blue file' blemished, but the Church of England has gone to great lengths to attempt to publicly disgrace and stigmatise me.
5. *Impacts on spouses and congregations – bringing the church into disrepute* – In my case, no consideration was given to the effect of the CDM on my wife, children and members of our congregation. For most of the time, our parishioners were left completely in the dark, isolated from me, and angry.

The briefing goes on to say,

> 'Conversations we requested with key players such as Clergy Discipline Commission president/members, ecclesiastical lawyers, Dean of Arches, Bishops and Archdeacons led us to believe that no-one had a comprehensive overview. In the course of our conversations and investigations we discovered;

1. CDM legislation contains NO provision for scrutiny of PRO-CESS – if a bishop is mishandling a case the only possible redress is to appeal at tribunal against the DETERMINATION.

'Suicide does not mean there is no killer.'

2. CDM operates largely in the dark. The ONLY statistics that are gathered are a once-yearly snapshot of case numbers and determinations published as the CDC annual report. Nobody knows what happens to people during or after CDM because nobody has asked the question.
3. There is NO comprehensive professional indemnity/defence scheme for clergy that would compare with, say, belonging to Medical Defence Union. Even taken all together, the Faithworkers branch of Unite, the Ecclesiastical Legal Aid and Ecclesiastical's insurance policy do not stack up to protect against the cost risks of being a CDM respondent.
4. The CDM is increasingly being used for purposes for which it was never intended and clergy are structurally exposed to high risk of vexatious and unfounded complaints.
5. There were people involved in the drafting of the 2003 Measure who had warned against exactly the problems we were seeing. They are a predictable consequence of badly framed legislation.'

The briefing paper goes on to say that they had identified 'further areas of enquiry that would merit investigation':

'1. The prevalence of PTSD in the aftermath of CDM
2. The prevalence of Moral Injury
3. The operation by bishops of 'irregular discipline' which is even less accountable than CDM
   We have also been aware of a degree of incredulity in our conversations. It can't really be possible that this has gone so badly wrong within the church – can it? Well, yes, and there are some specific reasons why this has arisen and needs to be remedied.

1. Clergy are office holders so the protections of employment law do not apply.

2. The bruising clerical sexual abuse scandals of the past decade take up the whole field of vision of the church hierarchy and promote a zero-risk defensive posture where a high degree of 'collateral damage' among clergy is tolerated as 'the price that has to be paid'.

3. The vulnerability of living in tied housing in the heart of the communities clergy serve.

4. Historical attachment to the primacy of the role of bishops in the discipline of clergy that is no longer tenable in a litigious culture and where episcopal training/resourcing is inadequate to the needs of safe implementation of the legislation.

5. Significant levels of conflict of interest among those handling the cases – many of these hard-baked into the roles prescribed by the Measure.

6. Clergy are more likely to fight for justice for other people than for themselves.

7. Until people have direct personal or second-hand knowledge of a case they generally believe 'it couldn't happen to me'.

8. Clergy are relatively non-unionised and professionally isolated which has mitigated against collective action.

9. There are ZERO sanctions for those who bring vexatious or unfounded complaints, not even suspension from holding office in the local church'.

After two years, the Sheldon Briefing has come to the conclusion that the Clergy Discipline Measure is 'so fundamentally flawed that starting over from first principles and completely replacing the Measure is essential.'

'Suicide does not mean there is no killer.'

I had suffered because of legislation that is 'fundamentally flawed', legislation which was known to be 'not fit for purpose' before it was implemented, and legislation that needs completely re-writing!

I am pleased that the Sheldon Briefing has identified some measures that need to be introduced to deliver 'consistent, timely and impartial justice', including:

- 'A mandatory and comprehensive insurance system for legal costs (at least part-funded centrally)
- Separation into two completely separate complaint tracks which are clearly demarcated.
  ○ Track A. Gross Misconduct. To handle allegations which, if proved, would warrant loss of home/livelihood. This would have a clear gateway process before being actioned, and would be professional, national, transparent, properly funded, evidence-based and not episcopally led.
  ○ Track B. Grievances. To handle all the other complaints. This would be episcopally led, local, focused on restoration of relationship and community, using resources such as mediation and training. Bishops would be able to sanction both clergy and laity.'

Had I had access to a Track A system, I believe I would have had a fairer and more transparent hearing and process. Sheldon are also recommending that Track A has an Ombudsman 'to oversee the process as well as a suitable appeals process against the judgement.' An Ombudsman is most definitely needed, so that clergy have an independent body to turn to, as we were able to with the Local Government and Social Care Ombudsman. Had I had recourse to an Ombudsman, the Diocese of Chichester would not have been allowed to get away with what they did. In taking Type A cases out of the hands of Bishops, Sheldon quite rightly states that this 'would enable bishops to support the clergy accused of gross misconduct instead of immediately isolating them at their time of greatest need, and the most troubling cases would be dealt with by people trained and resourced to administer good justice.'

I can only concur with Sheldon in that, if these changes and the others recommended in their Report were instigated, 'it would better reflect Christian Gospel values.' My experience to date has shown no reflection of Christian Gospel values at all.

The travesty and failing of this report is that the Church of England have put forward one of their own to be the chairman of a review, Bishop Tim Thornton, a Bishop at Lambeth Palace. I was also horrified to hear that Colin Perkins, the man who blatantly flouted the legislation in my case, is also a member of the review committee! Bishop Tim Thornton failed Lois and I, and ironically, he is the Bishop to the Armed Forces!

In my opinion, in order for real change to happen, there needs to be a completely independent investigation and recommendations implemented by a body outside of the Church of England.

'Tribunal'

The setup of the tribunal reminded me of the Court Martial I was involved with when I was in the army. The tribunal took place in a chapel in the heart of London, and the tribunal judge was elevated on the chancel of the chapel with the four other members of the tribunal panel sitting at a table, two on either side of the judge. My barrister and ecclesiastical lawyer sat at a table on the left side of the chapel facing the chancel, and on the opposite side of the chapel was the Church of England barrister and Archdeacon Edward Dowler.

'Suicide does not mean there is no killer.'

I sat in the pews with my therapist. My therapist had come to the tribunal not just as a tribunal witness but also to support me throughout the four-day hearing. Initially, there was no certainty that she would be allowed to accompany me throughout the hearing, but in the end, this was agreed to. A mere 'nod' to my mental health condition.

Holding the tribunal in a chapel was strange to me; this was, after all, the House of God. In the chapel and throughout the tribunal there was a constant loud humming noise. The noise made it difficult for anyone in the room to hear each other and was extremely irritating. For someone with PTSD, it was pretty much unbearable, and I sat throughout the tribunal in a pew using my 'Alpha-Stim' device. This is a device that calms the brain with electronic impulses.

My evidence consisted of me admitted the symptoms of my illness and taking full responsibility for the manifestations of my symptoms from my CPTSD and PTSD with dissociative subtype, although my medical team would say that, at the time of the dissociations, I was not responsible as the damage to my brain 'took over' and I was not in control of my actions. Nevertheless, I took full responsibility for what the consequences of these symptoms were for Lois who had been on the receiving end of my illness. This, I was told, would make it easier for everyone.

For four days, I sat and listened to the prosecuting barrister for the Church of England (the Designated Officer) call me a monster, a wicked, nasty and horrible person. I sat for four days listening to him repeat this over and over again. I felt like I wanted to walk out of the chapel, and jump off a bridge into the river Thames. He reminded me of a character in one of CS Lewis' stories. Under a low growling voice, the prosecutor repeatedly said, "He is a monster, he is cruel, he is wicked."

353

I had three witnesses who were there to testify concerning the medical evidence, attesting to the extensive research and understanding of the symptoms of CPTSD and PTSD with dissociative subtype, to testify to the damage that had been caused to my brain, and to testify that I could not be held responsible for my actions. One of my witnesses, an eminent professor, and amongst other things, an expert in the area of Military Mental Health, had diagnosed me with latent onset PTSD with dissociative subtype. The professor categorically stated that my episodes and behaviours resulted from my mental health condition.

My senior NHS Consultant Psychiatrist gave testimony and informed the tribunal panel that I have PTSD and I was not a risk to anyone. My therapist of some three years gave testimony, confirming my treatment for CPTSD and PTSD with dissociative subtype, and that my response to treatment meant I was asymptomatic.

The prosecution provided no medical experts, nor any witnesses to counter what my experts were saying. The prosecution was so certain of getting a result that they didn't bother to put up an opposing argument. Their case was merely, 'he did it, he's admitted it, he's a monster'!

Lois and I also gave testimony, but the decision was made before we even entered the court. When we returned home after the tribunal, we were told that a local clergyperson had, whilst we'd been in London, offered their services to 'cover' during the interregnum! Interregnums only happen when there is no clergyperson appointed to a post!

My barrister, in their summing up, said,

'This is an unusual and exceptional case that requires an exceptional and creative solution to help Mr Parks back into his ministry. The brain is a powerful and unpredictable organ. We have surely all had that experience where we have set our morning alarm for an important appointment, or an early flight to an overseas destination, only to find that we wake up suddenly, hours too early, because our brain is on alert not to miss the appointment or the flight. We have no control over that, it just happens. The tribunal members may not have encountered it before, but PTSD exists. It is described in psychiatric diagnostic manuals: DSM V and IV before and ICD 11 and L0 before it too. It is globally recognised. It is prevalent in the military. It can be severe and complex. It can involve sub-types including dissociation. Its manifestations can be hard to understand for those not affected. But I would invite the members of the tribunal to open their minds to the apparently inexplicable manifestations of it. To the layperson, what you have is unanimous evidence for Mr Parks that he suffers from a severe, chronic enduring PTSD with dissociation, and delayed onset starting around 2000, and getting progressively worse without treatment, leading to a crisis in 2017. I invite you to stand back and ask yourselves this question - why wouldn't a man or a woman who entered the army at 16 with a background of a dysfunctional family, prolonged bullying, witness to horrific events including men bleeding to death before his eyes, develop a serious psychological disorder in response?'

My barrister continued,

'There is no evidence contradicting the conclusion of PTSD, or its responsibility for six particularly serious episodes, and lesser conduct. If the tribunal concludes, as it must, on the available evidence, that PP does have PTSD and that it played at least some part in his conduct over the years, then it must consider a) the balance to be struck between penalising the misconduct, and b) the pastoral support, encouraging repentance, forgiveness, attempted reconciliation and moving on constructively from the past. The tribunal has a discretion to exercise in formulating a just penalty to fit the unique circumstances of this case. The reputation of the Church is protected by demonstrating compassion as well as punishing wrong-doing. In the context of severe mental disorder, this means not ostracising a member of the clergy or stigmatising him for having a mental disorder.'

Referring to the Professor's testimony, my barrister said,

'Dissociation is an unconscious act and means a person is 'not there', or is 'somewhere else', reliving other events. Easy to trigger. Automatic response, very severe, not aware of it, not responsible and then when told about it will be extremely upset.'

The barrister continued,

'I urge the tribunal to look deeply into the evidence provided by PP, LP and their witnesses. They are all professional witnesses, and have each worked with veterans for many years. Professor said this is about correlation not cause and effect. The significant episodes and the coercive and controlling behaviour can all be correlated with the

PTSD. This is sufficient for the Tribunal to take a more compassionate approach in this case and offer PP the opportunity to return to work with support. Anyone in this position will require a phased return. This is a routine type of response in cases of employees with a mental disorder. Dissociation, hypervigilance, anger, irritability, paranoia are symptoms of PTSD and Professor has explained their significance in relation to the behaviour of PP. It is hard to understand how someone can behave so appallingly and yet have no, or no complete understanding of what they have done afterwards. Yet this is well -recognised phenomenon. In this case, a proportionate penalty will strike a balance between punishing the Respondent for his admitted misconduct and supporting him to resume light duties with a timetable for monitoring, supervision, and periodic progress report. Returning to work will help his recovery and will not impact adversely on the reputation of the Church on the exceptional facts of this case. The Respondent is a military veteran. Major Stonestreet gave evidence of the prevalence of problems for veterans and it is right that this aspect of this case is properly reflected in the penalty.'

After both barristers had completed their summing up, and the panel had time to deliberate, we were all called back into the noisy chapel with the constant buzzing. The Church of England panel had made their judgement of me. Their judgement of me was that I was not allowed to return to work, to my job in Hastings, and I was not allowed to return to work for the Church of England for two years. This decision was in opposition to all the expert medical advice given, including the Church of England's own Occupational

Health Consultant Doctor. At the pronouncement of the decision, Archdeacon Edward Dowler couldn't hold back showing his delight and clenched his fist whilst saying, 'Yesssss'. Once he stood up, he then gave a little, rather childlike, jump for joy.

The lay panel had selected which parts of the medical evidence they chose to believe. They accepted that my behaviour during dissociative episodes was PTSD-related, but did not accept that the previous 'controlling' aspects of my behaviour were down to PTSD, although they had heard testimony from expert witnesses who gave evidence that hypervigilance and paranoia, symptoms of PTSD and, in particular, PTSD related to military service, causes 'controlling' behaviour.

'Journey home'

Lois and I thanked our barrister and expert witnesses and made our way to catch a train home to our children. We sat on the train next to each other, and both of us at the same time looked at each other and said, "I feel great, I feel free."

We both actually felt better than we had for many years knowing we would be free of the hypocrisy of Church of England life. No more controlling Bishops and Archdeacons, no more vexatious complaints from parishioners. We smiled and laughed together on the journey home to our children. We realised if I were to go back to work, what misery that would have brought us and our family. The Bishop would have made my life hell. I would never have been free from the senior staff's glare. We both realised that, although it was not in the way in which we had expected, God had looked after us.

On that day, my pay was stopped, and we were given four weeks to move out of our tied house. The diocese knew how much debt we were in. There was no compassion. Here we were, crushed by the diocese financially, now homeless, jobless, and no income.

In reality, Lois and I were not crushed; we still had our faith in God, our love for each other and for our children.

'Post-Tribunal'

We informed the diocese that we had no money, and we could not move out of the Rectory as we had no deposit for a house or money for rent. We had no money to pay a removal firm; we were completely stuck. We were even having to use the local food bank for food at this time. We told the Diocese that we were stuck unless they could help us with money for a removal firm and rent for a rental property. The response we got back from the Diocese was that they would help us to move, but it was on condition that I signed a Settlement Agreement, stating that in exchange for the financial help, I would not take legal action against any of the Officers of Chichester Diocese, and a whole list of legislation, some completely irrelevant, was given. I had no choice but to sign - we needed to move on and we had no other way of doing it.

Whilst this was going on, we were advised that the Church of England was going to publish the full decision of the tribunal on the web. This included precise details of what had happened during my dissociative episodes and was an extremely long document. It was only towards the end of the document that there was an acknowledgement that these episodes were as a result of PTSD and mental health. It made me out to be a monster, just what the Designated Officer had wanted! There is no Church of England regulation that says this must be done. The only requirement under ecclesiastical law was that the decision was pronounced in public, which happened on the 10th of January 2020.

My medical team were seriously concerned about the effect of such public humiliation on my mental health, and even contacted the National Safeguarding Team of the Church of England to advise them that, in their opinion, publication of the full details would be a safeguarding risk for me, and to ask them to intervene. They did nothing.

Under Ecclesiastical legislation, an appeal is not a right, you have to ask for leave to appeal to another branch of the Church of England legal system, and they decide if you are allowed to appeal the Church of England tribunal decision. Again, totally 'in-house'!

We were just too exhausted to appeal the decision of the tribunal and already had overwhelming debt. Even though we believe, as do our medical team, that the decision was wrong, we were just happy to be free of the Church of England.

We did, however, have to request leave to appeal the decision to publish on the internet the full decision of the tribunal. We, and my medical team which now also included our family GP, were concerned about the effect of the publication on myself and on our children and regarded it as a clear safeguarding risk.

Why would the Church of England want to harm our children?

We gave medical evidence to the Church of England and Chichester Diocese stating that I was still in recovery and part of PTSD is suicidal ideation, and publicly humiliating me could be damaging to me and hinder my recovery.

'Mum's Death'

I had sat with my older sister comforting her in her death. I had sat with my older brother comforting him in his death. I now, in 2020, soon after my Church of England tribunal had ended, had to sit with my mum and comfort her in her death. This psychopathic mum, my mum, was dying; at the age of 94, her life was coming to an end. I rushed up to Peterborough to see her. Mixed feelings swam around in my head. A mixture of anger, hate and love haunted me. I felt sorry for her. My life flashed by me with thoughts of pain and suffering at the hands of this elderly, frail person. Weirdly, I had popped up to see her a few days earlier and we laughed and cried together. "Could I see in her eyes a deep love for me? Was there a split second of softness in her eyes? Was there?"

Then, the normal mum, oblivious to the pain she causes and had caused to her children and many other people, was there. Oblivious!

Just a few months prior to her death, I had visited her out of pity and duty and, on that visit, she cut me to the heart and said to me, "You were always useless at school." It hurt so much, but it did not floor me. It hurt for a few minutes and not a few months as it would have done previously. Why? My therapy freed me. My faith freed me. I had forgiven her.

On the last visit, I stayed in a hotel overnight. The previous night, my daughter and some of my nieces spent time with each other in Mum's hospital room. Mum was full of morphine and unresponsive. I went back to my hotel, and at 4.00 am, I had a phone call from my younger sister to tell me that the hospital had 'phoned her to say that my mum would die soon. I went to the hospital on my own and sat by her bed. I held her hand until she took her final breath. I sat with her for 40 minutes or so, just me and her, dead.

I cried! I was numb! I was sad! Sad because it could have all been so different. Or could it?

'Public humiliation'

The Church of England's response to our request that the full decision of the tribunal not be posted on the internet, was that it was in the public interest to know what I had done. This is not true; it was in their interest of self-gratification, because I stood up to them.

The two Archbishops avoided being accountable for a decision to publish, so they sent my request to appeal to two judges. The judges upheld the Church of England's decision to publish and dismissed our concerns about it being picked up by the newspapers by saying that it might possibly make local news, if at all.

Soon after publication on the Church of England website, we received a phone call and messages from our older children, who were extremely distressed, telling us that it was in all the national newspapers, in print and online, and it was awful! The papers sensationalised the story and got pertinent details completely wrong, even saying that I had been defrocked! I haven't been, I am still an ordained priest and carry the title 'reverend'. Then the 'trolls' began, people who had no idea of what had gone on, branding me a monster and also having a go at Lois. It was an awful time for us, and I felt myself sinking back into depression and suicidal ideation. By this time, thank God, we had moved away from Hastings, and God had 'parachuted' us to the Isle of Man.

Lois was brought up on the Isle of Man, she had family there and I knew it was a place that she had longed to return to. We decided that the Isle of Man would be a good place to begin to convalesce and rebuild our lives, and we were so right! We packed up most of our belongings in the Rectory and lived out of boxes, waiting for our removal date in mid-March. News came to us that the Isle of Man was going to potentially close its borders due to Covid-19, so rather than being stuck in Hastings, we finished packing through the night, grabbed 2 hours sleep and got in our cars and drove to Heysham to catch the next boat! We already had a house to move into, thanks to the generosity of some good people on the Isle of Man who knew our story and understood mental health difficulties. God had been absolutely amazing. He had met all our needs!

The Isle of Man has been the perfect place for me to continue my therapy and healing. It was the perfect place for all of us, and Covid-19 and lockdown were a blessing to us as they gave us time just to 'be' and recover. Life on the Isle of Man is idyllic, coastal walks, canoeing and trips to many wonderful parks. We are so, so blessed!

Following the publication in all the daily papers, we were advised that it might be helpful to give an interview to a newspaper of our choice, to try and get our story across. This we did, and the response that we received was amazing. People from all over the world made contact, to show their support and understanding. We were overwhelmed by the love and care we received. At last, we felt that maybe things were turning for us.

PART SIX

'A Horse called ISIS'

2020
Age: 61

*"Dare to live the life you have dreamed for yourself.
Go forward and make your dreams come true."*

Ralph Waldo Emerson

Isle of Man

'Healing and Therapy'

ISIS, the therapy horse, a beautiful horse who I first encountered in the autumn of 2017, opened my mind to therapy, to the possibility of healing and helped me on the start of the long road to that healing. ISIS died earlier on this year (2020), but I will never forget the impact and effect that she had on mine and my family's life.

So, where am I now? I'm living on the Isle of Man with my wife Lois and my two youngest children. I am here, alive, because of a horse called ISIS, my faith in God and His choosing of me, and incredible therapy. I'm here because of Lois, her strength of character and unswerving faith in God, and the many 'angels' that God sent to help and support us along the way over the last three years.

My traumatology therapist is Emma Meyer of the Dare to Live Trust. Emma prefers to use the name 'Sun Tui', and as Lois and I explained to her one day the importance of the word 'Sunflower' in our lives, a huge smile broke out on her face, and she told us that 'Sun' is short for 'Sunflower'. How great are the goodness and promises of God!

Sun is absolutely incredible at what she does. Her knowledge of trauma and how it affects the brain, and her passion to see people, especially military veterans and first responders, healed and able to live a normal life again, is phenomenal. She is working at the cutting edge of the advancement of understanding just how trauma affects people's brains and lives, and not just the sufferer but also those around them.

My treatment has consisted of around 100 sessions of an integrated model of therapy including CBT (Cognitive Behavioural

Therapy), CPT (Cognitive Process Therapy), EMDR (Eye Movement Desensitisation Reprogramming), Rewind therapy and Trauma-Focused Regulation and Processing skills.

'Acronym'

This treatment has led me to many personal insights, and over three years of almost weekly therapy sessions, I have developed a sort of acronym, a bunch of letters which have developed in my mind, and I travel through this acronym, exploring the insights, every morning of every day.

Whilst I explore this acronym, I use a small device called an Alpha-Stim. Our brains naturally have electrical currents, and the Alpha-Stim sends a natural level of microcurrent, via small clips which I wear on my earlobes, through the brain to stimulate and regulate specific groups of nerve cells. This helps release positive chemicals into my brain.

It may seem rather strange, but the acronym I use is:

P S R R A A T T T O S F S M N S L D H Smile Stopp 'But I Chose You Paul' Baptism, filled with the Holy Spirit, White hard-wood windowsill.

Sounds a bit bizarre, I know, but to me, it keeps me grounded and ready to face the day.

Before I start to work my way through my acronym each morning, I listen to an audio daily reading of the Bible and a commentary on the section of the Bible I have listened to. I then listen to Christian worship music for around twenty minutes. Then I start with my acronym:

P = the word Piesss.

P - I scan my body and its physical sensations. I scan to see if I can feel, in my nervous system, muscles and body, a physical sensation which is a memory of a past trauma. What my nervous system, muscles and body physically remember can trigger a response in me of a past trauma. This could trigger a flashback, dissociation or an aggressive mood in me. This sensation I am scanning for is not a cognitive response. It is an instantaneous response to a body memory which I was not previously aware triggered me. This is the past distress of a trauma, bringing that trauma distress into my present. I am now aware of these sensations in my nervous system, muscles and body and I acknowledge their presence and I am able to tell my nervous system, muscles and body's memory, I am safe. It is a past experience, and I calm down. There is no immediate threat to my life. I remind myself through the day that my nervous system, muscles and my body may feel sensations and I calm my response before the sensation triggers a non-cognitive response. This scan grounds me into the here and now and reminds me of my now awareness of these traumas being in the past and not present.

I - I scan my intellect to discover how I am thinking. Am I negative and critical right now? Am I locked into negative recalling of paranoia? Am I feeling paranoia? Am I sharp and attentive? This scan helps me to be aware and in the present moment of how I am thinking. It makes me aware if I am in a thought process of past trauma. Am I being hypervigilant? This scan grounds my thoughts to the present. I am able to change any negative thinking by being aware of it and the potential consequences of this thinking. I evoke cognitive tools to change any negative thoughts such as thinking of a blue sky or a horse called ISIS. I break the downward spiral.

E - Emotional: I scan myself to see how I am feeling emotionally. Am I feeling depressed? Why? Am I feeling angry? If so, how can I be aware of how this affects other people? What is making me angry? How can I change feeling angry? I can go for a walk. Movement is helpful. Knowing I am feeling angry helps me be aware of my attitude to others. Am I feeling happy? Am I feeling agitated? What are my feelings saying? Scanning my feelings helps me to be grounded in the here and now. Where in my body am I feeling these sensations? This grounds me too. I apply tools to alleviate and change any negative emotions. Or I acknowledge them and own them so I don't blame others or project blame.

S - Suds. What are my anxiety levels on a scale of 1 to 10? What am I feeling in my body? Is it good 'butterflies'? Is it anxious stress? If they are a 1 to 3, then I'm ok. If they are above 3 then I can do some mindfulness exercises to bring my anxiety levels down.

S - Socially. How am I feeling with regards to socialising today? With my family? With other people? Am I feeling anxious? Am I feeling paranoid? Has something upset me and do I need to do a body scan and ground myself into reality? I need to be authentic to socialise and make steps to meet people. Calm myself.

S - Spiritually. How am I spiritually? Am I connected to my faith? Am I spiritually alert and awake?

R = Regulate. I regulate myself each morning by doing my acronym and I regulate myself throughout the day. This R reminds me about the importance of continued regulation and the insight I now have and the tools I have to regulate myself.

R = Resilience: I need to be resilient all the time. I also need to build on my physical resilience, mental resilience and spiritual resilience each day by walking, reading, socialising and resting. I realise resistance in life (difficulties), develops resilience.

A = Adult: I have come to learn that within me are three adults. There is the Adult. This is a mature, balanced and reasonable person. This adult is wise, considerate and thoughtful. This adult gives me peace. There is the Child adult. This adult sulks, manipulates like a toddler and feels like a victim. And there is the Sergeant Major adult. This adult gets angry easily, shouts and is aggressive to others. I have come to learn that I can consciously make a cognitive decision to stay in my mature adult. This adult brings me peace and calmness and a smile on my face. I can check myself throughout the day to see which adult I am being by the words I speak and my behaviour responses to people. I can pull back from Sergeant Major and Child adult because I am aware of them and their manifestations.

A = Authentic: I have had a personal insight into my life of hiding 'me', putting a smokescreen up to hide me and having many mirrors to be whoever people wanted me to be. I had never been the authentic 'me' in my life. The shame, guilt, depression, anger, rage, and outrage within my very soul were hidden by me from others. I was an expert at hiding. This stopped me ever living in a present moment of time. This stopped me being me. My head thoughts raced around putting up smokescreens to hide the true me from people, morphing me into who people wanted me to be. By meditating on the word 'authentic', a grounding of 'me' happens. The meditation brings me to be authentically in the present moment. I can be me. I do not need to hide, and throw up a smokescreen and mirrors to make me invisible. When I meet someone during the day, this cognitive thought of the word 'authentic' grounds me into a feeling and thought of being authentically me, in that moment.

I have nothing to hide anymore. I have dealt with my traumas, my shame and stigma. This gives me a sense of a wellbeing and a sensation of peace.

T = Trust: I have come to be aware that I have not been able to trust anyone in my life. This mistrust has fed my mental health condition and caused a breakdown of my relationships. Previously, I was never able to trust my wife Lois, and I would have always had doubts about people's motivation. My therapy, morning Bible Studies and acronym meditations, along with my journey to recovery, have brought me to a place of trusting God my Father. I know I have never seen my biological father but this growing trust in me for God my Father, the Loving Father who chose me, has now filled me with a sense of completely trusting God. I realise He has always been with me from my time in my mother's womb. This sense fills me with peace and calmness. Being able to trust my Father God has enabled me to trust Lois, my wife. I have never known trust before.

T = Truth: I have come to believe that the books, letters and stories in the Bible are the truth. They are truth in the message that each book, letter and story God uses to speak to us. The message is timeless. This grounds me to living a moral and spiritual life.

T = Thankfulness: I go through the many things for which I am thankful to God. This list could be what has happened in my life recently, to thanking God for my children, wife Lois and the very breath in my lungs. This has a positive effect on my wellbeing for the day and in that moment of thankfulness.

O = Obedience: I remind myself to be faithful to God in my walk through the day. I remember how obedient Jesus Christ was to God His Father.

S = Surrender: I recall my conversion experience in January 1991. I have a desire to kneel down before Jesus Christ crucified on the Cross. I desire to lay flat, prostrate at His feet, completely surrendered and submitted to Him. I experience the blood of His crown of thorns dripping His blood on to my head. I look up and His blood drips onto my face. I realise the depth of His love for me. He completely gave himself up for me. He died and suffered for me. He adores me. I imagine floating above Him on the cross and he looks up at me and He smiles at me with His crown of thorns cutting into his head. I realise and He realises I have come to understand He loves me so much, so deeply, that He raises me above Him. He totally surrenders and sacrifices Himself below me to lift me up. I realise I am loved, and I want to share His love with others.

F = Fear: I have come to understand I have nothing to fear anymore. I do not fear death because I trust God my Father and His promises of life after death. I do not fear guilt, shame and stigma from myself or others because He has forgiven me. I do not fear the condemnation of people because He is caring for me. I do not fear the experiences of trauma I've been exposed to. I understand and accept I am forgiven.

S = Slow down in work; slow down in this day. This grounds me into relaxing into the moment. I do not need to rush anything. I do not need to feel anxious about what needs to be done today. I am reminded to be in the present moment and to connect with Lois and my children. I am reminded to be in the moment to enjoy conversations with the people I meet today. This S removes anxiety. There is no rush.

M = Mountain: I am reminded to make 'top of the mountain' moments in the same way Jesus did. These are moments when

I either find time for myself to be on my own or go for a walk or bike ride. It keeps me grounded and healthy.

N = Not the first point of call: I am reminded to ignore paranoid thoughts that come into my head throughout the day. Thoughts that can change my mood. Thoughts that are not true. I am able to cognitively ignore these thoughts and replace them with positive thoughts by using wellbeing and traumatology tools.

S = Soft eyes, soft voice: I remind myself not to have angry eyes today. I am reminded to soften my voice. My hardened and aggressive eyes can scare and freeze people with a stare. My voice can demand and be controlling.

L = Live and don't exist: I remind myself that this new day is a gift and it should not be wasted. I have an optimistic feeling come over me and I desire to have a happy and positive day. It clears any depression hanging over me.

D = Dignity: I am reminded that all people are precious to God. Every person is special and filled with pain and joy. I am reminded to give everyone I meet dignity and respect and lift them up.

H = Horizon: I am reminded of a therapy session I did with ISIS, the horse, Lois, and Sun, my therapist. We ended the session with all of us standing in a straight line looking into the distance at a field with yellow flowers in. I imagined the flowers to be sunflowers. There was our horizon to reach. To me, the horizon was full of hope and the sunflowers represented people we could help. Looking at the horizon fills me with motivation and purpose. I want to get to that horizon.

Smile: Smile represents the first therapy session I had with the horse called ISIS. This is the therapy session that saved my life. It was Autumn 2017; I was personally finished, and death was calling me. The session started with me going into an area of a large circle of grass in a field. A thin ribbon marked out the circle. My therapist was kneeling down outside the circle and ISIS, the horse I was to work with, stood five feet away from me. ISIS was an old horse who looked to me like a thoroughbred horse. She did not look her age. Most days, ISIS roamed freely in the fields of the Dare to Live farm with other horses in a herd. Out of the blue, ISIS reared up onto her hind legs and kicked her two front legs into the air. All the time, ISIS was looking me in the eye. Her large gentle eye never broke her connection with my eyes. I had no idea what was happening. ISIS then walked over to me and stood to my left side with her shoulder next to my shoulder, still staring me in the eyes. My therapist told me to walk ISIS around the pen without any equipment. ISIS had no harness on, and I had nothing in my hands. I took a step forward and ISIS stood still. I stepped back and sensed I needed to wait for ISIS to connect with me on her terms. I sensed the time was right and I began walking forward and ISIS walked beside me, our shoulders about a foot in distance from each other. She kept looking at me with her big soft eye. She slowed down and I slowed down with her. We moved forward when each one of us was ready. We walked around the whole circle together and back to the start and stopped. My therapist asked me what had I learned? I stood there, thinking, with ISIS looking me in my eyes, and I sensed she was willing me on. After some thought, I said, "I learned that gentleness and patience are important in connecting with someone." ISIS had taught me this. I was then asked by my therapist to put some obstacles around the inside of the circle. ISIS and I would have to walk around the circle and step over the obstacles together. ISIS and I started walking forward once again. We moved forward only when we were connected together in mutual trust. Together we made our way over the obstacles to the finish again. My therapist asked me again, what did you learn? I thought it through again with ISIS staring at me and I said, "Gentleness and patience are needed to connect to and go through life with someone, and especially when there are obstacles in life. We can get over and through the obstacles together when connected by gentleness and patience." At that moment, ISIS looked me in the eye and I realised if I got healed of my mental illness and if I learned the language of gentleness and patience, I would be able to connect with Lois and my children. Hope, the first real hope I experienced, maybe in my whole life. This made me smile.

Stopp: This reminds me of the tool to help me stop triggering into CPTSD and PTSD with dissociative subtype symptoms. The S in Stopp means to stop. Stop right away any negative interactions with someone. Stop right away with any potential triggers. The T in Stopp means think, pause. Pause straight away. Do not hesitate to pause. The O in Stopp means observe. Observe what is going on for me. What is going on for the other person? This grounds me and gives me an understanding of myself in the present moment. The P in Stopp means pullback. Pull back from any engagement with someone else. Pull back from triggers I am aware just happened. The second P in Stopp means practise. I remind myself to apply this tool, stop, throughout the day when I need it.

'But I Chose You, Paul': I remind myself of the time, the only time, I have heard an audible voice from God. I was lying on my bed in the Rectory in Hastings, curled in the foetal position, a position I had spent most of my life in. Behind me and about a foot from me, a voice said to me, completely clearly, "But I chose you,

Paul." Over time, I have come to realise God chose me way back when I was in my mother's womb. He chose me then and He has been with me my whole life. This confirms to me that I am ok, and I will be ok in whatever life throws at me, because God chose me. This a wonderful reason for hope.

'Christ appearing to me crucified on the cross': I recall the moment I came to faith in Christ. Christ on the cross appeared to me and, at that moment, I was filled with the presence of the Holy Spirit. I was baptised in the Holy Spirit. I was filled with joy, love and peace. This memory gives me grounding, purpose and a desire for more of God.

A white hard-wood windowsill: This is a vision; a picture which came to me during therapy. It is a vision of a white hard-wood windowsill. Above the windowsill is a window and the window is open. I stand on the inside of this open windowsill. I am an adult and I am looking out of the window at me, a little boy, myself, aged about six years old. My boy image jumps off the windowsill, somersaulting and running up and down with complete joy. There is a blue sky above and lush trees and vegetation full of colour all around. My little boy self sprints up a long green grass run with trees on each side. At the end is a large door. He runs, jumps and skips in blissful joy. He is happy, really happy. My adult self is smiling with joy looking out of the window at me. When I imagine this vision in my meditation in the now, present, real time, I am filled with the chemical endorphins and it makes me ecstatically happy and joyful. These chemicals are released in me while I look at this vision and the chemicals make me happy. Over time, the 'little boy' me, in this vision, opened the door at the end of the long run of grass and he half-stepped in, and he waved back at me, the adult, looking at him. He did not go all the way in the door. After more time, the 'little boy' me opened the door and went inside the door. I do not see him anymore. I think this is because he can rest now. I have dealt with much of his pain. I can be free in my adult now. After re-imagining this vision, I am finished my morning meditation and I am ready for the day.

'Judah'

My step-daughter suggested I get a dog to help with my recovery. Judah, our Cockapoo, came into my life, our lives, in September 2017, and he has been such a blessing. Judah and I are now training together for him to be my Veterans with PTSD Assistance dog, my therapy dog. He knows how I am feeling and does whatever he needs to do to help me. He will jump on my lap, lick me and bother me until I recognise that I need to apply one of my 'tools' to change my mood or PTSD feelings. His ability to understand moods, feelings and emotion is quite incredible.

'How Trauma Physically Affects the Brain'

Aaron Meyer, of Aaron Meyer Law in California has written an article about how trauma physically affects the brain. Aaron Meyer was commissioned as a Marine Officer and Judge Advocate (JAG) in the United States Marine Corps in 2004. He wanted to help Marines protect innocent people. He quickly found that the warriors themselves were often the ones needing protection. When a Servicemember or veteran is broken in war, or merely suspected of a crime, he often becomes labelled as an inconvenience, distrusted, discarded, or abandoned by his leadership. This article helped me understand me, and I hope that anyone reading this book who is a veteran struggling with PTSD, or who supports a veteran struggling with PTSD, will find comfort and understanding in this article too.

'To understand the Legal Defenses surrounding Dissociative Reactions is to understand the Brain Before, During, and After Extreme Traumatic Exposure.

In basic terms, your Central Nervous System relies upon two systems: the "Inhibition Circuit" and the "Activation Circuit." In the healthy human adult brain, complex wiring/"white matter," robust regions, and groups of nuclei work to produce behavior appropriate to the given circumstances. This incredibly and intricately wired system makes us so uniquely human.

Understanding how this system works is essential to understanding how the PTSD brain loses the ability to cognitively function in a dissociative state. Our Central Nervous System is based on neurons. Under trauma, neurons die and the intricate system loses balance. Receptors that previously caught synapses and sent them through transmitters are "disregulated." The result can be extreme behavior.

The Amygdala Hijack

The amygdala is the catalyst of the brain's "raw emotion," as opposed to, say, the rational or thinking part of the brain. The amygdala sends information that triggers anxiety, fear, or a "rush." It arouses, for example, adrenaline, aggression, emotional intensity, and weakened self-control.

With a very powerful "emotional memory," the amygdala memorizes every painful or frightening event the brain has ever experienced. When the amygdala is stimulated by a new trauma or stressor that it matches to a previous "fight or flight"/life-or-death scenario in its memory Rolodex, it activates areas of the hypothalamus, adrenal cortex, and the "sympathetic" nervous system. Hormones and neurotransmitters like norepinephrine, dopamine, glucocorticoids, and adrenaline are then released.

One such hormone produced in the hypothalamus is the Corticotropin Releasing Factor (CRF). During stress, CRF release causes pure panic, fear, loss of appetite, rage, and depression. If the amygdala were to be likened to a rider whipping horses into a frenzy, then CRF would be the whip. The more intense the stress, the higher the CRF level. The higher the CRF level, the more norepinephrine and dopamine run wild. At higher levels, the brain is hijacked. The brain is running on pure emotion and instinct, potentially to the point of unconscious behavior.

The controlled rush of this activated circuit can prove valuable to warriors in combat, athletes, bystanders reacting to an emergency, etc. With release of endorphins, the body feels little pain in the moment. Focus is intense, and actions are swift. But amygdala hijack may also bring irrational behavior, tunnel vision, panic, and blind aggression.

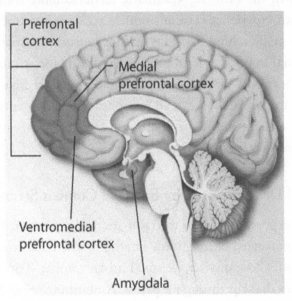

The Hippocampus - Reining in the Amygdala

By contrast, a healthy Inhibition Circuit serves to rein in the amygdala, contextualizing events for the brain to process rationally. The prefrontal cortex and hippocampus also use recorded memory and strongly-held beliefs to rationalize and intervene before the amygdala can dominate with pure emotion.

The Hippocampus contextualizes experiences, saying, "This is not life or death. Everything's ok. We've seen this before." It's your control center. In the sense of "Houston, we have a problem," it's Houston. Just as the Activation Circuit activates hormones and neurotransmitters, the "Inhibition Circuit" releases serotonin to rein in the norepinephrine and dopamine. Serotonin increases senses of well-being, control, and self-tolerance. In cases of chronic, severe PTSD, drugs (described below) are often prescribed to simulate and increase serotonin levels necessary for regulation.

Thus, in the ordinary traumatic scenario more mundane to the human experience (a minor vehicle accident, argument with a spouse, a grade school fistfight, intense sports participation, etc), the rational brain is able to process the traumatic stimuli, put it into context, and prevent an irrational amygdala hijack. Since it is also important to have an appropriately active amygdala in even these more mundane traumatic scenarios, this integrated system requires a fine balance.

Cell Death Caused by Extreme Combat Stressors

Combat exposes the brain to traumatic information it has never before experienced or imagined. Firefights where life could end at any second. Close-quarter, personal urban combat. Triple-stacked IED blasts that rip through a patrol. Ambushes. Sniper fire. The sensations involved in taking the life of another. The rational brain (hippocampus) has no memory that can contextualize the sights, smells, sounds, and depraved experiences and say, "It's ok, we have seen this before." Dissociative reactions may happen for the first time even in these moments.

Even in the non-kinetic experiences, those previously-held subconscious beliefs about reality in the hippocampus are overwhelmed. The sight of children and animals living in unthinkable conditions. Handling body parts of the dead. "Anticipatory anxiety." Immense guilt over what your mind later determines to be "avoidable" tragedies. Chronic fatigue. Indeed, war, in every sense, is a "violation of everything your mind thought was right."[12]

Post-traumatic stress does not affect every individual exposed to these stressors. But regardless of the degree of training, intestinal fortitude, or mental toughness, a constellation of additional factors from childhood experiences to frequency to the introduction and timing of TBI can uniquely combine to have residual effects in any brain.

Extreme Stress Re-Wires the Brain

If the rational mind cannot comprehend a scenario, it shuts down. Our minds want desperately to compartmentalize and make sense of each experience. When the brain cannot contextualize extreme trauma, the hippocampus and prefrontal cortex experience neuronal cell death. Cells die.

Extreme stress is toxic to the brain. In chronic, severe PTSD and TBI, damage is physically manifested. Physical damage in neurons, degraded connectivity (white matter), "hypofunction," and atrophy (shriveling) of the hippocampus and prefrontal cortex have been observed and measured through tools such as brain scans, functional neuroimaging, new variations on CT scans, high definition nerve fiber tracking, and single-voxel proton MR spectroscopy.

Not only have images shown withered hippocampus in these cases, but the brain studies have linked the increased size of the amygdala to PTSD severity. The primitive parts of your brain physically take over- in measurable ways. The higher the degree of atrophy, the more likely, frequent, and severe dissociative symptoms become in the individual positive for that subtype.

The severity of previously-believed "invisible" wounds can be observed, measured, and quantified through advanced brain imaging. This technology, as it pertains to PTSD and TBI imaging, is still developing and not in wide use. The military has dedicated large amounts of money to developing and testing these tools, but actual centers that provide adequate imaging and treatment are all still very new. Mere CT Scans or MRIs are simply unable to demonstrate the neuron-level damage involved in the brain with severe PTSD, TBI, and/or dissociative symptoms. Despite what we saw after Vietnam, despite Iraq and Afghanistan, we are still in relatively early stages of understanding, identification, and treatment.

Trauma is Cumulative

Traumatic events are "cumulative." The more you experience trauma, the more severe your brain's physiological reaction to stress becomes, and the chemical composition changes.

Ok, so we know that in an extremely traumatic event, the Rational/Inhibition Circuit is overwhelmed by the extreme information it receives, and thus, fails to oppose (calm) the amygdala/"Activation circuit." The amygdala then goes from zero to 100 on the activation scale, igniting the rest of the circuit. The CRF hormone is released, acting like a whip to a horse. Dopamine and Norepinephrine are those horses. The result is a mind acting on raw and irrational stimulus, not cognitive reasoning, and these moments of "hijack" can physically kill neurons.

But, is the balance then restored thereafter? Not exactly. When the mind dissociates during an extreme stressor, the amygdala records all subsequent experiences, feelings, and information for the duration of the dissociation, storing those sensations as life-threatening events without any associated contextualized, calming thoughts. Thus, those "memories" in the amygdala remain strongly in place as powerful unconscious future generators of panic or rage. From that time forward, unless properly treated, mitigated, and controlled, the amygdala is vulnerable to "triggers" that conjure those same images, feelings, and sensations from that experience. The later experiences do not have to even be the same subject-matter as the original trauma, just sensations that remind the amygdala of how it felt in that first dissociation. When that happens, "fear memories" in amygdala become triggered without conscious control and "fight or flight" can be engaged.

Since cells die and the amygdala grows with each amygdala hijack, it becomes increasingly easier for the switch between the two circuits to become "disregulated." The veteran experiences "circuit modulation" at a more rapid rate. The hippocampus is shrinking. The amygdala is growing. The more he endures, the more the control center loses control or is compromised. If dissociative symptoms are present, the dissociative "disregulation" will be easier and more severe the next time, and the next.

Feedback Loop

The brain also becomes predisposed to the release of CRF, glucocorticoids, and adrenaline. It's a vicious cycle known as the "feedback loop." As instability increases, more trivial reminders serve to trigger the release of these chemicals that are toxic to the brain in excessive doses. And the more traumatic episodes that are triggered, the more the amygdala records new traumatic experiences, multiplying the scope of experiences that could potentially ultimately trigger a dissociation. A rough example would be a traumatized skunk that panics and sprays at any stimuli in its environment.

The brain's intricate threat-response mechanisms erode to reflect a more primitive, animalistic system. For instance, the tiger or the mouse can tolerate very little stimuli before they instinctively enter "survival mode," choosing either to attack or flee. Their circuit modulation is immediate. Their brains release adrenaline or dopamine in less sophisticated ways. The hippocampal memories and beliefs are not strong. The fish or the snake has even fewer working mechanisms, causing immediate, instinctive, and intense response to even minor perceived threats. There is very little "white matter." The response is not malicious, hateful, or intentional. It's simply the brain's, albeit irrational, reaction to a perceived threat.

As time wears on and the feedback loop repeats over and over, the structure of the Rational Circuit is wearing down, almost like a knee loses cartilage with prolonged stress, soon to be bone-on-bone if not mitigated.

Combat Veterans are not Ticking Time Bombs

As I said before, I want to note that, while these phenomena are important to understand when analyzing a case after-the-fact for intent and mental responsibility purposes, the described injuries to the PTSD suffering brain are not permanent. They do not mean that the sufferer is without hope of recovery. In the overwhelming majority of these cases, the criminal episode triggered by PTSD/ TBI came at a time when the veteran was either (1) not properly diagnosed or treated, (2) not receiving proper treatment, trying to fight through the wounds, unwilling to admit there were problems due to a well-founded fear of social and professional stigma or (3) at a vulnerable time of transition between medications or treatment.'

'Final Thoughts'

My final thoughts? My final thoughts are for the veterans and families of veterans who suffer from PTSD. We are ignored; the institutions, the government - they ignore us. I now completely get the theme tune from the 1970s/80s TV Programme M*A*S*H, 'Suicide is Painless'. Painless for the person wanting to commit suicide maybe, but for those we leave behind when we commit suicide, it is completely painful.

There is another way.

It has been exceedingly difficult for me up to this point, for my longing for peace in my life. It is exceedingly difficult for veterans or any person who suffers from a mental health condition. Our wives, our partners, our families suffer immensely with us on our journey. We suffer a lifetime of waiting and hoping for healing, for sanity. We wish, we pray, we beg God for help, for understanding from others, for the shame and stigma to go, to disappear. Just to have one day of peace in our minds.

Yet, until we begin our journey of healing, our illness heaps shame and stigma onto us from others. Time after time, we are slapped in the face. We try but we cannot do it. The longing for healing in us is, at times, too painful, and we know people around us do not get the depth of our pain. It is hard for us to listen to the gossip and observe the wagging fingers or the vicious stares.

I have found that we cannot deny our illness; we cannot look away from ourselves in denial and hope things will get better. We cannot skip over the painful parts of the symptoms of our illnesses. We cannot skip over the consequences of our symptoms for the other people in our lives.

The pain matters; it all matters.

Our pain is essential to the process of healing ourselves and our relationships. I realise this with all of my heart. Pain is essential to the process of healing. Why? Because it is in the process. When you are at the end of the process, the past pain will feel like only minutes in a lifetime. It will seem like minutes when the joy of healing comes.

After the pain of peeling back the layers of trauma and hurt, you will find the little boy or the little girl within you crying out with rage and outrage, and hug them so much that their pain is squashed right out of them.

For you who are suffering right now, it might seem easy for me to write this, but I have lived through it. I have lived through my longing and I have endured the different seasons of my life, and I have survived. I have come out on the other side of the darkness. I can say that the pain, all of it matters, and is essential. We must not look away and skip over important parts of our lives. We must sit with the pain, and the discomfort, and face our illness. We must rid ourselves from denial once and for all.

For me, I invited Jesus into my pain. For me, I opened up to a horse called ISIS. For me, I faced shame and stigma and I roared in its face. I roared, "No more! I am Paul! I am a good man! I am chosen by God!" I will never again lose my intimacy with Jesus in pursuit of my healing in my own strength. I will not skip over the painful parts of my story.

My bitterness, my pain, my regret, my sorrow, my loss, my trauma are all essential to my story, as rotten as it is and as hurtful as it is.

You see, God is writing my story with me.
I will not look away from myself!
I embrace Him as He embraces me.

If you would like to contact the author of this book, Rev Paul Parks,
his email address is: hidelittleboy2020@gmail.com

Lightning Source UK Ltd.
Milton Keynes UK
UKHW040642241120
373998UK00001B/47

9 781913 704810